Feeling
GOOD
Together

D1421474

Also by Dr David Burns from Vermilion

10 Days to Great Self-Esteem

When Panic Attacks

Feeling
GOOD
Together

The Secret to Making Troubled Relationships Work

Dr David Burns

1 3 5 7 9 10 8 6 4 2

Published in 2009 by Vermilion, an imprint of Ebury Publishing
First published in the USA by Broadway Books, an imprint of
The Doubleday Publishing Group, in 2008

Ebury Publishing is a Random House Group company

Copyright © David Burns 2008

David Burns has asserted his right to be identified as the author of this Work in
accordance with the Copyright, Designs and Patents Act 1988.

All rights reserved. No part of this publication may be reproduced, stored in a retrieval
system, or transmitted in any form or by any means, electronic, mechanical, photocopying,
recording or otherwise, without the prior permission of the copyright owner.

The Random House Group Limited Reg. No. 954009

Addresses for companies within the Random House Group can be found at
www.rbooks.co.uk

A CIP catalogue record for this book is available from the British Library

The Random House Group Limited supports The Forest Stewardship
Council (FSC), the leading international forest certification organisation. All our
titles that are printed on Greenpeace approved FSC certified paper carry the FSC logo.
Our paper procurement policy can be found at:
www.rbooks.co.uk/environment

Mixed Sources
Product group from well-managed
forests and other controlled sources
www.fsc.org Cert no. TT-COC-2139
© 1996 Forest Stewardship Council
FSC

Printed in the UK by CPI Mackays, Chatham, ME5 8TD

Book design by Michael Collica

ISBN 9780091929619

Copies are available at special rates for bulk orders. Contact the sales development team
on 020 7840 8487 for more information.

To buy books by your favourite authors and register for offers, visit www.rbooks.co.uk

The information in this book has been compiled by way of general guidance
in relation to the specific subjects addressed, but is not a substitute and not
to be relied on for medical, healthcare, pharmaceutical or other professional
advice on specific circumstances and in specific locations. Please consult your
GP before changing, stopping or starting any medical treatment. So far as the
author is aware the information given is correct and up to date as at March 2009.
Practice, laws and regulations all change, and the reader should obtain up to date
professional advice on any such issues. The author and publishers disclaim, as
far as the law allows, any liability arising directly or indirectly from the use, or
misuse, of the information contained in this book.

The names and identities of the people in this book have been disguised extensively,
and any resemblance to any person, living or dead, is purely coincidental.

Contents

Acknowledgments

I would like to thank my daughter, Signe Burns, who was my editor in chief for this book. Signe's contributions were brilliant and extensive. Working with my daughter on this project has been absolutely wonderful!

Several other editors have also helped me tremendously along the way, including Amy Hertz, Marc Haeringer, and Sarah Manges. I am deeply indebted to all of them. Finally, I would like to thank my editor at Broadway Books, Rebecca Cole. Wow! Your contributions were awesome!

Introduction

Troubled relationships hurt. Most of us base our feelings of self-worth, at least in part, on our relationships with other people. It's no fun to argue or fight with someone you care about. Even a feud with someone you don't care about can eat away at you and rob you of energy and joy.

If you're not getting along with someone, I've got some good news for you: I can show you how to develop a far more rewarding relationship with that person. It makes no difference whether the person you've been battling is your spouse, sibling, parent, neighbor, or friend, or even a complete stranger. No matter who it is, I can show you how to transform feelings of frustration and resentment into warmth and trust, and it can happen much faster than you think. In fact, sometimes it only takes a few minutes.

However, it will require some hard work on your part, and you may have to look at some things about yourself that you didn't want to see. The path to intimacy is nearly always painful. If you can muster up some courage and humility, and you're willing to roll up your sleeves and do the work, I can show you something truly amazing—something that will change your life.

David D. Burns, MD
Adjunct Clinical Professor Emeritus, Department of Psychiatry
and Behavioral Sciences, Stanford University School of Medicine

Part One

Why Can't We All
Just Get Along?

Chapter 1

What the Experts Say

We all want friendly, rewarding relationships with other people, but we often end up with the exact opposite—hostility, bitterness, and distrust. Why is this? Why can't we all just get along?

There are two competing theories. Most experts endorse the *deficit theory*. According to this theory, we can't get along because we don't know how. In other words, we fight because we lack the skills we need to solve the problems in our relationships. When we were growing up, we learned reading, writing, and arithmetic, but there weren't any classes on how to communicate or solve relationship problems.

Other experts believe that we can't get along because we don't really want to. This is called the *motivational theory*. In other words, we fight because we lack the motivation to get close to the people we're at odds with. We end up embroiled in hostility and conflict because the battle is rewarding.

The Deficit Theory

Most mental health professionals, including clinicians and researchers, endorse the deficit theory. They're convinced that we wage war simply because we don't know how to make love. We desperately want loving, satisfying relationships but lack the skills we need to develop them.

Of course, different experts have different ideas about what the most important interpersonal skill deficits are. Behavior therapists, for example, believe that our problems with getting along result from a lack of communication and problem-solving skills. So when someone criticizes us, we may get defensive when we should be listening. We may pout and put the other person down instead of sharing our feelings openly, or we may resort to nagging and coercion in order to get our way. We don't use systematic negotiation or problem-solving skills, so the tensions escalate.

A related theory attributes relationship conflict to the idea that men and women are inherently different. This theory was popularized by Deborah Tannen in her bestselling book *You Just Don't Understand: Women and Men in Conversation* and by John Gray in his bestselling book *Men Are from Mars, Women Are from Venus*. These authors argue that men and women can't get along because they use language so differently. The idea is that women use language to express feelings, whereas men use language to solve problems. So when a woman tells her husband that she's upset, he may automatically try to help her with the problem that's bugging her because that's how his brain is wired. But she simply wants him to listen and acknowledge how she feels, so she gets more upset when he tries to "help" her. They both end up feeling frustrated and misunderstood. You may have observed this pattern in yourself and someone you're not getting along with, such as your spouse.

Cognitive therapists have a different idea about the deficits that lead to relationship problems. They emphasize that all of our feelings result from our thoughts and attitudes, or *cognitions*. In other words, the things other people do—like being critical or rudely cutting in front of us in traffic—don't actually upset us. Instead, we get upset because of the way we think about these events.

This theory may resonate with your personal experience. When you're mad at someone, you may have noticed that your mind is flooded with negative thoughts. You tell yourself, "He's such a jerk! He only cares about himself. He *shouldn't* be like that. What a loser!" When you feel upset, these negative thoughts seem overwhelmingly valid, but they actually contain a variety of thinking errors, or *cognitive distortions*, listed on pages 6–7.

One of the most interesting things about the cognitive theory is the idea that anger and interpersonal conflict ultimately result from a mental con. In other words, you're telling yourself things that aren't entirely true when you're fighting with someone. However, you don't notice that you're fooling yourself because the distorted thoughts act as self-fulfilling prophecies, so they seem completely valid. For example, if you tell yourself that the person you're annoyed with is a jerk, you'll treat him like a jerk. As a result, he'll get angry and start acting like a jerk. Then you'll tell yourself that you were right all along and that he really *is* a jerk.

Cognitive therapy is based on the idea that when you change the way you think, you can change the way you feel and behave. In other words, if we can learn to think about other people in a more positive and realistic way, it will be far easier to resolve conflicts and develop rewarding personal and professional relationships.

This theory sounds great on paper, but it's not that easy to change the thinking patterns that trigger anger and conflict. That's because there's a side of us that clings to these distortions. It can feel good to look down on someone we're angry or annoyed with. It gives us a feeling of moral superiority. We just don't want to see that we're distorting our view of that person.

Some experts claim that the most important deficit that leads to relationship problems is a lack of self-esteem. In other words, if you don't love and respect yourself, you'll have a hard time loving anyone else because you'll always be trying to get something from the other person that you can only give yourself. This theory has been popular in our schools. The idea is that if we help children develop greater self-esteem when they're growing up, they'll be able to develop warm, trusting relationships with others and won't be so attracted to violence, crime, and gang membership as they get older.

Other experts believe that relationship distress results from a different kind of deficit called *relationship burnout*. You may have noticed that when you aren't getting along with someone, the negativity nearly always escalates over time. You and your spouse may criticize each other more and more and stop doing all the fun

The Ten Distortions That Trigger Conflict

	Distortion	Description	Example
1.	All-or-Nothing Thinking	You look at the conflict, or the person you're not getting along with, in absolute, black-and-white categories. Shades of gray do not exist.	You tell yourself that the person you're mad at is a complete zero with no redeeming features. Or if your relationship breaks up, you may think that it was a total failure.
2.	Overgeneralization	You view the current problem as a never-ending pattern of frustration, conflict, and defeat.	You tell yourself, "She'll *always* be like that."
3.	Mental Filter	You catalog the other person's faults, dwell on all the negative things he or she has ever done or said to you, and filter out or ignore all the other person's good qualities.	You tell your spouse, "This is the tenth time I've told you to carry out the trash." Or, "How many times do I have to remind you not to leave your dirty socks on the floor!?"
4.	Discounting the Positive	You insist that the other person's good qualities or actions don't count.	If someone you're fighting with does something positive, you tell yourself that she's trying to manipulate you.
5.	Jumping to Conclusions	You jump to conclusions that may not be warranted by the facts. There are three common patterns:	
		Mind-Reading. You assume that you know how the other person thinks and feels about you.	You tell yourself that a friend is totally self-centered and only wants to use you.
		Reverse Mind-Reading. You tell yourself that the other person should know what you want and how you feel without your having to tell him or her.	You tell your spouse, "You should have known how I was feeling!"
		Fortune-Telling. You tell yourself that the situation is hopeless and that the other person will continue to treat you in a shabby way, no matter what.	You tell yourself that the person you're not getting along with will *never* change.

things you did when you first met and began to date. Pretty soon, your marriage becomes a source of constant stress, frustration, and loneliness, and all the joy and caring you once experienced has disappeared. At this point, separation and divorce begin to seem like highly desirable alternatives.

Therapists who endorse the burnout theory will encourage you

Distortion	Description	Example
6. Magnification and Minimization	You blow the other person's faults way out of proportion and shrink the importance of his or her positive qualities.	During an argument, you may blurt out, "I can't believe how *stupid* you are!"
7. Emotional Reasoning	You reason from how you feel, or assume that your feelings reflect the way things really are.	You *feel* like the other person is a loser and conclude that he really *is* a loser.
8. *Should* Statements	You criticize yourself or other people with *should*s, *shouldn't*s, *ought*s, *must*s, and *have to*s. There are two common patterns:	
	Other-Directed *Should*s. You tell yourself that other people *shouldn't* feel and act the way they do, and that they *should* be the way you expect them to be.	"You've got *no right* to feel that way!" Or, "You shouldn't say that. It's unfair!"
	Self-Directed *Should*s. You tell yourself that you shouldn't have made that mistake or shouldn't feel the way you do.	
9. Labeling	You label the other person as a "jerk" or worse. You see his or her entire essence as negative, with no redeeming features.	"She's such a bitch!" Or, "He's an asshole!"
10. Blame	Instead of pinpointing the cause of a problem, you assign blame. There are two patterns:	
	Other-Blame. You blame the other person and deny your own role in the problem.	You tell your spouse, "It's all your fault!" Then you get angry, frustrated, and resentful.
	Self-Blame. You feel guilty and worthless because you blame yourself for the problem, even if it isn't entirely your fault.	You tell yourself, "It's all my fault!" Then you use all your energy beating up on yourself instead of finding out how the other person is feeling and trying to solve the problem.

and your partner to accentuate the positive. For example, you could schedule more fun, rewarding activities together so you can begin to enjoy each other's company again. You might also do several loving, thoughtful things for each other every day, such as calling your partner from work just to say hello, or bringing your partner a cup of coffee in the morning to show you really care.

Many therapists believe that relationship problems ultimately result from a lack of trust and the fear of vulnerability. Let's say that you're ticked off because of something that a colleague or family member said to you. On the surface, you're angry, but underneath the anger, you feel hurt and put down. You're reluctant to let the other person know that you feel hurt because you're afraid of looking weak or foolish. Instead, you lash out, get defensive, and try to put the other person down. Although the tension escalates, your anger protects you because you don't have to make yourself vulnerable or risk rejection. In other words, the basic deficit is a lack of trust—we fight because of our fears of intimacy. Therapists who endorse this theory will encourage you to accept and share the hurt and tender feelings that are hiding underneath all the anger, hostility, and tension.

Psychoanalytic and psychodynamic therapists believe that all of these interpersonal deficits and problems with loving each other ultimately stem from painful experiences and wounds we endured when we were growing up. The idea is that if you grew up in a dysfunctional family, you may subconsciously re-create the same painful patterns over and over as an adult. For example, if your father constantly criticized you and put you down, you may have felt like you were never quite good enough to earn his love. As an adult, you may be attracted to men who are equally critical of you because you feel like your role in a loving relationship is to be put down by someone who's powerful and judgmental, and you may still be desperately trying to get the love you never got from your father.

When I first began treating people with relationship problems, I believed all of these deficit theories, so I naturally tried to help my patients correct the deficits that were causing their conflicts. I enthusiastically taught troubled couples how to communicate more skillfully, how to solve their problems more systematically, and how to treat each other in a more loving way. I also taught them how to boost their self-esteem and modify the distorted thoughts and self-defeating behavior patterns that triggered all the anger and resentment. Sometimes we analyzed the past to try to trace the origins of these patterns.

I was surprised to discover that none of these techniques worked very well. It wasn't that they weren't ever effective—individuals who learned to listen, shared their feelings more openly, and treated others with greater love and respect often experienced immediate and dramatic improvements in their relationships with other people. But these individuals were few and far between. Most of the people who complained about their relationships with other people didn't actually seem motivated to use any of these techniques. In fact, many of them didn't seem interested in doing anything whatsoever to develop more loving, satisfying relationships with the people they were at odds with. They claimed that they sincerely wanted a more loving and satisfying relationship, but what they really meant was, "I want you to agree that my wife (or husband) is a loser."

These experiences were quite different from my experiences treating people who were suffering from depression and anxiety. They were also plagued by distorted negative thoughts that constantly flowed across their minds, such as, "I'm no good. I'm such a loser. What's wrong with me? I'll *never* get better." When I showed them how to challenge and dispute their self-critical thoughts, the feelings of depression and anxiety disappeared and they were thrilled. But when I tried to help individuals who were angry and having trouble getting along with others, it was a different kettle of fish entirely. They didn't seem interested in changing the way they thought about, communicated with, or treated the person they weren't getting along with. They seemed far more interested in bashing each other's heads in! At first, this came as a shock, and I was confused. Before long, I began to question the so-called deficit theories, and my understanding of the causes of conflict took a sudden turn in an unexpected direction.

"Why Should *I* Have to Change?!"

The following is typical of the cases that began to shift my thinking. Mickey was a forty-five-year-old businessman who was referred to me by a colleague for the treatment of depression. Mickey had been treated with every known antidepressant, but none of them had made a dent in his mood. I took Mickey off his medications, because they obviously weren't working, and used cognitive therapy techniques instead. Within a few weeks, his depression disappeared. I thought that he might be done with therapy, because he seemed to be free of symptoms. To my surprise, Mickey asked if he could keep coming to see me "for growth purposes." I said I'd be happy to continue working with him, but I needed to know what else he wanted help with.

Mickey explained that he was dissatisfied with his marriage and had a long list of complaints about his wife, Margie. He said that he'd lost all respect for her because:

- She wasn't his equal intellectually and never had anything interesting to say.
- She never read anything challenging. Instead, she wasted time reading fashion magazines and trashy newspapers like the *National Enquirer.*
- She wasn't affectionate and was never in the mood for sex.
- She didn't seem to appreciate all his hard work to earn a good living for their family.
- She constantly nagged and criticized him.
- She never seemed happy to see him when he came home from the office.
- She rarely cooked his favorite foods for dinner.
- When she was upset, she got back at him indirectly by buying overpriced jewelry and clothing behind his back. Then he'd get socked with a huge credit card bill at the end of the month.
- They constantly argued about their twin daughters, who were in Year Seven.

Mickey was so annoyed that he'd kept a journal documenting all of Margie's faults for the past fifteen years. Each day, he'd record all the things she'd said or done that had frustrated him. He started bringing the journal to his therapy sessions so he could read lengthy excerpts out loud, giving me blow-by-blow accounts of this or that argument. For example, eleven years earlier, while he and Margie were driving, they'd had an argument about whether to keep the car windows open or use the air-conditioning. While he was reading his account of the argument, Mickey would look up from his journal every now and then and mutter, "Isn't that terrible?" or "Don't I deserve better?" or "Can you believe she'd say something as ridiculous as that?"

During our sessions, Mickey seemed perfectly content just to read from his journal and tell me about all of Margie's shortcomings, but after several weeks of listening, I began to wonder where the therapy was going. What were we trying to accomplish? I pointed out that Mickey had three options:

- If he was unhappy about his marriage, and felt that things were hopeless, he might want to consider a trial separation or even file for divorce.
- If he still loved Margie and wanted to make his marriage better, we could try couples therapy.
- He could maintain the status quo and make sure that nothing changed.

Mickey definitely wasn't interested in the first option. Separation was out of the question. He explained that he felt obligated to live at home until their daughters had graduated from secondary school. He didn't trust Margie's mothering skills and felt that the girls needed to have their father at home until they were safely off to college.

Mickey also rejected the second option. He said that he definitely wasn't interested in marital therapy because he was convinced that Margie could never change. In addition, he didn't see any reason why *he* should have to change, given how poorly she'd treated him over the years.

Mickey seemed committed to the third option—maintaining the status quo. It struck me as odd that someone would complain so bitterly about his marriage and still choose to maintain the status quo. However, this choice is common. In fact, of the three options I described—leaving the relationship, working to make the relationship better, or making sure that nothing changes—the third option is by far the most popular.

I told Mickey that I wanted him to do a thought experiment. I said to imagine that we could wave a magic wand and make all his problems vanish in the blink of an eye. Suddenly, Margie has become the woman of his dreams. She's loving, thoughtful, sexy, and admiring. Every evening when he comes home from work, she greets him with a smile and a kiss, asks about his day, and has a wonderful dinner waiting for him. She's also a super mother and brags about what a great father and husband he is whenever they're out with friends.

One day, a member of the local Mafia approaches Mickey with an unusual business proposal. He tells Mickey that he and his associates will give Mickey $50,000. All he has to do is to turn his wonderful, loving wife into a nagging, whiny, hostile bitch within one month. If Mickey succeeds, they'll give him the money. But if he fails, they'll put out a contract on his life and give the $50,000 to a hit man who will break Mickey's kneecaps and put a bullet through his head.

I told Mickey that between now and our next session, I wanted him to list at least five things he could do during that month to ruin his marriage and save his life. Mickey seemed excited about the assignment and promised to bring his list to the next session.

The following week, Mickey enthusiastically read the list he'd prepared. He explained:

First, I could stop at a bar on the way home from work every night and have several drinks. If I came home drunk and smelling of alcohol, it would really upset Margie. She *hates* alcohol because her father was an alcoholic who got violent and ugly whenever he was drunk. If Margie protested that there was alcohol on my breath, I could just pour myself another drink right in front of her and tell her she was being uptight.

Second, I could have affairs with women when I'm traveling on business trips around the country. I could have a girlfriend in Denver, a girlfriend in Cleveland, and another in Nashville. Then I could come home with lipstick on my collar or leave the stubs of show tickets on the dresser so Margie would discover them and catch on that I was having affairs behind her back. That would devastate her.

Third, Margie feels inferior because she never finished college. When we're out with friends, she always comments on current events and tries to sound intelligent. When she tries to make conversation, I could make sarcastic comments and point out that she gets her information from real scholarly sources like the *National Enquirer*. That would humiliate her in front of our friends.

Fourth, whenever Margie tries to discipline our daughters, I could sabotage her by saying, "Don't listen to your mother. You girls can do whatever you want."

Finally, I could come home late without calling to let her know I was delayed. That would definitely make her feel rejected and upset.

I asked Mickey if he thought these activities would be enough to ruin his marriage and save his life. He replied, "Oh, absolutely! Any *one* of them would be enough. I'm sure of it!"

Then I asked Mickey how many of these things he was already doing. His chest puffed up with pride and he exclaimed, "*All* of them, Doctor!"

So here's a man who's convinced that he's the victim of a bad marriage. He feels sorry for himself and tells himself that he's stuck with a cold, unloving wife, and he's been documenting all the things that she's been doing wrong for the past fifteen years, almost like an attorney preparing a case for court. He blames her for their problems and his own unhappiness. But he's been knowingly treating his wife in a shabby way and intentionally doing things that are certain to demoralize her and ruin their marriage the entire time that he's been complaining about her.

What are we to make of a man like Mickey? It would be easy to put him down, claiming that he's a rare case of stubbornness or ignorance. But far from being an isolated example, Mickey was actually fairly typical of what I was seeing in my office every day. Though many individuals and couples came in complaining of frustration in their relationships with other people, very few of them seemed ready, willing, or able to do anything about it. This resistance to change had nothing to do with gender. Men and women were equally likely to protest and say, "Why should I have to change? It's all his (or her) fault!"

Can Couples Therapy Help?

Research studies began to confirm what I was seeing clinically. Dr. Don Baucom, from the University of North Carolina, is one of the most highly regarded marital therapy researchers in the United States. In fact, he's conducted more couples therapy studies than any other living researcher. Dr. Baucom also reviews the results of all the studies on couples therapy that are published in scientific journals throughout the world and publishes reviews in scholarly journals and textbooks. Every year he comes to the same startling conclusion: there is no truly effective form of marital therapy in the world at this time.*

These findings aren't limited to any particular type of therapy. It makes no difference whether your therapist emphasizes communication training, cognitive therapy, problem-solving training, venting your feelings, exploring the roots of your problems in your childhood experiences, boosting your self-esteem, or scheduling more loving and rewarding activities with your partner. None of these approaches, alone or in combination, seems to be especially effective. In other words, correcting the so-called deficits that seem to cause relationship problems will *not* reliably lead to satisfying, loving relationships.

---

* Epstein, N. B., & Baucom, D. (2002). *Enhanced Cognitive-Behavioral Therapy for Couples: A Contextual Approach*. Washington, DC: American Psychological Association.

That doesn't mean that no one can be helped with these treatment methods. In most studies, roughly 50 percent of the couples report some improvement in the short term, but that's not an impressive success rate. A fair number of them would have improved without treatment, either because of their own efforts or simply because of the passage of time. The long-term results are even less encouraging. Many of the couples who initially report some improvement eventually end up in separation or divorce.

There's definitely something missing—something important. We're just not hitting any home runs when it comes to treating people with troubled relationships. Most marital therapists will privately acknowledge that what I'm saying rings true. They're painfully aware that many troubled couples, as well as angry individuals who can't get along with others, are tremendously resistant to change and almost impossible to treat.

Negative research studies can be unsettling because they indicate that our treatment methods aren't nearly as effective as we'd hoped, and that our theories may not be valid, either. At the same time, negative studies can be exciting because they mean that we've probably been looking for the solutions in the wrong places and overlooking something tremendously important. If we simply listen to what our research studies and clinical experiences are trying to tell us, it can trigger new discoveries and lead to the development of far more effective treatment methods.

When we fight, there's no doubt that we *do* think about the person we're at odds with in a negative, illogical, and self-defeating way, and we *do* get defensive and frustrated and make demands that drive the other person further away. But what if these distorted thinking patterns and dysfunctional behaviors are just the symptoms, and not the true causes, of conflict? After all, people with pneumonia cough like crazy, but coughing doesn't cause pneumonia. And you can't cure pneumonia by telling the patient to stop the coughing. You have to kill the bacteria that have invaded the lungs.

Chapter 2

The Dark Side of Human Nature

Although experts have different theories about the causes of relationship problems, they all seem to agree on one idea: human beings are inherently good. We all have strong needs for intimacy and deep, instinctual yearnings for loving, rewarding relationships with other people. So why, then, do we fight with each other so much? Is it because we lack the skills we need to develop loving relationships? That's what nearly all the experts believe—that we *want* to be close, but just don't know how.

This idea is tremendously appealing because it allows us to think of our aggressive, destructive urges as thwarted desires for love. We're all painfully aware of how much horrific violence and hostility there is in the world today, and how much there's been throughout human history, so it's comforting to think that human beings are inherently good. It's not so much that we *want* to fight and hurt each other; it's just that we don't know a better way.

If this theory were correct, there would be a simple solution to relationship problems. If we just developed healthier attitudes and more effective interpersonal skills, we'd all stop fighting and enjoy greater love and intimacy. But what if the experts are wrong? What if we *aren't* simply inherently good, but have negative, destructive motives as well? And what if these negative motives are just as basic to our nature, and just as powerful, as the positive, loving motives?

If this were true, then our problems getting along with each other might result less from the fact that we don't know how to love each other, and more from the fact that *we don't want to*. Maybe we sometimes *choose* conflict and hostility because they seem far more appealing and desirable than getting close to the person we're at odds with. Is it really possible that we're secretly attracted to conflict and hostility?

A Look at the Dark Side of Human Nature

Let's do some research of our own and check it out. I'm going to tell you about Harry and Brenda, a couple with a troubled marriage. If we can figure out why they're at odds, maybe we can learn something about the causes of troubled relationships in general.

Brenda initially sought treatment with me because she was struggling with chronic feelings of depression and inadequacy. She was an intelligent young woman who completed two years of college after graduating from secondary school. She had a straight-A average and an interest in biology. One of her teachers encouraged her to complete her undergraduate degree and go on to graduate school in veterinary medicine because of her intense love for animals. However, Brenda didn't have a great deal of self-confidence and didn't know if she could cut it at the university level. In addition, she didn't want to ask her parents for any more financial support, so she went to work as a receptionist for a dentist instead.

About that time, Brenda and Harry began dating. Harry had begun working as a carpenter after graduating from secondary school five years earlier. He was ambitious and had started his own construction company. The day he started his company, he proposed to Brenda. She wasn't sure that she was in love with Harry, but told herself that she could learn to love him over time.

Shortly after they were married, Brenda got pregnant and

delivered their first child, a boy they named Jack. Brenda returned to work because they needed both salaries to make ends meet. Two years later, they had a second child, a boy named Zachary. Although Brenda and Harry didn't have the most dynamic or exciting relationship, things were more or less okay for the first five years of their marriage. Then things took a turn for the worse. During an argument about how to discipline their sons, Harry started shouting and called Brenda a stupid bitch, and he threatened that if she didn't shut up, he'd let her have it. Brenda was devastated and humiliated.

The next week it happened again. They started arguing and Harry suddenly launched into a tirade laced with insulting obscenities and told her to shut up. Before long, six more years had passed, and the same thing had been happening almost every week.

Brenda felt depressed, ashamed, and deeply hurt. She thought about leaving Harry but was afraid that she could never make it on her own. She told herself that if she just hung in there, things would eventually get better. She was also concerned about Jack and Zachary, who were now eleven and eight years old. They were both starting to hang out with the wrong crowd, wouldn't study, and were flunking several classes. Whenever Brenda asked them to do their homework or clean up their room, they made insulting comments and refused to do anything she asked.

Harry and Brenda didn't agree on what to do about Jack and Zachary. Harry told Brenda that the boys didn't respect her because she was so insecure. But Harry never supported her efforts to discipline the children. In fact, he always watched and said nothing while they insulted their mother.

Why does Harry berate Brenda? What motivates him? Why does Brenda put up with it? What motivates her? What triggers their fights?

I saw some evidence for most of the deficit theories that we reviewed in chapter 1. Harry and Brenda don't communicate very skillfully, and they don't seem to know how to solve the problems that are plaguing them. Brenda suffers from low self-esteem, and they both grew up in dysfunctional families. Harry and Brenda are definitely experiencing marital burnout out as well. They almost never do anything fun together and rarely treat each other in a kind or loving way. And when Brenda expresses her feelings, Harry insults her or tells her that she shouldn't feel that way, so they both end up feeling frustrated. At this point, we might be tempted to conclude that if we could simply teach them how to communicate more skillfully, schedule more rewarding activities together, and resolve their childhood traumas, they'll stop fighting and start loving each other.

Before we jump to this conclusion, maybe we need to peek behind closed doors so we can examine what actually happens when Harry and Brenda fight. Here's a typical example. It's a Saturday morning, and Brenda is busy in the kitchen, baking a cake for Zachary's birthday party. Harry walks in and enthusiastically explains that his best buddy, Bret, and his wife just bought an older home on the east side of town. They got a nice-sized fixer-upper on a large lot for a really good price. Harry says that he and Brenda should go over and check it out later in the day because there are other homes for sale in the same neighborhood. They've been talking about moving out of their apartment and buying a house for some time, and he seems excited.

Brenda is less than enthusiastic. She interrupts him and points out that anyone familiar with real estate knows that property values on the east side are plummeting because of all the prostitutes and drug dealers who hang out in that area. She says that buying property on the east side is like flushing your money down the toilet, and that anyone with half a brain would know that.

Harry gets flustered and tries again. He suggests that they could at least visit Bret and his wife later in the day and check out the neighborhood. He explains that Bret told him that the police have been cracking down on crime, and the area is a lot nicer than Brenda thinks. In fact, Bret said it was an up-and-coming neighborhood with a tremendous potential for appreciation.

Brenda points out that the politicians have been promising to clean up the east side of town for years, but everyone knows that it's never going to happen. Harry protests, but Brenda shoots him down every time he tries to speak.

Why is Brenda doing this? She feels tired, resentful, and

humiliated because of the way Harry has been treating her for years. Physically, she's no match for Harry, but she's a lot brighter, so she uses her mind as a weapon. This is her way of fighting back. She's not consciously aware that she's putting him down, and she's not intentionally provoking him. It happens automatically.

The longer they argue, the more frustrated Harry gets. The veins on his neck begin to bulge and suddenly he boils over. He starts shouting and tells Brenda to shut up. Suddenly, there's no more arguing. In fact, there's hardly any communication until the next week, when the same thing happens again.

Now how will we understand the problems that plague Harry and Brenda? Although their problems seem devastating, the popular theories about relationship problems might allow us to cast their difficulties in a more positive, optimistic light. For example, we could argue that although Harry treats Brenda shabbily, he does it because of his unsatisfied needs for intimacy. He wants Brenda to listen and admire him, but he simply doesn't have the proper tools to bring this result about. In other words, his aggression might simply be the result of his frustrated desires for love and respect. That's why he treats her in such a mean-spirited manner. He puts her down and threatens her because he just can't think of any other way to get his point across. Brenda uses her intelligence as a weapon, and Harry fights back with threats and obscenities. In other words, underneath all this aggression, they both just want to feel close to each other. And if we give them some communication training, help them develop more positive attitudes, and encourage them to schedule more fun activities together, the hostilities will disappear and they'll enjoy the love and respect that they've always wanted.

Do you buy this analysis? It's certainly an optimistic way of thinking about a difficult situation. Let's look at another scenario before we decide. One Saturday night, Harry invited several of his buddies over for beer and poker. Brenda was relegated to the role of waitress, bringing them crisps and beer while they got more and more drunk. She didn't hear a whole lot of *thank yous*—mainly just demands for more beer. Harry was clearly the ringleader. When

Brenda was in the kitchen, she overheard them complaining about what bitches women are and boasting about how they have to put their wives in their place from time to time, sometimes with a little persuasion from their fists. They were all laughing and seemed to be having a wonderful time.

Now how are we going to think about the problems that Harry and Brenda are experiencing? Is it possible that Harry actually *enjoys* intimidating his wife? Maybe the fighting turns him on and makes him feel like a winner. Maybe his needs for power and control are greater than his desires for intimacy and tenderness. Maybe he *likes* to intimidate Brenda.

These negative rewards may be more desirable to Harry than the rewards of mutual love and respect. His troubled marriage may actually be a great source of excitement and self-esteem. In fact, we're the ones who are labeling his relationship with Brenda as a "problem."

Of course, if you asked Harry about this, he'd deny having any negative motives and insist that he doesn't *really* enjoy humiliating his wife. He'd tell you that he's the victim and that the problems in their marriage are all Brenda's fault. As far as he's concerned, she gets exactly what she deserves. Brenda makes him so mad that he flies off the handle and can't control himself. She provokes him with her complaining, and he just starts shouting before he realizes what's happening.

In fact, that's essentially what Harry did say. After Brenda and I met for several sessions, I asked if she was interested in couples therapy. She said it sounded wonderful but doubted that Harry would be interested. She asked if I'd be willing to call and invite him to join us, because she was afraid of what might happen if she asked him.

Her prediction was accurate. Harry told me that he had no interest in therapy and thought his marriage was fine. He said he didn't really believe in "shrinks," or all that touchy-feely communication training, but realized that his wife had problems and hoped I could fix her. He didn't seem at all concerned about the hostilities in his marriage and he definitely wasn't interested in developing a more loving relationship with his wife. He was perfectly happy to maintain the status quo.

You may be thinking, "But I'm not like Harry." You may see him as a crude guy who's somehow different from the rest of us. That's a comforting way to look at it, because then we won't have to think about any evil or hostile motives that might be hiding inside us. But what if Harry and Brenda aren't really so different? What if there's a little bit of Harry and Brenda in all of us?

Chapter 3

Why We Secretly Love to Hate

Let's do a little thought experiment. Think about one person you don't like or get along with. Picture that person in your mind's eye and try to remember all the things about that person that turn you off. Maybe he was mean to you when you needed some support. Perhaps she was critical, stubborn, or self-centered. Maybe he talked about you behind your back.

Do you have someone in mind? I do, too. I'm thinking about a colleague I don't care for. Now, imagine that you have a magic button on your desk. If you press the button, you'll have a wonderful, close, caring relationship with the person you're thinking about. No effort will be required to bring this change about. Just push the button, and the person you're feeling annoyed with will suddenly become your closest friend. Will you press that button?

When I do this exercise in my Intimacy Workshops, I ask for a show of hands. How many of you are going to press the button? There's a lot of giggling and almost no hands go up.

That's where most of us are at. Sometimes we just don't *want* to get close to the person we're at odds with. I'm no exception to the rule. I don't want to press the button, either. The colleague I'm thinking about has treated me abusively over the years, and I don't see him as particularly trustworthy. A close relationship with him is the last thing in the world I want. What I *really* want is for him to admit how self-centered and dishonest he is. I'm embarrassed to say it, but that would give me some real satisfaction.

The point I'm trying to make is very basic. Sometimes we just don't want to feel close to the people we're not getting along with, and there are many reasons why. Let's examine some of them.

Twelve Motives That Compete with Love

1. **Power and Control.** Power and control top my list. Consider Harry and Brenda. Harry seems more interested in power and control than intimacy. The control is far more important to him than getting close to her. Love isn't at the top of his priority list because he finds aggression and domination so gratifying. Harry is getting *exactly* what he wants out of his marriage.

2. **Revenge.** It's natural to want to get back at someone who has treated us badly, and the urge for revenge can overwhelm any desires for a warm, caring relationship with the person who hurt us. The desire to get even with someone who's wronged us can be almost irresistible. However, we don't usually think of our revenge fantasies as bad because we're convinced that we have the *right* to get back at the other person.

3. **Justice and Fairness.** I recently saw a television report about road rage that featured a man named Neil who got annoyed when he noticed that a car was tailgating him in the fast lane of the motorway. Instead of switching lanes so the other car could speed ahead, Neil slowed down to thirty miles an hour. He was determined to force the car to go around him and show the other driver how wrong he was for tailgating. Instead of going around him, the other driver crept up within a foot of Neil's rear bumper and started honking repeatedly. Neil could see that the driver and his passenger were making obscene gestures.

Neil wasn't about to take any abuse, so he pulled over to the edge of the motorway, hoping to provoke a confrontation. The other driver obligingly pulled over behind him and stopped. Neil watched in his rearview mirror as two menacing young men jumped out of the other car, angrily shouting. Neil wasn't the type of guy who was easily intimidated, and he wasn't about to back down. He stepped out of his car, opened the boot, and removed his crossbow. He smiled, calmly aimed the crossbow, and pulled the trigger. One of the young men fell and bled to death on the hard shoulder of the road when the arrow severed his aorta. Neil reloaded and pulled the trigger again. The other young man ended up a paraplegic when Neil's second arrow severed his spinal cord.

Neil fled the scene but was eventually arrested and convicted of first-degree murder. In a television interview from prison, he proudly declared that he had no remorse whatsoever and that those young men had gotten exactly what they deserved. He viewed himself as a hero and a crusader for justice, and said he'd do it all again if he had the chance.

4. **Narcissism.** Some people are tremendously self-absorbed and preoccupied with their own ambitions. Narcissists have big egos. They feel superior to others and see people as objects to be manipulated for their own purposes. They typically become enraged at the slightest hint of criticism and are far more interested in using people to advance their own agendas than in getting close to them.

   Of course, narcissism isn't always bad. In fact, a little bit of narcissism can be healthy. But sometimes we get so preoccupied with promoting ourselves and pursuing our own goals that our relationships with other people suffer. Narcissism competes intensely with our desires for intimacy and frequently wins the battle.

5. **Pride and Shame.** Intimacy requires humility and the willingness to examine your own failures in your relationships. This can be painful because feelings of shame get in the way, espe-

cially when we care about the person who's criticizing us and we sense that her criticisms are true. We don't want to hear it. So instead of listening and acknowledging the truth in the criticism, we put up a wall and get defensive. We tell ourselves that the other person doesn't know what she is talking about. Of course, this annoys the other person, and she intensifies her attack. What might have been a golden opportunity for intimacy simply becomes an endless battle of egos.

6. **Scapegoating.** Families, religious and ethnic groups, and even nations can get seduced by scapegoating. It can be deeply rewarding to label some person or group as inferior or defective. It makes you feel like you're okay and gives you a crystal clear explanation for the problems that are plaguing you. For example, in a dysfunctional family, a spouse or a child may get labeled as the "bad one." The scapegoated family member gets blamed for all the family's problems. This allows the other family members to feel better about themselves and gives them a convenient excuse for all the tension and unhappiness that everyone is experiencing. Scapegoating is a little like gossip—we don't want to admit that we enjoy it when in fact, we really do.

7. **Truth.** In my workshops, I often say that Truth is the cause of nearly all the suffering in the world today. Of course, this is an exaggeration, but if you think about relationship problems, or even international conflicts, you'll see that a battle over Truth nearly always fuels the hostilities. When you're at odds with someone, there's an overwhelming tendency to tell yourself that you're right and he's wrong. If you look at any troubled couple who are arguing, you'll find that every sentence that comes out of their mouths is some version of, "I'm right and you're wrong, and you'd better admit it!" Of course, the partner feels exactly the same way and says, "No, I'm right and you're wrong. Any idiot can see that!" Around and around they go, endlessly beating up on each other in the name of their Truth.

If you can recall an argument or disagreement you've had with someone you're at odds with, I can show you what I mean. Ask yourself this question: In your opinion, who was right, and who was wrong? The odds are high that you believe that you were right and she was wrong. It seems like we all get hooked by our view of "Truth." In fact, right now you may be thinking, "But I really *was* right, Dr. Burns." Of course you were!

It may seem strange to think of Truth as a major cause of suffering and hostility, because we usually think of Truth as something good. Even the Bible says, "The truth shall make you free." But more often than not, Truth is just a club that we use when we beat each other up.

8. **Blame.** Blame usually walks hand in hand with Truth. It can be extremely tempting to blame other people for the problems in our relationships with them. This mind-set makes you feel self-righteous and morally superior. In addition, it lets you off the hook because you don't have to examine your own role in the problem, and you don't have to feel guilty.

   Sometimes the real problem is not so much that the other person really is to blame, but rather, the fact that you're blaming him. The moment you blame the other person, he'll blame you right back. It's like a game of hot potato—no one wants to get stuck with the potato. Blame is arguably the most toxic and addictive mind-set of all. It competes fiercely with our desires for love.

9. **Self-Pity.** Blame often triggers self-pity because you begin to see yourself as the innocent victim and you view the other person as the bad guy. After all, if it's all his or her fault, you don't have to examine your own role in the problem. You can feel like a martyr or hero and tell yourself that life is unfair and that you've been singled out for punishment. There's a certain emotional rush associated with feeling like a deprived and downtrodden martyr, fighting against impossible odds. Self-pity is painful but addictive.

   When I was doing my research fellowship in psychiatry, I felt snubbed by a more experienced colleague named Roger who

I'd been hoping would mentor me. Roger was an extremely gifted researcher, and I really wanted to study with him. He was world-famous. Unfortunately, Roger was overwhelmed with his own responsibilities, and I had to fend for myself. I felt hurt and disappointed.

One day, a colleague I admired mentioned that there was going to be an important research meeting later in the day and asked if I was planning to attend. I told him that I hadn't been invited, so I wouldn't be there. I didn't know why I hadn't been invited, but I felt resentful and started feeling sorry for myself. I sat alone in my office, puffing on a cigar and wallowing in a puddle of misery.

Later in the afternoon, Roger walked by my office and I immediately felt a surge of annoyance. He looked in and cheerfully announced, "We're going to have a research meeting in a few minutes in room 701. Are you planning to come?" I still felt so mad that I growled that I was busy with my research and didn't have time to attend. I wasn't about to give up the role of victim that easily, even if it meant turning down the chance to do what I wanted to do in the first place!

10. **Anger and Bitterness.** No discussion of the forces that compete with love would be complete without including anger. It isn't wrong to feel angry, and anger isn't always a bad thing. Some anger can be healthy, especially if you use it constructively and channel it in a positive direction. But sometimes anger turns into chronic resentment and hostility and sours your outlook on life. Letting go of anger can be extremely difficult because it gets tied up with our sense of pride, identity, and personal values. Anger can be exhilarating. It can make you feel powerful and alive.

Although troubled relationships are incredibly draining and demoralizing, anger can be energizing. It can provide us with a sense of purpose and meaning. Of all the negative emotions— including depression, hopelessness, anxiety, panic, guilt, and feelings of inferiority—anger is by far the hardest to overcome because it makes us feel powerful and self-righteous.

11. **Competition.** When you're at odds with someone, you may tell yourself that one of you is going to win and the other is going to lose. Obviously, you don't want to be the loser, so you pour all your energy into making sure that you're the winner. Winning is exciting. We all want to be winners. However, the desire to win keeps the battle alive because the other person will be equally determined to defeat you.

A woman named Maureen told me how frustrated she was because her husband, Vic, never did the things she asked him to do. Whenever she bugged him to do something he'd "forgotten," he'd tell her to stop bugging him and being such a control freak. Then she'd insist that she *wasn't* being a control freak but was just asking him to follow through on his commitments. Of course, her denial convinced him that his criticism was absolutely valid, and so the battle raged on.

I asked Maureen if she thought there might be a grain of truth in Vic's comment and whether it might help to acknowledge that so they wouldn't be constantly at each other's throats, arguing about who was "right." Maureen said, "I'd rather *die* than let Vic gloat and feel like he's won."

12. **Hidden Agendas.** You may prefer to keep your partner at a distance because of a hidden agenda. There may be something you want more than love and intimacy, but you're keeping it a secret. For example, if you have a lousy marriage, you may feel that your extramarital affairs are justified. We saw an example of this in chapter 1. If Mickey's marriage improved, he might have to give up the exciting romantic adventures he pursues on his business trips.

A businessman named Nick told me that he felt discouraged about his marriage. Although he was totally devoted to his wife, Marianne, they almost never spent any time together. Nick explained that every time he invited her to do something fun together, Marianne always had other plans.

The week before, Nick's accountant had tipped him off that Marianne was spending an enormous amount on purchases from mail-order catalogs and eBay auctions. Apparently, she was addicted to shopping, and their home was totally cluttered with knickknacks and decorative items that she'd purchased. She'd also purchased more than sixty pairs of designer shoes. I told Nick that it sounded like some couples therapy might help, so he eagerly brought Marianne to his next session.

Marianne agreed that they needed to spend more time together. She said that there were no real problems in their relationship and explained that she'd just gotten overly involved with her own activities, such as her tennis team and a variety of activities at the country club. As a psychotherapy homework assignment, I suggested that they could schedule some time together doing things they both enjoyed, such as hiking or going to a movie. Marianne agreed that this made perfect sense, but when they returned the next week, she apologetically explained that she'd "forgotten" all about their homework assignment. We tried again the next week, with similar results. Marianne said that something had come up at the last minute, so she had to cancel her plans with Nick. We kept trying, but every week Marianne had a new excuse.

I asked Nick and Marianne for permission to videotape one of our sessions so I could show it to my colleagues at our weekly couples therapy conference. I was hoping that their input might help me break the logjam in the therapy. When my colleagues watched the tape, they confirmed my assessment of why the therapy was failing. Marianne didn't really seem to love Nick, but didn't want to admit it. She seemed perfectly happy to remain in the marriage as long as she had access to his bank account and didn't have to spend any time with him. From Nick's perspective, their lack of intimacy was a problem, but from Marianne's perspective, things were exactly the way she wanted them.

If we fight because the battles reward us, then the key to resolving any conflict might ultimately have to start with a personal decision. The first step would be to answer this question: What do I want more—the rewards of the battle, or the rewards of a close, loving relationship?

Chapter 4

Three Ideas That Can Change Your Life

I once treated a fifty-two-year-old woman named Allison who came to me for help with depression. Allison had been in treatment for decades, but nothing had ever helped her. At our very first session, Allison said that she was already feeling a bit better because she'd just read an article titled "Loneliness in Marriage" in a popular women's magazine. The article stated that men and women have trouble communicating because they're inherently different. When boys are growing up, they play with trucks and learn to solve problems and achieve goals. In contrast, when girls are growing up, they play with dolls and learn to talk about their feelings so they can develop emotional bonds with each other. Allison said she was relieved to discover that millions of women throughout America felt just as lonely and frustrated as she did because their husbands couldn't deal with feelings or intimacy.

She explained that her husband, Burt, was exactly like that—he was an accountant and understood numbers, but didn't understand a single thing about emotions. She said that he was a cold fish who couldn't, or wouldn't, express his feelings. In fact, she'd tried to get Burt to open up for more than thirty years, but nothing had ever worked. Now she finally understood why she'd been so depressed and lonely all those years. It was all because of Burt.

I suggested that if Burt had trouble expressing his feelings, some couples therapy might help them learn to share their feelings more openly and develop a more loving relationship. Allison seemed taken aback. She said that it would be a total waste of time because she'd already tried everything and she knew that nothing worked. She said that Burt was a hopeless case who could *never* learn how to express his feelings.

I asked Allison if she'd be willing to give it a try just once in spite of her doubts. I pointed out that even if they decided not to pursue couples therapy, I'd at least have the chance to see what she was up against. Allison reluctantly agreed, and she and Burt came to the next session together. I was curious to see what kind of fellow Burt was, and was surprised when he didn't fit my stereotype of a rigid, obsessive accountant. Instead, he seemed open and friendly. He said that he knew that they'd been having problems for a long time and seemed eager to participate in the therapy.

I told Allison and Burt that good communication requires three things. First, you have to be able to express your feelings openly and directly. Second, you have to be able to listen nondefensively when your partner talks. Third, you have to treat your partner with respect, even if you feel angry or frustrated. This doesn't mean that you have to hide or deny your angry feelings. It simply means that you share them in a respectful way without demeaning or insulting your partner.

Bad communication is just the opposite. Instead of opening up, you hide your feelings or act them out aggressively. Instead of listening to your partner, you argue defensively and insist that he or she is wrong. And instead of conveying caring and respect, you go to war and try to put your partner down. Allison and Burt agreed that these ideas made perfect sense.

I suggested an exercise called the One-Minute Drill so I could diagnose what went wrong when they tried to talk things over. I explained that when you do the One-Minute Drill, one of you is the Talker and the other is the Listener. When you're the Talker, you get 30 seconds to express your feelings. You can say anything you want and get your feelings off your chest.

When you're the Listener, you sit quietly and respectfully and concentrate on what your partner is saying. Look directly into your partner's eyes and convey receptive body language. Avoid frowning, folding your arms, or shaking your head in a judgmental way. When your partner has finished talking, summarize what she or he said as accurately as possible. The goal is not to agree or disagree, but to paraphrase what your partner said and acknowledge how she or he was probably feeling.

Allison wanted to be the Talker first and Burt agreed to be the Listener. Allison launched into an angry diatribe about how frustrated she was because Burt never talked about his feelings. She told him that no matter what she did or how often she tried, he simply wouldn't open up. She said she'd felt lonely and miserable for decades because he was such a cold fish, and that she'd finally given up on him. She said that he was a hopeless case, a kind of emotional cripple, and that he was to blame for her depression and for their horrible marriage as well.

Burt listened attentively while Allison was speaking. When she was done, I asked him to paraphrase what she'd just said with two goals in mind. First, I wanted him to summarize the ideas Allison had just conveyed as accurately as he could. Second, I wanted him to tell Allison how he thought she might be feeling inside, given what she'd just said. Burt turned to his wife and said:

> Allison, you just told me that you feel lonely and frustrated because I've never done a good job of expressing my feelings, in spite of your best efforts to get me to open up. You also feel angry and depressed because I'm such a cold fish. You've tried everything you can think of but nothing has ever worked. As a result, you've decided that I'm a hopeless case and you've given up on me. In fact, you think of me as an emotional cripple. In addition, you feel like I'm entirely to blame for your depression and for the problems in our marriage. I think you must feel tremendously resentful, discouraged, and alone. And you're probably feeling hopeless, too.

I asked Allison how accurate Burt's summary was, between 0 percent and 100 percent. Did he do a good job of listening? Did he accurately summarize what she'd said? Did he acknowledge how she was feeling inside?

Allison seemed surprised and conceded that Burt had done an excellent job. She gave him an accuracy rating of 100 percent. I explained that we'd learned several things so far. First, we'd learned that Allison could express her feelings clearly and openly and didn't pull any punches. Second, we discovered that Burt was a superb listener, because he'd accurately summarized Allison's comments and received a perfect rating. Third, we saw that Burt could treat Allison with respect, because there was no hint of sarcasm or hostility when he summarized her comments.

I explained that it was time for a role reversal so we could find out if Burt could express his feelings, and if Allison could listen. I reminded Allison to listen attentively, using receptive body language, and not to agree or disagree with anything Burt said. Instead, her job was to concentrate on what he was saying and how he was feeling inside so she could accurately summarize his comments when he was done.

Burt explained that he also felt lonely and frustrated, and wished that they were closer. He said that he had many thoughts and feelings that he wanted to share with her. In fact, he'd tried to tell her how he felt every day for many years, but felt that he was stuck between a rock and a hard place. On one hand, she constantly demanded that he open up, but every time he tried to share his feelings, he felt criticized and belittled. He said that this was upsetting and confusing to him and made it hard to open up because he felt that he was getting mixed messages from her. He pointed out that he was trying to share his feelings right at that very moment but was afraid she was going to shoot him down again.

While he was speaking, Allison began to frown. Her eyes darkened and she shook her head back and forth. Suddenly, she stood up, leaned forward, and started shaking her finger at Burt's nose. She shouted, "You've got *no right* saying stupid things like that! That's a lot of lies! You shut up! I won't put up with this crap!" She stormed out of the office and slammed the door.

I was dumbfounded and opened the office door to see what was happening. Allison was sitting in the waiting room with her arms

　　　　　　　　　FEELING GOOD TOGETHER

folded defiantly across her chest. I asked if she wanted to return to the session so we could process what had just happened and how she was feeling, but she flatly refused. Burt and I tried to use the remaining time as best we could, but it felt pretty awkward.

The next week, Allison returned without Burt. She said that the session had been a total waste of time, just as she'd predicted, and that Burt had been completely unable to express his feelings all week long, in spite of my best efforts to help him during our session the previous week. She said this proved what she'd been trying to tell me all along—Burt was a hopeless case. She told me she was willing to keep coming to see me on one condition—that I'd agree never to let Burt participate in another therapy session.

I asked Allison if she thought there might be any connection between her behavior and Burt's difficulties opening up. She snapped and said that if I insisted on pursuing that theme, this would definitely be our *last* session. She warned me that she'd had to fire her three previous therapists because they'd wrongly and foolishly implied that *she* might be contributing to the problems in her marriage.

Allison seemed oblivious to the fact that she was causing the very problem that was bothering her. If she'd tried to design a behavior modification program to make sure that her husband would *never* share his feelings with her, she couldn't have done a better job. She punished him every time he tried to express his feelings, and she'd been doing this to him for decades. The impact of her behavior wasn't exactly subtle.

At the same time, she had no interest whatsoever in examining her role in the problem. She made it clear that this topic was strictly off-limits. Perhaps the pain of self-examination was more than she could endure.

You may feel annoyed with Allison, but don't be too quick to throw stones at her. We all do these kinds of things when we're not getting along with other people, but owning up to it can be very painful. I know that when I'm at odds with someone, I hate to examine my role in the conflict because I feel *certain* that it's the other person's fault. When it finally dawns on me that I was actually provoking the problem, it feels embarrassing and shameful.

Over time, the following fact has become clearer and clearer to me: you can provide people in troubled relationships with all the interpersonal skills in the world, but it won't do them a bit of good if they aren't strongly motivated to develop greater intimacy or get close to the person they're at odds with. In most cases, hostility and conflict probably do *not* result so much from skill deficits, but rather from overpowering motivational factors. The skill deficit theories sound great on paper, but they just don't cut it in the real world.

The Basic Principles of Cognitive Interpersonal Therapy

I've developed a radically different approach that I call cognitive interpersonal therapy (CIT). CIT is based on three simple but powerful ideas:

1. We all provoke and maintain the exact relationship problems that we complain about. However, we don't seem to realize that we're doing this, so we feel like victims and tell ourselves that the problem is all the other person's fault.
2. We deny our own role in the conflict because self-examination is so shocking and painful, and because we're secretly rewarded by the problem we're complaining about. We want to do our dirty work in the dark so we can maintain a façade of innocence.

These two principles of CIT may sound pretty negative. The third principle is far more positive:

3. We all have far more power than we think to transform troubled relationships—*if* we're willing to stop blaming the other person and focus instead on changing ourselves. The healing can happen far more quickly than you might think. In fact, you can often reverse years of bitterness and mistrust almost instantly—but you'll have to be willing to work hard and experience some pain along the way if you want to experience this kind of miracle.

I'm going to show you how CIT works by asking you to identify one person you're not getting along with. It can be your spouse or partner, but that's not necessary. It can be anyone at all, such as a friend, neighbor, colleague, or customer. This will be a vitally important part of your learning, and I'd encourage you to begin thinking about who that person might be right now.

As I walk you through the solution, you'll learn about CIT in a very real and practical way. I'll be asking you to do some exercises on paper, and not just in your head. These exercises will lead you to an understanding of the precise cause of the problem, as well as the solution. If you do these exercises, your understanding of CIT will be far deeper and more dynamic than readers who simply read without doing the exercises. I have to warn you, however, that the process will require some work on your part, and it may be painful at times. Of course, our ultimate goal is not pain but joy and intimacy.

In the next chapter, you're going to take the Relationship Satisfaction Test (RSAT). This brief but exceedingly accurate instrument will show you exactly how satisfied—or dissatisfied—you feel about any relationship. It can be someone you care about or someone you're at odds with. You can take the RSAT repeatedly as you read this book to chart your progress.

Then I'm going to ask you some questions about your troubled relationship. Do you want to settle for the status quo, end the relationship, or make it better? If you decide that you want a better relationship, I'm going to ask you who's more to blame for the problem, and who should do most of the changing. Is it you, or the other person? I'm also going to ask if you're willing to pay the price of intimacy. What would it be worth to you if I could show you how to develop a far more rewarding relationship with the person you're at odds with?

Then we'll focus on one upsetting interaction with that person and diagnose precisely what went wrong. You'll suddenly discover exactly why you're fighting and arguing. You'll also understand the cause of all the problems in all your relationships. So although we'll focus on just one brief moment in one troubled relationship, our goals will be fairly lofty.

Finally, I'll show you how to transform that relationship into one of warmth and trust using the Relationship Journal and Five Secrets of Effective Communication. These techniques can lead to a profound change in the way you relate to the people you care about—as well as the ones you don't. You'll learn how to deal with criticism, pouting, and defensiveness, and how to convert hostility into intimacy and trust.

Part Two

Diagnosing Your Relationship

Chapter 5

How Good Is Your Relationship? The Relationship Satisfaction Test

Think about any person you're involved in a relationship with. It could be your spouse, mother, sister, or boss. Anyone at all will do. Now complete the Relationship Satisfaction Test (RSAT) overleaf. The RSAT asks how satisfied or dissatisfied you feel about your relationship in seven different areas. You can complete the RSAT in less than a minute.

Once you've answered all seven questions, add up your score and put the total in the box at the bottom. The total will be between 0 (if you answered "very dissatisfied" in each of the seven relationship areas) and 42 (if you answered "very satisfied" in each area).

The scoring key shows how to interpret your score. Low scores indicate that you're unhappy with the person you rated, and high scores indicate that you're satisfied with your relationship. A score of 39 would mean that you're very satisfied, and a score of 42 would mean that you have a phenomenal relationship.

Lots of my patients have low scores on the RSAT. Scores of 20 or lower are common, and scores of 10 or lower mean that you're probably feeling pretty miserable and unhappy with your relationship. I've seen many people with scores of 0. The good news is that there's plenty of room for improvement.

| Relationship Satisfaction Test (RSAT)

Instructions: Use ticks (✓) to indicate how satisfied or dissatisfied you feel about your relationship. Please answer all the items.	0–Very dissatisfied	1–Moderately dissatisfied	2–Slightly dissatisfied	3–Neutral	4–Slightly satisfied	5–Moderately satisfied	6–Very satisfied
1. Communication and openness		✓					
2. Resolving conflicts and arguments	✓						
3. Degree of affection and caring					✓		
4. Intimacy and closeness				✓			
5. Satisfaction with your role in the relationship			✓				
6. Satisfaction with the other person's role			✓				
7. Overall satisfaction with your relationship					✓		

Date:_____   TOTAL ➜

Copyright © 1989 by David D. Burns, M.D. Revised 2005. Therapists who wish to obtain a license to use the RSAT in their clinical work or research can visit my website at www.feelinggood.com for more information about the *Therapist's Toolkit*.

Scoring Key for the RSAT			
Total Score	Satisfaction Level	Percentage of People with Troubled Relationships Who Are More Satisfied	Percentage of People with Successful Relationships Who Are More Satisfied
0 - 10	Extremely dissatisfied	75%	100%
11 - 20	Very dissatisfied	35%	95%
21 - 25	Moderately dissatisfied	25%	90%
26 - 30	Somewhat dissatisfied	15%	75%
31 - 35	Somewhat satisfied	5%	50%
36 - 40	Moderately to very satisfied	1%	10%
41 - 42	Extremely satisfied	<1%	<1%

You probably want to know how your score compares with other people who've taken the RSAT. For example, if you were thinking about your spouse, is your marital satisfaction level below par, average, or superb? Where do you stand? I've given the RSAT to more than 1,200 people throughout the United States and asked them if they felt their relationship was:

- successful overall.
- troubled but not needing professional help.
- troubled and needing professional help.

When you look at the scoring key, you can see how your relationship compares with people with successful or troubled relationships.

For example, if your score was 5, it means that you're extremely dissatisfied with your marriage. The scoring key tells you that 100 percent of the people with successful relationships scored higher than this. In addition, 75 percent of the people with troubled relationships also scored higher. This means that you're less satisfied than most of them as well. Although low scores are a matter of concern, it doesn't necessarily mean that the outlook for your relationship is grim or that you and your partner are hopelessly mismatched. It simply means that you're extremely unhappy and that your relationship is not meeting your needs.

Now let's assume that your score was 34. This means that you feel somewhat satisfied. The scoring key indicates that only 5 percent of people with troubled relationships score this high. This means that you're doing much better than most of those people. However, the scoring key also shows that 50 percent of the people with successful relationships scored higher than 34. This means that your level of satisfaction is only average in comparison with that group. There's definitely room for improvement, but you probably need only a marital tune-up and not a major overhaul.

The Relationship Satisfaction Test won't tell you who's to blame for the problem. It only shows how satisfied or dissatisfied you feel. It also won't tell you how good or bad your relationship is. There is no such thing as an inherently "good" or "bad" relationship. The quality of any relationship is completely personal and subjective. We all have to judge for ourselves whether our relationships are meeting our needs.

How high should your score on the RSAT be? Some people may feel that an RSAT score of 32 ("somewhat satisfied") is good enough. In contrast, someone with a score of 41 ("extremely satisfied") may feel the desire for greater closeness and intimacy. That's okay, because there are lots of things you can do to make a great relationship even better. It's all a matter of your goals and expectations.

The RSAT is not just a pop psychology quiz. It's been used in studies published in scientific journals and has been validated against the most highly regarded research instruments.* In fact, it's arguably the most accurate relationship satisfaction scale ever developed.

Research studies indicate that the RSAT measures relationship satisfaction with 97 percent accuracy. This means that your total score will be accurate within a range of 3 percent. You may find it hard to believe that something as inherently subjective as intimacy or relationship satisfaction can be measured so accurately. Perhaps that's because we all know how we feel. Other people, including experts, cannot judge the quality of your relationship or the amount of satisfaction or dissatisfaction that you might be feeling at any moment—but most of the time, you know very well how you're feeling.

If the person you rated is someone you're close to, such as your husband, you can ask him to take the same test so you can find out how he feels about the relationship. The information can be unsettling. I recently saw a depressed man named Dale who had a score of 42 on the RSAT. This meant that he thought his marriage was absolutely wonderful. Perfect scores on the RSAT are fairly rare, so I asked Dale how he thought his wife felt about their marriage. He said that she felt exactly the same way, and that they had a tremendous relationship. I asked Dale if he'd be willing to take a copy of the RSAT home so his wife could fill it out. He was happy to do so.

Dale brought her completed RSAT to his session the following week. She'd scored a 0! This is the *worst* score you can possibly have. She was completely dissatisfied in every single category.

I subsequently discovered that she was also quite depressed. This was another big surprise for Dale, because he thought she

---

* For example, see Burns, D. D., Sayers, S. S., & Moras, K. (1994). Intimate relationships and depression: is there a causal connection? *Journal of Consulting and Clinical Psychology*, 62(5), 1033–1042.

was perfectly happy. Armed with this information, Dale decided to invite his wife to participate in the treatment, which proved helpful to both of them.

You may think that the extreme discrepancy between how Dale and his wife felt about their marriage is unusual, but it's not. My research indicates that these emotional disconnections between husbands and wives are common, especially if the relationship is troubled. The more troubled the relationship is, the more extreme the discrepancies tend to be. In the most troubled marriages, there's no significant correlation between how husbands and wives rate their relationship. Their feelings don't match up at all. Sometimes the husband's rating will be much higher, and sometimes the wife's rating will be much higher. This means that they're actually living in different worlds. In contrast, in happy, successful relationships, both partners typically rate the relationship in almost the same way, indicating that they're emotionally connected with each other.

Dale's misperception of how his wife was feeling illustrates a rather mind-boggling phenomenon; namely, that our ideas about how other people feel, including our loved ones, are frequently way off base, but we don't realize this. We'll talk about solutions to this problem a little later in the book when we discuss empathy.

When to Seek Treatment

If you have a low score, I don't want to alarm you but to nudge you. Relationships aren't likely to change through wishful thinking or waiting for your partner to change. Ultimately, the fate of your relationships will be up to you. If you have a strong desire to make a troubled relationship better, I can show you how.

When should you consider going to a therapist for a relationship problem, and when should you try to work things out on your own? Some relationships are so dysfunctional that you should enlist the help of a therapist. Your therapist can provide much-needed support and help you decide whether it makes more sense to try to repair or end a troubled relationship. Professional treatment may be needed if your partner is abusive or violent, engaged in criminal activity, or addicted to drugs or alcohol. Professional treatment may also be needed if:

- You're addicted to drugs or alcohol.
- You feel severely depressed, overwhelmed, or suicidal.
- You're having violent fantasies or urges, or losing control and hurting other people.
- You've tried unsuccessfully to apply the techniques in this book on your own.

Sometimes it's hard to see how you come across to other people, or how well you're doing when you try to change the way you relate to other people. In this case, objective feedback from someone you like and trust can be invaluable.

You can take the RSAT as often as you like to track your progress as you read this book. I recommend taking it once a week. You can photocopy the RSAT on page 258 in Your Intimacy Toolkit. Make sure you leave this page blank so you can make extra copies for your own personal use.* If you evaluate the same person each time you take the test, changes in your scores will show how much progress you're making.

---

* Therapists who wish to obtain a license to use the RSAT in their clinical work or research can visit my website at www.feelinggood.com for more information about the *Therapist's Toolkit*. Numerous assessment and treatment tools are available.

Chapter 6

What Do You REALLY Want?

Think about one person you're not getting along with, and try to picture what happens during a conflict or argument. Perhaps:

- Your husband is relentlessly critical and finds fault with everything you do.
- Your wife clams up and refuses to talk to you when she's upset.
- Your son pouts, slams doors, and insists that he's not mad.
- Your daughter claims you don't love her when you know you really do.
- Your friend whines and complains, but refuses to listen to your advice.
- Your most difficult customer argues whenever you try to make your point.

Three Options for Dealing with a Troubled Relationship

These interactions can be incredibly frustrating. When you're at odds with someone, you have three choices: you can maintain the status quo, you can end the relationship, or you can work to make the relationship better. Which option appeals to you the most? Before I can work with you, I need to know how you're going to answer this question. Think about it for a moment before you continue reading.

1. Maintaining the Status Quo

Believe it or not, the first option—maintaining the status quo—is the most popular. Most people with troubled relationships don't seem to be motivated to do anything about the problem. You might choose this option because you feel unsure about what you want, so you're buying a little time. For example, if you have a troubled marriage, getting divorced might seem overwhelming, frightening, or shameful, but working on your relationship may not seem very appealing, either. You may feel convinced that your spouse is a hopeless case because you tried to make things better in the past, but nothing worked, or it may seem unfair that you should have to do all the work. You may think that the costs of leaving the relationship would be greater than simply putting up with the situation, and you tell yourself that a bad relationship is better than none at all. So you may decide just to tread water for a while and see what happens.

2. Ending the Relationship

The second option, ending the relationship, is also popular, and there's no rule that says we're obligated to try to get along with everyone. I can think of several people whom I don't particularly like or trust, and I don't have any desire to get close to them. If you said, "David, I can show you how to improve your relationship with so-and-so," I'd tell you that I wasn't interested. Trying to develop close, loving relationships with certain kinds of people can be a drastic mistake. This includes con artists as well as individuals who are violent, reckless, alcoholic, addicted to drugs, hopelessly self-centered, or psychopathic.

3. Making the Relationship Better

If you chose the third option—working to make the relationship better—I'm thrilled because it means that we can work together. But now I have a new question for you: How are you going to make the relationship better? You can:

- Wait for the other person to change.
- Try to change the person you're not getting along with.
- Focus on changing yourself.

Lots of people patiently wait for the other person to change. If you choose this option, you may be in for a long wait. Although we all have the capacity to learn and grow, it can take years for people to become more loving and open, and it may never happen. Waiting for someone to change is essentially the same as choosing to maintain the status quo.

That's why so many people get frustrated and try hard to change the person they're not getting along with. For example, if your husband has trouble opening up and expressing his feelings, you could remind him that men have feelings, too, and point out that communication is an important part of any loving relationship. Or if a colleague constantly criticizes you, you could tactfully point out that she's wrong and explain your own thinking so she'll understand where you're coming from. Or if a depressed friend constantly complains and puts a negative spin on everything, you could encourage him to cheer up and look at the positive side of things. Or if you're fed up because your wife never listens, you could be assertive and tell her that your ideas and feelings are just as important as hers. And if you have a friend who uses you, you could tell him that you're not going to put up with his self-centered behavior any more.

How well do these strategies work? You probably know the answer to that question. When you try to change someone you're not getting along with, he'll nearly always dig in his heels and resist. This is a fact of human nature. You could even say that trying to change someone *forces* him to remain exactly the same. So if you're trying to change the other person, you're also choosing to maintain the status quo.

If you want to develop a more loving or satisfying relationship with anyone, we're going to have to approach the problem from a radically different angle. You're going to have to focus entirely on changing yourself. This requires courage, and it may be painful, but it can lead to some amazing results. Let's find out how hard you're willing to work to achieve intimacy.

Chapter 7

The Price of Intimacy

Think about the person you're not getting along with, and ask yourself this question: In your opinion, who's more to blame for the problems the two of you are having? Who's being a bigger jerk? Is it you or the other person? Answer this question from your heart of hearts before you continue reading. I want to know how you really feel.

If you're like most people, you're convinced that the other person is to blame. When I ask this question at my Intimacy Workshops and ask for a show of hands, 90 percent of the people in the audience say it's the other person's fault.

It's not surprising that so many of us feel this way. There are lots of good reasons to blame the other person for the problems in your relationship. In fact, we can evaluate them with the Blame Cost-Benefit Analysis (CBA) on page 53.

Think about someone you're not getting along with, and list the advantages of blaming that person in the left-hand column of the CBA. For example:

- You can tell yourself that you're being honest, because the other person probably *is* acting like a jerk. "Truth" will be on your side.
- You can look down on the other person.
- You can feel a sense of moral superiority.
- You won't have to feel guilty or examine your own role in the problem.
- You can play the role of victim and feel sorry for yourself.
- You won't have to change.
- You can try to get back at the other person. After all, he or she deserves it.
- You can be angry and resentful—anger is empowering.
- You won't have to feel guilty or ashamed.
- You can gossip about what a loser the other person is and get sympathy from your friends.

I'm sure you can think of a few other advantages as well. List all the advantages of blame you can think of in the left-hand column opposite before you continue reading. I strongly recommend that you do this exercise on paper, and not just in your head. Don't worry about messing up the Blame Cost-Benefit Analysis by writing on it, because I've included fresh blank copies of all the important forms and charts in Your Intimacy Toolkit on page 257.

When you're done, ask yourself if there are any disadvantages of blaming the other person. Is there a downside? For example, if you blame the other person:

- You'll feel frustrated and resentful because nothing will change.
- The other person will feel judged and insist that it's all *your* fault.
- The conflict will be demoralizing and exhausting.
- You won't be able to get close to the other person.
- You won't experience any spiritual or emotional growth.
- People may get tired of your complaining.
- You won't experience any joy or intimacy because you'll be hopelessly enmeshed in the conflict.

Blame Cost-Benefit Analysis	
Advantages of Blaming the Other Person	Disadvantages of Blaming the Other Person

Copyright © 1984 by David D. Burns, M.D.

I'm sure you can add to that list. Please take a minute to list all the disadvantages of blame in the right-hand column on page 53.

Once you've completed your lists of advantages and disadvantages, weigh them against each other on a 100-point scale. Assign the larger number to the list that feels more compelling, and put your ratings in the two circles at the bottom of page 53. For example, if the advantages of blame seem a lot greater than the disadvantages, you could put a 70 in the left-hand circle and a 30 in the right-hand circle. If the advantages and disadvantages of blame feel about the same, you could put a 50 in each circle. And if the disadvantages seem slightly greater, you might put a 45 in the left-hand circle and a 55 in the right-hand circle. The numbers you choose will be entirely up to you.

When you're weighing the advantages of blame against the disadvantages, think about how the lists feel as a whole. You don't need to get terribly obsessive about it. Just review your lists and then ask yourself whether the advantages or disadvantages of blame feel greater. It won't always be a matter of which list is longer. Sometimes one advantage will outweigh many disadvantages, or vice versa. Put two numbers that add up to 100 in the two circles at the bottom of page 53 now.

Were the advantages or disadvantages of blame greater? If the advantages were greater, I'm afraid that I've got some bad news for you—I probably won't be able to help you with this relationship. Blame is too powerful an adversary for me. It's the atom bomb of intimacy. It destroys everything that gets in its way. I'm not aware of any techniques that are powerful enough to help people who blame others for the problems in their relationships. I don't want you to stop reading, but you might do better to focus on a different relationship with someone who's more important to you.

If the advantages and disadvantages were equal, I'd have to say the same thing. Asking the other person to shoulder half the blame may sound perfectly reasonable, and it's definitely the politically correct approach, but it doesn't work very well in the real world. If you want a better relationship, you'll have to focus on your own role in the problem and work entirely on changing yourself. Waiting for the other person to do his or her share will simply keep you stuck.

The Key to a Loving Relationship

Several years ago, I did a series of studies to identify attitudes that lead to happy and unhappy marriages. More than 1,200 individuals participated in the study, including men and women from a variety of educational, ethnic, religious, and socioeconomic backgrounds. Some were receiving therapy, and others were simply people who had attended my lectures and volunteered to help out with the study. Gay and heterosexual couples were included, as were married, separated, and divorced individuals, as well as couples who were living together.

Everyone in the study completed the Relationship Satisfaction Test (RSAT) that you took in chapter 5. Some of the participants took these tests again three months later so I could track changes over time. I was curious to see if I could predict which couples would be feeling more loving and satisfied three months later, and which troubled couples would still be at each other's throats. I also asked about feelings of satisfaction or dissatisfaction with the handling of finances, sex, recreational activities and leisure time, the sharing of duties and household chores, the raising of children, and relationships with friends and relatives so I could get a complete picture of their relationships. In addition, I asked the participants how much love they felt for their partners; how committed they were to their relationships; and how guilty, anxious, trapped, depressed, inferior, frustrated, or angry they felt.

Finally, the participants completed an intimacy inventory. The chart overleaf assesses a variety of attitudes and beliefs about personal relationships and self-esteem. The patterns on the top half of the table—Submissiveness and Demandingness—have to do with how you see your role and your partner's role in your relationship. The patterns on the bottom half of the table— Dependency and Detachment—have to do with how you measure

Beliefs That Trigger Conflict	
Submissiveness	Demandingness
1. **Pleasing Others.** I should always try to please you, even if I make myself miserable in the process.	5. **Entitlement.** You should always treat me in the way I expect. It's your job to make me happy.
2. **Conflict Phobia/Anger Phobia.** People who love each other shouldn't fight. Anger is dangerous.	6. **Justice/Fairness.** If you don't meet my expectations, I have every right to get mad and punish you.
3. **Perceived Narcissism.** You can't tolerate any criticism or disagreement without falling apart.	7. **Truth.** I'm right and you're wrong and you'd better admit it!
4. **Self-Blame.** The problems in our relationship are all my fault.	8. **Other-Blame.** The problems in our relationship are all your fault.

Dependency	Detachment
9. **Love Addiction.** I can't feel happy and fulfilled without your love.	13. **Achievement Addiction.** My self-esteem depends on my achievements, intelligence, or income.
10. **Fear of Rejection.** If you rejected me, it would mean I was worthless. I can't be happy if I'm alone.	14. **Perfectionism.** I must never fail or make a mistake. If I fail, it means I'm worthless.
11. **Approval Addiction.** I need your approval to feel happy and worthwhile.	15. **Perceived Perfectionism.** You won't love or accept me as a flawed and vulnerable human being.
12. **Mind Reading.** If you really love me, you'll know what I need and how I feel without me always having to explain myself.	16. **Disclosure Phobia.** I can't tell you how I really feel inside. I have to keep my true self hidden.

Copyright © 2008 by David D. Burns, M.D.

your self-esteem. Many people base their self-esteem on love and approval, whereas other people are more perfectionist and focused on achievement.

Each self-defeating belief, such as Other-Blame, was represented by several statements, such as "My partner is to blame for most of the problems in our relationship." Participants indicated how strongly they agreed with each statement, with response options ranging from "not at all" (scored 0), "slightly" (scored 1), "moderately" (scored 2), "a lot" (scored 3), or "completely" (scored 4). This allowed us to develop a unique profile of beliefs for each person in the study.

FEELING GOOD TOGETHER

When I analyzed the data from the study, I was interested in the answers to these kinds of questions:

- What are the keys to a successful marriage? Do certain attitudes lead to loving, rewarding relationships?
- What causes troubled relationships? Do certain attitudes lead to conflict and misery?
- How important are demographic variables, such as gender, age, ethnicity, marital status, length of the relationship, religious affiliation, education, number of children, and socioeconomic status?
- Whose attitudes and feelings will have a bigger impact on your relationship, your own or your partner's?
- Are certain combinations of husband and wife attitudes especially toxic? Which combinations lead to loving, satisfying relationships?

My colleagues and I made a variety of predictions before we analyzed the data. For example, what will happen if an extremely demanding husband is paired with a very submissive wife? They might get along reasonably well because their roles will be complementary and clearly defined. However, it's also possible that the demanding husband will be happy and satisfied—because his submissive wife is constantly catering to his every whim—while she feels frustrated and unhappy because of the "give-get imbalance" in their relationship. In other words, she keeps giving, giving, giving, and he keeps taking, taking, taking. Before long, she ends up feeling used, bitter, and burned out.

But what would happen if the roles were reversed, so that an extremely demanding wife was married to a submissive husband? And what would happen if two demanding individuals were paired? I predicted that this combination would be associated with intense feelings of anger and low relationship satisfaction scores because both partners would feel that the other one wasn't living up to expectations or behaving as he or she "should" behave. In contrast, I predicted that two partners with high scores on the Conflict Phobia/Anger Phobia scale might report low levels of anger—because they'd almost always avoid fights or arguments—but they might also report low levels of intimacy because they'd have fears of opening up and talking about the problems in their relationship.

Because there were so many potentially important pairings of husband-wife attitudes, a colleague and I programmed the main-frame computer at the University of Pennsylvania medical school to evaluate every conceivable combination. The computer gener-ated and tested several thousand theories per second, based on patterns in our data.

What were the results? First, we examined the demographic variables. As it turned out, it makes little difference whether you're old or young, male or female, rich or poor. Education and religious affiliation were also unimportant. These variables ap-peared to have little or no impact on how happy or depressed the participants were, or how satisfying or conflicted their relation-ships were. The presence or number of children and the length of the relationship didn't seem very important either.

Some results were completely unexpected and hard to believe at first. None of our predictions about the pairings of husbands' and wives' attitudes appeared to be valid. There weren't any combina-tions that had anything whatsoever to do with the success or failure of any of these relationships. Instead, each partner's feelings seemed to depend entirely on their own attitudes, and not their partner's.

Which attitudes were the most important? Other-blame was by far the most important mind-set. People who blamed their part-ners (or people in general) for the problems in their relationships were angry, frustrated, unhappy, and intensely dissatisfied with their relationships. In addition, this mind-set accurately predicted what would happen in the future. Individuals who blamed their partners for the problems in their relationship were even more miserably unhappy three months later. Things were clearly going downhill for this group. In contrast, people who were willing to assume complete personal responsibility for solving the problems in their relationships, and who felt a strong commitment to mak-ing their partners happy, not only reported the most satisfying and loving relationships at the time of initial testing, but their positive feelings seemed to increase over time.

At first, I was disappointed by these results. The findings just seemed too simple. I had been convinced that certain patterns of interactions between husbands and wives would account for whether their relationships were successful or troubled. However, the study clearly indicated that this notion wasn't valid. The only thing that really seems to matter is this: Do you blame your partner for the problems in your relationship? If so, you may be in for a tough time. However, if you're willing to examine your own role in the problem and you feel that it's your job to make your partner happy, the prognosis for a rewarding, successful relationship is extremely positive—now *and* in the future. These appear to be the real keys to success in any relationship. It makes no difference whether the other person is your spouse, a family member, a neighbor, a friend, or even a complete stranger.

Although I was initially skeptical about the results of the study, my clinical work soon convinced me that the findings were valid. I noticed that individuals who complained and blamed others for the problems in their relationships never seemed to get better. They just kept arguing and fighting with other people, no matter what therapy techniques I tried. In contrast, individuals who focused on changing themselves, rather than blaming or trying to change the person they were at odds with, were usually able to work wonders in their relationships. In most cases, it didn't take long at all.

Is Self-Blame the Answer?

A word of warning is in order. When you stop blaming other people, you may think you're supposed to start blaming yourself. Be careful. Self-blame can trigger depression. It won't help you solve relationship problems any more than blaming the other person will.

I once treated a woman named Hilda who was concerned because her relationship with her husband, Charles, seemed distant and lacked any passion or intimacy. She explained that most of their conversations were superficial. In fact, it sometimes felt like they were just roommates who coexisted and barely knew each other.

I suggested that some couples therapy might help them share their feelings more openly. This made sense to Hilda, and Charles was eager to join us as well. I quickly noticed an alarming pattern during their sessions. Whenever Charles said anything even slightly negative or critical, Hilda began sobbing uncontrollably. Between tears, she'd blurt out that she was a failure as a wife and that everything was her fault. She said that Charles would be better off if she just committed suicide and got it over with. Of course, Hilda's statement was extremely disturbing to Charles, who immediately shut up, apologized, and awkwardly tried to reassure her.

Hilda looked helpless and inadequate, but she was actually controlling her husband in a powerful way. Her self-blame was her not-so-subtle way of keeping Charles in a straitjacket. She was really saying, "I can't bear to hear what you're telling me. Don't say anything critical or I'll make you pay!" She was so fragile that I had to discontinue the couples therapy so I could work with her individually.

Hilda's self-blaming tendencies were a huge barrier to intimacy. She simply couldn't endure the pain of getting close to the man she loved because she didn't know how to love and accept herself.

Fortunately, the story had a happy ending. I showed Hilda how to talk back to her relentless self-criticisms, and she soon broke out of her depression and developed a much stronger sense of self-esteem. Then we were able to resume the couples therapy with far more positive results.

Self-blame is not the antidote to blaming your partner. As you can see in the table on page 62, self-blame triggers guilt, anxiety, depression, and giving up. It won't lead to love or to meaningful solutions to the problems in your relationships with other people. Personal responsibility, without any blame at all, is the mind-set that leads to intimacy.

Lots of people have trouble distinguishing self-blame, other-blame, and personal responsibility, even though they're worlds apart. A colleague named Christina told me that she'd been treating a severely depressed man named Manuel who'd been struggling with chronic pain and drug addiction. He was also diagnosed with borderline personality disorder. Patients with this diagnosis can be very challenging and are sometimes difficult to treat.

One day, during a staff meeting, a psychiatric colleague said, "Your treatment of Manuel is worthless. He hasn't improved one iota the entire time you've been treating him. All he does is try to manipulate the staff to try to get prescriptions for tranquilizers and narcotics, and he's just faking most of his symptoms so he can get on disability."

Christina was devastated but said nothing. There was a long, awkward silence. She left the meeting feeling demoralized and resentful. She avoided her colleague but couldn't stop obsessing about his comment, oscillating back and forth between self-blame and other-blame. When she was in self-blaming mode, she told herself, "I'm totally inadequate. I'm a failure as a therapist. What if I get fired?" These thoughts made her feel worthless, guilty, and anxious. Then she'd suddenly switch to the opposite extreme and blame her colleague, telling herself, "He's an asshole. He doesn't know what he was talking about." These thoughts made her feel resentful and bitter.

Self-blame and other-blame aren't very productive. Self-blame paralyzes you, demoralizes you, and defeats you, and other-blame leads to a never-ending battle with the person you're at odds with. In both cases, your negative thoughts will be flooded with all the cognitive distortions we discussed in chapter 1. The only difference is that when you blame yourself, the distortions will be directed against yourself instead of someone else.

I asked Christina if she could spot any distortions in her thoughts of "I'm inadequate" and "I'll probably get fired." She was surprised to see that she was involved in All-or-Nothing Thinking, Overgeneralization, Mental Filtering, Discounting the Positive, Magnification, Emotional Reasoning, hidden Should Statements, Labeling, and Self-Blame (see the list of distortions on pages 6–7). And when she told herself that she was on the verge of getting fired,

Self-Blame vs. Other-Blame vs. Personal Responsibility		
	Self-Blame	Other-Blame	Personal Responsibility
What you tell yourself	Your mind is flooded with distorted thoughts about yourself, such as, "I'm no good. It's all *my* fault. Things are hopeless."	Your mind is flooded with distorted thoughts about the other person, such as, "He's such an asshole. It's all *his* fault. He's got *no right* to feel that way."	Your thoughts are objective and non-judgmental. You try to pinpoint any specific errors you made so you can learn from the situation and take steps to resolve the conflict.
How you feel	You feel guilty, ashamed, inferior, anxious, or hopeless.	You feel angry, resentful, irritated, frustrated, or hurt.	You have a sense of self-respect and curiosity that's mixed with healthy sadness, concern, or remorse (if indicated).
How you communicate	You withdraw because your self-esteem is on the line and you can't stand to hear anything critical.	You argue defensively, insisting that the other person is wrong.	You listen and try to find the truth in the other person's criticism. You share your feelings, but tactfully, and you convey respect.
What you do	You give up and avoid the other person.	You put up a wall and do battle, trying to "win" or get back at the other person.	You actively engage the other person so you can both develop greater understanding.
Your body language	You look demoralized, defective, discouraged, and defeated.	You look hurt, defiant, adversarial, sarcastic, or judgmental.	You appear open, receptive, interested, respectful, and caring.
The result	Isolation, depression, and loneliness	Endless fighting, blaming, bitterness, and arguing	Greater intimacy, trust, and satisfaction

she was involved in Fortune-Telling. She realized that her thoughts about her colleague contained the same kinds of distortions.

I asked Christina if she could challenge her negative thoughts. For example, was there any evidence that she was inadequate as a therapist or on the verge of getting fired, aside from the criticism about her treatment with Manuel? She admitted that in the eight years that she'd been working at the hospital, this was the only time she'd ever received any criticism about her work, and that her evaluations from patients and colleagues had been stellar.

I also asked her if it was terribly unusual to get stuck with some patients, and she said all the therapists on their team struggle with especially difficult patients. I asked her how strongly she now believed that she was inadequate and on the verge of getting fired. She said that her negative thoughts didn't seem to make sense, and no longer seemed credible.

To make sure she really grasped this, I told her that I'd play the role of the negative voice in her mind, and I'd try to make her feel anxious, inadequate, and bitter, and she could play the more objective, positive, self-loving voice. I call this technique the Externalization of Voices. It's one of the most powerful techniques ever developed for changing negative thinking patterns at the gut level. Here's how our dialogue went:

David (as Christina's negative internal voice): You know, Christina, I'm that voice in your brain that makes you feel miserable, and I just want to remind you that your treatment of Manuel has been totally ineffective and worthless. In fact, you've wasted the past six months. This shows that you're an inadequate therapist.

Christina (as Christina's positive internal voice): That's ridiculous. I am stuck with Manuel, but I have lots of other patients I've helped.

David: Yes, but your colleagues heard the criticism that your treatment of Manuel was worthless, so the word will spread that you're no good and you'll get fired.

Christina: That's also ridiculous. I've done great work at the hospital. My evaluations have been outstanding for the past eight years. And all my colleagues get stuck with some of their patients, too. But if I did get fired, which seems extremely unlikely, it might be a blessing in disguise—I could make twice as much in private practice!

David: Well, that could be, but you've got every right to feel enraged with the psychiatrist who criticized you. He's a total asshole and he *never* should have said that.

Christina: I wish that he'd expressed himself a little more tactfully, but he was basically right. I *have* been stuck with Manuel. He's very manipulative and he's not getting better. He seems to be more interested in getting prescriptions for narcotics and tran-quilizers, and getting on disability, than getting well. Perhaps I should see if my colleague has any helpful suggestions on what I could do differently.

Christina felt immediate relief. In fact, we both started giggling during the role-playing because she was blowing me out of the water. She said that her feelings of guilt, anxiety, depression, and resentment disappeared almost completely. Then we discussed how she might approach her colleague in a way that would lead to collaboration and respect, rather than hostility and mistrust. We practiced again, using role-playing.

The next day, Christina approached her colleague and said,

I've been thinking about your comment that my treatment of Manuel was worthless. At first, I was upset when you said that because your criticism seemed harsh. In fact, to be hon-est, I felt defensive and hurt. But then I got to thinking about what you said and realized that you were absolutely right. I've been stuck. Manuel is very manipulative and he hasn't made a bit of progress. I've also questioned his motivation. Would you be willing to share your ideas about how I might work with him more effectively? I think we're actually on the same page, and I think I need some help.

Christina said that her colleague was touched by this comment. He admitted that he'd been feeling stuck, too, and didn't have any good ideas about how to treat Manuel. He apologized for his sharp tone of voice and said that he'd always admired Christina. Christina told me that at the end of their conversation, she felt like she'd found a new friend and ally. Several weeks later, they decided to co-lead a weekly therapy group that became one of the most successful programs at their clinic.

Chapter 8

The Relationship Journal

S everal years ago, I conducted an Intimacy Workshop for the general public. The workshop was sponsored by a local hospital as part of its public outreach program. At the start of the workshop, I encouraged the people in the audience to think of one person they couldn't get along with so we could diagnose the cause of the problem and talk about how to develop more loving and satisfying relationships. Then I asked if some of the participants would like to tell us about the problem they were thinking about. A woman named Hannah enthusiastically raised her hand. She said that the difficult person in her life was her husband, Hal. She said that he constantly criticized her, and she asked, "Why are men like that?"

I told Hannah that there were lots of theories about the causes of relationship problems, but researchers don't really know why people have so much trouble getting along with each other (or why men are the way they are!). However, if she'd be willing to describe one specific interaction she'd had with Hal, we might be able to diagnose the problem. All I needed was one thing that Hal had said to her, and exactly what she said next. Could she think of one thing that Hal had said to her that was hurtful or upsetting?

Hannah said she had plenty of examples. In fact, earlier that day, Hal had said, "You never listen!" She said he'd been saying that to her for the past thirty-five years. I asked how she felt when he said that she never listened. She said she felt hurt, resentful, lonely, discouraged, and put down.

I asked Hannah what she said to Hal next. She replied, "Oh, I just ignored him." There was a lot of laughter from the people in the audience, because they could see something obvious that Hannah could not see.

Do you remember the first principle of cognitive interpersonal therapy? We cause the exact relationship problems we complain about, but we don't realize we're doing it, so we feel like victims and tell ourselves it's all the other person's fault. Hannah's conflict with Hal is a perfect example of this idea. She ignores him and then wonders why he always criticizes her and claims that she never listens.

Hannah's conflict also illustrates something amazing: when you're having trouble getting along with someone, the entire conflict will nearly always be embedded in any one brief exchange between the two of you. When you understand why the two of you were butting heads at that moment, you'll understand the cause of *all* the problems in your relationship with that person. In fact, you'll probably discover the cause of all the problems in all of your other relationships as well. In addition, when you learn how to resolve the problem you were having at that moment, you'll know how to resolve most, if not all, of the problems in your relationship with that person—or with anybody, for that matter.

Let's Get Specific

Although that might seem hard to believe, you'll see what I mean when we examine a specific interaction you've had with someone you aren't getting along with on a form called the Relationship Journal. Take a look at the Relationship Journal on page 68 now. As you can see, there are five steps. When you do Steps 1 and 2, you'll write down one thing the other person said to you and exactly what you said next. Make sure you choose an interaction that didn't go very well. This will be our raw data. When you do Steps 3 and 4, you'll examine that interaction and analyze what went wrong. This will help you develop a crystal-clear understanding of the cause of the conflict, and you'll understand exactly why you and that person aren't getting along very well. The information you can gain can be surprising—and upsetting. When we do Step 5, I'll show you how to turn the problem around.

Here's how the first two steps of Hannah's Relationship Journal looked.

Step 1. S/he said.

Write down *exactly* what the other person said to you. Be brief:

Hal said, "You never listen!"

Step 2. I said.

Write down *exactly* what you said next. Be brief:

I just said nothing and ignored him.

Now I want you to do Steps 1 and 2. Think of a specific interaction you've had with someone you're not getting along with, and visualize what happened during the conflict. Maybe your son lashed out at you when you were trying to set some limits and lay down the law. Perhaps your depressed friend said that you just don't understand when you were trying your best to help. Maybe a colleague got defensive when you tried to explain that he was wrong, or your spouse pushed you away when you were trying to get close. Perhaps your girlfriend said that she needed more space when you were trying to tell her how much you loved her.

When you do Step 1, all you have to do is write down one thing that the other person said to you. Make it brief—one or two sentences will be enough. Don't put a description of the other person's behavior, such as, "My husband, Ron, always criticizes me" or, "My friend Diane constantly complains about everything." Instead, simply write down exactly what Ron said when he was being critical or what Diane said when she was complaining. If you're drawing a blank and can't remember what the other person

Step 1. S/he said. Write down *exactly* what the other person said to you. Be brief:

But what was stevens reason
for telling you.

Step 2. I said. Write down *exactly* what you said next. Be brief:

What has that got to do with
it. You betrayed me. You hurt me.

Step 3. Good Communication vs. Bad Communication. Was your response an example of good communication or bad communication? Why? Use the EAR Checklist or the list of Common Communication Errors on page 73 to analyze what you wrote down in Step 2.

Bad, no empathy, dismissed comment.
No assertiveness - You You You
No respect - what has that
got to do with it.

Step 4. Consequences. Did your response in Step 2 make the problem better or worse? Why?

No, worse because lisa was being defensive
because I believe she is lying. My comments
angered her. Upset her. I completely
dismissed what she said.

Step 5. Revised Response. Revise what you wrote down in Step 2, using the Five Secrets of Effective Communication (see page 98): Remember to note which techniques you're using in parentheses after each sentence you write down. If your Revised Response is still ineffective, try again.

Copyright © 1991 by David D. Burns, M.D. Revised 2007.

said, just write down the type of thing that she or he typically says when you're not getting along with each other.

Now write down exactly what you said next. This is Step 2. If your boss criticized you for missing a deadline, don't put, "I tried to explain why I was behind schedule." This is a description of what happened. Instead, write down what you actually said to your boss.

Doing this exercise on paper is vitally important. Doing it in your head won't work. Please complete Steps 1 and 2 now, before you continue reading.

Before we continue, I have a question for you. In the last few chapters, I've asked you to do several written exercises. Have you actually done them? Or are you just reading along? You might skip over the written exercises because you think the person you're not getting along with is too stubborn to change, or because you're not convinced that what I'm offering has real value. Or you may not be used to doing written exercises when you read a book.

I can't blame you for not doing the written exercises. However, I can say this with confidence: if you don't do them, your chances of learning these techniques will be very low. Mastering these skills in real time when you're feeling upset will have to be an active process, much like learning to swim, play tennis, or ride a bicycle. Simply reading about these methods won't get the job done.

If you haven't already done so, I'd like you to stop and complete the first two steps of the Relationship Journal now. It will take only a minute, and it will make all the difference in the world when you read the next few chapters. You're about to learn some things that may be disturbing, but you're also taking the first steps toward greater intimacy and understanding.

Chapter 9

Good Communication vs.
Bad Communication

Throughout history, mystics and philosophers have told us to look within ourselves if we want to find the answers to life's deepest questions. That sounds intriguing, but how do you look within? Socrates said that the unexamined life is not worth living. How do you examine your life? Do you close your eyes and meditate? Do you lie on an analyst's couch and free-associate? And what are we supposed to discover that's so exciting and important? Is it some form of enlightenment? And will the answers we've been searching for *really* make our lives better?

When I began working with people with troubled relationships, I began to see what the mystics and philosophers might have meant. You *can* discover something inside that feels a lot like enlightenment. In the next two chapters, I'm going to show you exactly how to develop this kind of understanding in a clear, step-by-step way that won't seem like a lot of mumbo-jumbo. If you follow the steps I describe, you can achieve a fantastic and unique understanding of yourself and other people. But I have to warn you: enlightenment can be painful.

If you've read this far, you're probably willing to consider a new approach in which you stop blaming the other person and focus instead on your own role in the problem. But how do you do this? I'll assume that you've completed Steps 1 and 2 of the Relationship Journal on page 68. In Steps 3 and 4, we're going to diagnose why you and the other person aren't getting along. However, we'll focus exclusively on the errors you're making, and not on the errors the other person is making, even though she or he is undoubtedly making lots of them.

When you do Step 3, you examine what you said to the other person (i.e., what you wrote down in Step 2) and ask yourself whether your response was an example of good communication or bad communication. In order to do this, we'll have to define good communication and bad communication. What do these terms mean?

Essential Ingredients of Good Communication

Good communication involves three components: skillful listening (Empathy), effective self-expression (Assertiveness), and caring (Respect). The acronym, EAR, will help you remember these three components: E = Empathy, A = Assertiveness, and R = Respect. Bad communication is just the opposite. You don't listen, you don't express your feelings openly, and you don't convey any caring or respect.

Empathy is the first characteristic of good communication. Empathy means that you listen and try to see the world through the other person's eyes. You find some truth in what the other person is saying, even if his criticism of you seems unfair or his point of view is very different from yours. You also acknowledge how he's thinking and what he's probably feeling, given what he just said to you.

Most people don't do a very good job of listening. When they're upset, they don't acknowledge how the other person is thinking and feeling or try to find any truth in what the other person said. Instead, they defend themselves and insist that the other person is wrong.

Assertiveness is the second characteristic of good communication. You express your feelings openly and directly, using "I Feel" Statements, such as "I'm feeling a bit uncomfortable right now" or "I'm feeling sad." In addition, you share your feelings tactfully so the other person won't feel belittled, attacked, or put down.

In contrast, in bad communication, you hide your negative feelings or act them out aggressively instead of sharing them openly. For example, you might resort to name calling or lash out at the other person by saying, "You're a jerk. Go screw yourself!" Although this statement expresses anger, it does not qualify as an "I Feel" Statement because it sounds hostile. It's classified as a "You" Statement because you're putting up a wall and attacking the other person. "You" Statements trigger more conflict and fighting.

Respect is the third characteristic of good communication. You treat the other person with an attitude of kindness, caring, and respect, even though you may feel frustrated and annoyed. In contrast, in bad communication, you treat the other person in an adversarial, condescending, or competitive way, as if she were an enemy that you want to defeat or humiliate. Your goal is to put the other person down rather than to get close.

The three characteristics of good and bad communication are highlighted on the EAR Checklist on page 73. You'll also find a list of Common Communication Errors. I photocopy these lists on the back of the Relationship Journal. That makes it easy to pinpoint the communication errors in the statement you recorded for Step 2. You can just turn your Relationship Journal over and take a look at the two lists. You'll find a blank copy on page 261.

Let's do Step 3 now. We'll start with Hannah and Hal, the couple you read about in the last chapter. When Hal told Hannah that she never listened, she ignored him and said nothing. Take a look at the EAR Checklist and ask yourself whether her response was an example of good communication or bad communication.

The answer is pretty obvious. Did Hannah empathize with Hal? Although we don't know exactly how Hal was feeling, we can make an educated guess. When Hal said, "You never listen," he was probably feeling ignored, frustrated, angry, lonely, and shut out. Hannah didn't acknowledge any of his feelings or try to find any truth in what he said.

The EAR Checklist

Instructions: Review what you wrote down in Step 2 of the Relationship Journal. Use ticks to indicate whether it was an example of good communication or bad communication.

👂	Good Communication	✔	Bad Communication	✔
E = Empathy	1. You acknowledge the other person's feelings and find some truth in what he or she is saying.		1. You don't acknowledge the other person's feelings or find any truth in what he or she is trying to say.	
A = Assertiveness	2. You express your feelings openly, directly, and tactfully, using "I Feel" Statements.		2. You argue defensively or attack the other person.	
R = Respect	3. You convey caring and respect, even if you're feeling frustrated or annoyed with the other person.		3. You belittle the other person or treat him or her in a cold, competitive, or condescending way.	

Copyright © 2008 by David D. Burns, M.D.

Common Communication Errors

Instructions: Review what you wrote down in Step 2 of the Relationship Journal. How many of the following communication errors can you spot?

1. **Truth.** You insist that you're right and the other person is wrong.	10. **Diversion.** You change the subject or list past grievances.
2. **Blame.** You imply that the problem is all the other person's fault.	11. **Self-Blame.** You act as if you're awful and terrible to prevent the other person from criticizing you.
3. **Defensiveness.** You argue and refuse to admit any flaw or shortcoming.	12. **Hopelessness.** You claim that you've tried everything but nothing works.
4. **Martyrdom.** You claim that you're the innocent victim of the other person's tyranny.	13. **Demandingness.** You complain that the other person "should" be the way you expect him or her to be.
5. **Put-Down.** You use harsh or hurtful language and try to make the other person feel inferior or ashamed.	14. **Denial.** You deny your role in the problem or insist that you don't feel upset when you really do.
6. **Labeling.** You call the other person a "jerk," a "loser," or worse.	15. **Helping.** Instead of listening, you give advice or "help."
7. **Sarcasm.** Your attitude, words, and tone of voice are belittling or patronizing.	16. **Problem Solving.** You ignore the other person's feelings and try to solve the problem that's bothering him or her.
8. **Counterattack.** You respond to criticism with criticism.	17. **Passive Aggression.** You say nothing, pout, or slam doors.
9. **Scapegoating.** You imply that the other person is defective or inadequate.	18. **Mind Reading.** You expect the other person to know how you feel without having to tell him or her.

Copyright © 2008 by David D. Burns, M.D.

Was Hannah being assertive? Did she share her feelings openly? Not really. She told me that when Hal criticized her, she felt sad, hurt, criticized, resentful, lonely, frustrated, discouraged, and put down, but she said nothing to him, essentially keeping her feelings hidden.

You might argue that she expressed her feelings indirectly when she ignored Hal, and her body language probably spoke volumes. Her arms may have been folded across her chest and she probably had a huffy, indignant expression on her face. She might have sighed and rolled her eyes toward the ceiling. But this is not the same as sharing your feelings openly. Hannah acted out her feelings in a passive-aggressive manner. She froze Hal out and gave him the silent treatment. This approach certainly didn't convey any caring or respect. In fact, she acted like Hal didn't even exist. Her silence conveyed the message, "You're not even worthy of a response." So Hannah scores zero for three on the EAR Checklist.

When Hannah came to my Intimacy Workshop, she was convinced that everything was Hal's fault and wanted to find out why he was so critical of her. Now that we've turned the spotlight on her, we can see that she's made some serious communication errors.

The discovery that you've been screwing up big-time can be painful, especially if you were convinced that the other person was to blame. If you want to get close to someone you've been at odds with, you're going to have to examine your own role in the conflict, and that may be uncomfortable for you, too. If you're willing to endure the uncomfortable process of self-examination, you'll be on the path to interpersonal enlightenment and personal empowerment. After all, you can't change other people—their thoughts, feelings, and actions are beyond your control—but you can learn to change yourself.

Turning the Spotlight on Yourself

When you do Step 3 of the Relationship Journal and examine how you responded to the other person, you'll need to turn a critical eye on yourself. It may be hard to spot your missteps, especially at first, but the list of Common Communication Errors on page 73 will help you identify where you went wrong.

Let's practice using this list. A woman named Nan told me that she was upset about her relationship with her daughter, Jill. Jill had recently gotten married, and Nan said that she and Jill seemed to be drifting apart. Every time they spoke, there was tension in the air.

I asked Nan for a specific example of the problem. What was one thing Jill had said to her, and what did she say next? Earlier in the week, Jill had said, "You're putting my husband down." Nan felt hurt, defensive, frustrated, and embarrassed when she heard this, so she replied, "I feel like I'm working hard to have a good relationship with him." On the surface of it, that response doesn't sound too bad, but it flopped big-time. Nan told me that the tension in the air was palpable.

Review the list of Common Communication Errors on page 73 and see if you can pinpoint some of Nan's errors. When you're done, you can continue reading.

Here are some of the errors I spotted:

- **Truth.** Nan implies that she's right and Jill is wrong. She's not acknowledging that her attitude and behavior toward her son-in-law may have seemed negative, critical, or off-putting, or that their relationship may be strained.
- **Blame.** Nan seems to think that the problem is her son-in-law's fault. When she says, "I feel like I'm working hard to have a good relationship with him," it makes it sound like he's extremely hard to get along with.
- **Defensiveness.** Nan isn't admitting her own role in the problem. She's putting up a wall and pushing her daughter away. She might as well have said, "Stop bugging me! I'm doing my best to get along with the jerk you married."
- **Martyrdom.** Nan's statement makes it sound like she's a hero who's fighting the good fight in spite of impossible odds.
- **Put-down.** Nan implies that her son-in-law is the one with the problem.

- **Scapegoating.** She also implies that her son-in-law is a boor.
- **Demandingness.** Nan probably thinks that her son-in-law *shouldn't* be the way he is and *should* be easier to get along with.
- **Denial.** Nan clearly denies her own role in the problem.

If we'd used the EAR Checklist, we would have concluded that Nan didn't empathize. Jill was feeling hurt, annoyed, disappointed, protective, and frustrated, but Nan didn't acknowledge any of these feelings or try to find any truth in what Jill was saying. Nan didn't express her own feelings either. She felt hurt, guilty, and upset, but didn't tell her daughter how she was feeling. And she definitely didn't convey any caring or respect. In fact, Jill probably felt discounted or put down when Nan said, "I feel like I'm working hard to have a good relationship with him." So Nan scores zero for three on the EAR Checklist as well.

You might argue that she did use an "I Feel" Statement when she said, "I feel like I'm working hard to have a good relationship with him," but this is not a description of her feelings. It was just a subtle way of telling Jill that she was wrong. In fact, Nan was feeling hurt, embarrassed, put down, and ashamed, but she carefully kept all of her feelings hidden.

On the surface, Nan and Jill are talking about the conflict between Nan and Jill's husband, but there's another important conflict that they're both ignoring. Nan and Jill are clearly upset with each other. They both feel hurt, frustrated, and rejected. These feelings are heavy and obvious, but nobody's talking about them. If Nan continues to ignore Jill's feelings, she'll end up with two problems for the price of one—a conflict with her son-in-law, and a conflict with her daughter as well.

Now I want you to focus on the conflict you described earlier. Ask yourself if the statement you wrote down in Step 2 of your Relationship Journal was an example of good communication or bad communication. You can use the EAR Checklist or the list of Common Communication Errors to analyze your response to the other person.

Summarize your analysis in Step 3 of your Relationship Journal. Don't do this analysis in your head—do it on paper on page 68. For example, you might write something like this: "I got zero for three on the EAR Checklist, because I didn't acknowledge my husband's feelings or tell him how I was feeling. Instead, I argued and insisted that he was wrong. I certainly didn't convey any caring or respect."

When you do Step 3, remember to focus on what *you* said (Step 2) and *not* on what the other person said (Step 1). The other person probably made lots of errors as well, but pointing them out won't do you any good. I can guarantee that the person you're arguing with won't be the least bit interested in hearing you describe his or her communication errors!

I've found that some people can't "see" their own communication errors when they first use the EAR Checklist. For example, some people feel convinced that they acknowledged the other person's feelings and expressed their own feelings when they really didn't. Mental health professionals also have trouble with this at first. It might seem strange to say this, but their communication skills actually aren't much better than the average person's.

Feeling Words

If you're having trouble, the list of Feeling Words overleaf can help you analyze what you wrote down in Step 2. See if you can find any of these words in your response. If the other person seemed frustrated or upset with you, did you say something like, "Wow, Bob, it sounds like you might be frustrated or upset with me right now. Can you tell me more about how you're feeling?" That would be a good example of an empathic response because you're acknowledging how Bob is probably feeling.

If you can't find any Feeling Words in the statement you wrote down in Step 2, then you probably didn't acknowledge the other person's feelings. You probably didn't share your feelings directly and openly, either.

This statement would be a good example of Empathy and Assertiveness: "Simone, I can see that you're upset, and I want you

Feeling Words			
Feeling	Words That Express This Feeling		
Angry	mad resentful upset irate	pissed off irritated furious annoyed	ticked off incensed enraged bitter
Anxious	worried apprehensive panicky nervous	afraid uptight fearful concerned	scared tense frightened uneasy
Bored	uninterested	unmotivated	
Criticized	picked on judged	put down blamed	insulted
Embarrassed	foolish humiliated awkward	self-conscious mortified	flustered shy
Frustrated	stuck exasperated	thwarted	defeated
Guilty	ashamed	at fault	bad
Hopeless	discouraged	pessimistic	desperate
Inferior	inadequate useless second-rate	worthless undesirable defective	flawed intimidated incompetent
Jealous	envious		
Lonely	abandoned unwanted	alone unloved	rejected
Paranoid	mistrustful	suspicious	
Sad	blue depressed hurt disheartened	down disappointed lost low	unhappy despairing dejected miserable
Stressed	overwhelmed pressured	burned out overworked	tense frazzled
Tired	exhausted drained sleepy	weary worn out burdened	fatigued lethargic wiped out
Vulnerable	weak	fragile	exposed

Copyright © 1989 by David D. Burns, M.D. Revised 1992, 2006.

to know that I'm also feeling hurt and frustrated right now." This statement acknowledges Simone's feelings and expresses your own as well.

If you did try to express your feelings, ask yourself if you used "I Feel" Statements or "You" Statements. Consider this statement: "You're pissing me off right now!" Would you say that this is an open and direct expression of your feelings? You might say yes, because you used a form of the phrase *pissed off*, which appears on the list of Feeling Words. However, this is a "You" Statement, and it sounds hostile because you're blaming the other person for the way you feel. This will put the other person on the defensive. You don't get credit for "You" Statements.

Statements such as, "You're wrong," or "I feel like you don't know what you're talking about," are not expressions of your feelings, either. These statements are put-downs. You're attacking with your feelings instead of sharing your feelings openly in the spirit of respect.

This brings us to the final distinction between good and bad communication. Ask yourself if your response in Step 2 conveyed warmth, caring, or respect. Was your tone of voice critical, sarcastic, defensive, competitive, or patronizing? How will the other person feel, based on what you said? It's perfectly okay to feel angry and frustrated, but the way you convey your feelings will make a huge difference in what happens next. You can use your anger as a weapon and do battle, or you can share your feelings respectfully so you can develop a deeper and more meaningful relationship with the other person.

The discovery that your response was an example of bad communication can be shocking, especially if you were convinced that the problem was the other person's fault. If you have the courage to identify and acknowledge your own communication errors, you've taken a painful but vitally important step toward more rewarding relationships with other people.

Chapter 10

How We Control Other People

You'll remember that the first principle of cognitive interpersonal therapy is that we actually cause the problems in our relationships with other people, even though we're not consciously aware of it. When you do Step 4 of the Relationship Journal, the impact of your behavior on the other person will become clear.

Hannah's response to Hal is an obvious example of this idea. When Hal said, "You never listen," Hannah ignored him. What effect will Hannah's response have on Hal? How will he feel? What will he conclude? What will he say or do next?

Hal will conclude that his criticism was correct because she's *still* not listening. How will he feel? Ignored and frustrated. What will he do next? He'll keep criticizing her. He'll have to keep knocking on the door because Hannah refuses to let him in. Hannah complains that Hal is relentlessly critical, but she's provoking this exact behavior.

When Hannah came to the workshop, she wanted to know why her husband had been so critical of her throughout their entire marriage. She asked, "Why are men like that?" The answer may not be the one that Hannah was hoping to hear. Hal is relentlessly critical because she forces him to be like that. And she's probably been doing the same thing for the past thirty-five years.

The answer to Hannah's question is both good news and bad news. On the one hand, the finger of blame suddenly rotates 180 degrees and points directly at Hannah. That's going to feel pretty lousy. On the other hand, it means that she has far more power than she thinks because she's constantly creating her own inter-personal reality. If she wants, she can use that power to create the loving relationship she's been longing for.

How is Hannah going to feel about this analysis? It's bound to be uncomfortable. It's easy for us to examine Hannah's role in the prob-lem, but from her perspective, these new insights may feel shameful and humiliating. The discovery that you're causing the problem that you've been so upset about can be a shock to the system.

So Whose Fault Is It Anyway?

You may want to come to Hannah's defense. Doesn't Hal also con-tribute to the problem? Isn't he just as much to blame as she is?

Hal *does* play a role in the problem. In fact, if Hal had come to me with complaints about his marriage, we would have used the Relationship Journal to examine his behavior. This analysis would undoubtedly show that he hadn't listened, expressed his feelings openly, or conveyed any warmth or respect. In fact, he'd discover that he was provoking the precise reactions from Hannah that he was complaining about. Then we'd conclude that *Hal* was 100 percent responsible for the problems in their relationship!

How can this be? How can Hannah be 100 percent responsible for their problems if Hal is also 100 percent responsible for them? It's because they're enmeshed in a system of circular causality. When Hal criticizes Hannah in a loud, hostile tone of voice, she feels anx-ious, hurt, and angry, so she clams up. So we could say that he *forces* her not to listen. But when Hannah ignores him, she forces him to keep criticizing her, because she still hasn't "gotten it."

Where do we punctuate this series of interactions? This is like asking what came first, the chicken or the egg? Hannah is always looking at Hal's behavior, and not her own, so she feels certain that she's the victim and he's to blame. Hal is always looking at Hannah's behavior, so he feels equally certain that she's to blame and he's the victim. Who's right? They're both right.

However, focusing on the other person's errors won't do you any good. In fact, the more you try to blame or change another person, the harder they'll fight and resist you. But if Hannah accepts the fact that she *can't* change Hal, and focuses instead on changing herself, he *will* change. He'll change at the exact moment that she changes. This is a paradox. We change other people every time we interact with them—but we're just not aware of it.

Let's revisit Nan. You may recall that when Nan's daughter, Jill, said, "You're putting my husband down," Nan replied, "I feel like I'm working hard to have a good relationship with him." We've already seen that Nan has made numerous communication errors. Now let's examine the consequences of her response. How is Jill going to feel when Nan says, "I feel like I'm working hard to have a good relationship with him"? What will Jill conclude? What will happen next? Will Nan's response make the problem better or worse? Why?

When Nan denies her role in the problem, she puts up a wall and sounds defensive. She implies that she's *not* putting her son-in-law down. Of course, if this were true, it would mean that Jill and her husband were foolishly misinterpreting Nan's loving behavior. So that's another put-down. Here's the bottom line: when Nan defends herself, she proves that Jill's criticism is valid. In fact, Nan *is* putting Jill and her husband down.

How will Jill feel when Nan responds like this? She'll probably feel hurt, frustrated, and annoyed with her mother, and she'll also feel the need to stick up for her husband. This will lead to more tension and disagreement. Eventually, Jill may give up and withdraw. Of course, this was Nan's concern in the first place. She wondered why she and Jill had been drifting further and further apart. Now we see why. When Jill tried to open up and talk about the tension she and her husband had been feeling, Nan got defensive. Essentially, she shut Jill out and pushed her away.

Why in the world would Nan behave in such a self-defeating way? Maybe we don't want to admit that there's a grain of truth in what our loved ones are saying to us when the feelings of tension are high. Maybe it's just too painful to examine our own role in these problems. Self-examination requires courage.

Let's examine the conflict you described on page 68. Think about the consequences of what you wrote down for Step 2 and ask yourself these kinds of questions:

- What effect will my statement have on the other person?
- How will my response make him or her feel?
- What will she or he conclude?
- What will she or he say or do next?

Complete Step 4 of your Relationship Journal now. Here's a tip that will make this step easier and more interesting. Ask yourself what the other person is doing that you find upsetting. For example, the person you're not getting along with might be rigid, stubborn, defensive, or argumentative. She might refuse to listen, whine and complain, or put you down. She might make endless demands on you, or have trouble opening up and telling you how she feels inside.

Now examine the consequences of what you wrote down in Step 2 and see if you can figure out how your statement will actually cause the other person to be the exact way you don't want her to be. For example, let's assume that the other person constantly argues and never listens to what you have to say. When you examine what you said in Step 2, you may also discover that you didn't listen or acknowledge any truth in what the other person was saying. Instead, you may have insisted that she was wrong.

If so, what will happen next? The other person will get frustrated and will keep trying to make her point. When you think about it from this perspective, you may suddenly realize that you're practically *forcing* the other person to be argumentative, even though you feel like she *should* listen to you and *shouldn't* be so defensive.

There are infinite variations on this theme. If your best friend seems to have trouble expressing her feelings, you may discover that whenever she tries to open up, you criticize her or tell her that she *shouldn't* feel that way. If she feels judged, she obviously won't feel motivated to open up. Or you may rush in and offer to help instead of listening and encouraging her to open up and tell you more about how she's feeling.

Here's another tip that might help when you do Step 4. Ask yourself how you want the other person to treat you. For example, let's say you want your wife to be a better listener without constantly *yes-but*ting you and getting defensive. Now examine what you wrote down in Step 2. You may discover that you blurted out, "You're wrong and you should admit it! Any idiot could see that!" What will happen next? Will your wife feel motivated to listen and acknowledge the truth in your point of view? Will she say, "Oh, thank you, dear! You are so right!"?

If you're beginning to understand your own role in the problem, then you're off to a tremendous start, and I'm proud of you. Although Steps 3 and 4 can be extremely interesting from an intellectual perspective, they can be very difficult emotionally. Right now, you're paying your dues. If you're willing to do this kind of work and you can endure the pain of self-examination, there will be a reward for you when we complete Step 5 of your Relationship Journal.

When I do my Intimacy Workshops, some people get restless and want to jump to Step 5 without doing Steps 3 and 4. They say, "Well, what *should* I have said to my son (or boss, etc.)?" They want to know the solution without examining what they wrote down in Step 2. This doesn't work.

Similarly, lots of my patients want to talk in general terms about the people they aren't getting along with. That's human nature, and it's understandable. We all need to vent. But if you want things to change, you'll need to focus on one specific interaction. Do the analysis on paper, using the Relationship Journal. If you try to do it in your head, I can guarantee that it won't work. Write down one thing the other person said to you (Step 1), and exactly what you said next (Step 2). Then ask yourself whether your response to the other person was an example of good communication or bad communication (Step 3) and examine the consequences of your response (Step 4). Will it make the problem better or worse? Why? This process may seem simple, but it can trigger some profound insights.

Chapter 11

Three Troubled Couples

Before we move on to Step 5, let's practice what we've learned so far. In this chapter, we're going to diagnose the relationship problems of three troubled couples. These couples have problems many people can identify with, such as nagging or a lack of sexual intimacy. It's always easier and less painful to pinpoint the errors someone else is making than to focus on your own. Hopefully, this chapter will make it a little easier for you to analyze the problems in your relationship.

Jed and Marjorie

A contractor named Jed told me that his wife, Marjorie, constantly criticized him and was never interested in sex. The previous evening she'd said, "I'm mad. You got drunk on the way home from work again. You choose alcohol over me. You'll probably sit on the sofa in a stupor and channel-surf all night long. You stink, too, and it pisses me off." Jed felt a flash of anger and said, "I might as well get drunk. You're about as warm and cuddly as an ice cube. *Nothing* turns you on!"

Now that we know what Marjorie said, and exactly what Jed said next, we can do Step 3 of the Relationship Journal. Would you say that Jed's response was an example of good communication or bad communication? Did he listen? Did he share his feelings openly and directly? Did he convey caring and respect? When you've completed your analysis of his response, I'll share my thinking with you.

Step 3. Good Communication vs. Bad Communication

Jed's response to Marjorie was a classic example of bad communication. He was zero out of three on the EAR Checklist. He certainly didn't empathize. Marjorie was feeling frustrated, angry, and lonely, but he didn't acknowledge how she felt or admit that there might be some truth in what she said. Jed didn't express his feelings, either. He was feeling controlled, put down, hurt, and angry. He also felt rejected because Marjorie didn't seem interested in sex, but he didn't share any of his feelings, either. Instead, he tried to get back at her by labeling her as an ice cube. His response sounded disrespectful and rejecting.

Jed's communication errors are obvious. He plays the role of a helpless, innocent victim who simply can't control his drinking because of the abuse and neglect he has to endure from his horrible, nagging, unloving wife.

Now let's do Step 4. This will be a little more challenging. Jed's big complaint is that Marjorie isn't warm or sexually responsive. But why is Marjorie like this? Think about the consequences of what Jed said to her. How will his comment make Marjorie feel? What will happen next? Put your analysis on a separate piece of paper before you continue reading.

Step 4. Consequences

It's pretty easy to see why Marjorie isn't sexually responsive. When Jed gets drunk on the way home from work every night and walks in the front door with alcohol on his breath, Marjorie feels lonely, hurt, and rejected. When she tries to express her feelings, Jed puts her down and implies that everything is her fault. This makes her feel angry, frustrated, and defensive. Obviously, she won't feel very loving or want to be with him sexually. Most of us don't feel sexually aroused when we're feeling hurt, angry, and put down. Jed practically forces her not to love him.

Jed wanted to know if there was any hope for his marriage. Was there any chance that Marjorie would change? This is the wrong question. The real question is this: Is Jed willing to change? Once you've pinpointed the errors you're making, and you understand the impact of your statements and actions on the person you're not getting along with, then you can decide to change the way you respond to him or her. The moment you change, the other person will change as well. We'll talk about how to do that shortly.

Harriet and Jerry

A piano teacher named Harriet told me that her husband, Jerry, absolutely fell apart whenever she tried to express anything even mildly critical. She said that Jerry just couldn't deal with negative feelings, and this prevented them from enjoying a close, loving relationship. She explained that he was a minister and thought that people should always be nice to each other. She said that religion was fine, but sometimes it felt like she wasn't allowed to be genuine.

I asked Harriet for a specific example of the problem. Could she recall one thing Jerry had said to her, and exactly what she said next? Earlier in the week, Jerry had said, "I feel hurt and blamed when you judge me." Harriet responded, "It seems like anytime I disagree with you or say anything negative, you get upset. I feel like I have to be super careful about what I say, and sometimes I feel like I have to keep quiet just to keep the peace. But I don't want false peace." She recorded these two statements as Steps 1 and 2 on her Relationship Journal.

Let's do Step 3. Was Harriet's response an example of good communication or bad communication? Did she acknowledge how Jerry was feeling? Did she express her own feelings openly and directly? Did she convey caring or respect? Examine her response to her husband and see what you think before you continue reading.

Step 3. Good Communication vs. Bad Communication
Here's what Harriet put on her Relationship Journal:

> My response was an example of bad communication because I didn't acknowledge how Jerry was feeling. He was trying to tell me that he felt blamed and judged, but I implied that he was wrong instead of finding some truth in what he said. I didn't express my feelings, either. I was feeling frustrated and lonely, but instead of telling him how I felt, I put him down and implied that he was to blame for our problems, since I always have to be "super careful" when we interact. My comment sounded self-righteous and certainly didn't convey respect.

Now let's examine the consequences of Harriet's response in Step 2. How will he feel? What will he conclude? Put your analysis on a separate piece of paper before you continue reading.

Step 4. Consequences
Here's how Harriet analyzed the impact of her response:

> When Jerry tried to express his feelings, I put him down. When he told me that he often felt judged, I jumped right in and judged him again. I blamed him and implied that he was wrong. This proved that he was right. I want to feel closer to him, and I want our relationship to be more emotionally open, but I punished Jerry and pushed him away when he tried to open up.

Notice the shift that's occurred. Harriet wanted to know why Jerry couldn't deal with negative feelings without falling apart.

This makes it sound like he's defective and the problems are all his fault. But when you examine an actual interaction between them, you suddenly see things in an entirely different light. Harriet actually discouraged him when he tried to express his feelings.

You may have noticed that Harriet avoids negative feelings as well. She didn't acknowledge any of Jerry's feelings or express her own. But this is exactly what she's accusing him of. Instead of trying to figure out why Jerry can't deal with negative feelings, Harriet might do better to ask herself why *she* can't deal with negative feelings. And perhaps more to the point, is she willing to learn how to do this?

Barry and Richard

A software engineer named Barry told me that his partner, Richard, was very controlling and constantly nagged him. For example, the previous Friday night, they'd decided to see a film. As Barry was parking the car, Richard got annoyed and said, "Why didn't you park over there instead of driving around the car park three times?"

Barry tried to sound upbeat and replied, "I wanted to get a really good parking place." Barry's response sounds harmless enough. Would you say that it was an example of good communication or bad communication? Here's how Barry analyzed his response when he did Step 3 on his Relationship Journal:

> My response was an example of bad communication because I didn't listen, express my feelings, or convey respect. Richard seemed frustrated and annoyed, but I ignored his feelings. I felt belittled but hid my feelings and tried to act chipper. When I said I wanted to find a really good parking place, I sounded defensive. I was secretly ticked off and implied that he was wrong. My tone of voice and body language probably betrayed how I felt. I certainly didn't convey any genuine warmth since I was faking it.

Step 4. Consequences

What are the consequences of Barry's statement? How will Richard feel? What will happen next? Give this some thought before you continue reading.

Richard will probably feel frustrated and annoyed because Barry deflected his criticism. Pretty soon, Richard will criticize him about something else. Barry feels like a victim but encourages Richard to nag him when he doesn't acknowledge Richard's feelings or share his own. They're both sweeping their feelings under the carpet, so their feelings come out indirectly, as a cycle of nagging and defending.

Many people try to avoid conflict by changing the subject or by trying to smooth things out as quickly as possible. I call this mind-set Conflict Phobia or Anger Phobia. Subconsciously, you may be afraid that something terrible will happen if you express any negative feelings openly or fight with someone you care about. Or you may believe that people who really love each other shouldn't ever argue or get mad at each other. Or you may see yourself as a basically *nice* person, so you're always sweeping your feelings under the carpet and pretending they're not there.

Of course, we don't all avoid conflict. Some people love a good battle, so they jump right in and defend themselves. They want to win. Either way, the negative feelings escalate.

Barry complains that Richard nags him and constantly picks on him. But he fuels the fire when he ignores Richard's mean-spirited tone of voice, acts like everything is just fine, and defends himself. This is why Richard keeps picking on him—because Barry doesn't acknowledge the fact that they're both feeling annoyed. There's an elephant in the room, but they're both pretending that it isn't there. If Barry's willing to bring the hostility to conscious awareness in a direct but gentle way, he can put an end to the game they're playing and encourage more open and honest communication.

Now you've learned how to complete the first four steps of the Relationship Journal, and you've seen how easy it is to diagnose the precise cause of any relationship conflict simply by examining one exchange between two people who aren't getting along with each other, including the conflict that you described earlier. Now you're ready for Step 5—that's where you learn to transform troubled relationships into loving, rewarding relationships.

Part Three

How to Develop Loving Relationships with the People You Care About

Chapter 12

The Five Secrets of Effective Communication

S hortly after my first book, *Feeling Good*, was released, I received a call from a man named Chris who lived in Atlanta. Chris had bipolar (manic-depressive) illness and was taking lithium, but was still struggling with depression. He explained that he'd been to some of the top psychiatrists in the country, but no one had been able to help him. When he read *Feeling Good*, he suddenly realized that I was the guy he'd been looking for. He said that if I'd be willing to see him, he'd fly to Philadelphia every week for sessions with me.

As you can imagine, I was pretty excited. I'd been in private practice for only a few years, and this was the first referral I'd received because of my book. I scheduled a double session for Chris because he was coming from such a great distance.

I couldn't wait to meet him; however, when he walked into my office a few days later and I introduced myself, he looked crestfallen. I asked if there was a problem. He apologized and explained that when he'd read *Feeling Good*, he'd had the impression that I was an older man with gray hair. He said I was clearly too young to be his doctor.

The air went out of my balloon fast! I'd been looking forward to the session, and it suddenly felt like the race was over before

I'd even gotten out of the starting gate. I felt embarrassed and frustrated, and I wanted to persuade Chris to give the treatment a try. I pointed out that although I might seem young, I'd been in practice for several years and had extensive experience treating bipolar illness. I explained that I'd even run a lithium clinic while I was a research fellow, and that I also had expertise in all the new treatment techniques he'd read about in *Feeling Good*.

Have you ever noticed that when you try to defend yourself from criticism, you're rarely successful? Well, Chris's response was, "Doctor, I've been treated by the chief of the National Institute of Mental Health, but he couldn't help me. Then I flew out to the University of California, Los Angeles (UCLA) and saw the chairman of the Department of Psychiatry, but he couldn't help me, either. I saw the top bipolar expert in Chicago, and even he couldn't help me. But at least those doctors had a good bedside manner. You don't even seem to have that!"

Things weren't going well, but I was convinced that I could help Chris if he'd just give me a chance. I pointed out that if he had a ruptured appendix, he'd probably want to be treated by the most skillful surgeon he could find, and it wouldn't make a whole lot of difference whether the doctor had a good bedside manner. I said that the same thing was true in psychiatry. You could have the nicest shrink in the world, but if he didn't have the tools to help you, it wouldn't do you a bit of good.

That comment went down like a lead balloon. Chris got more and more frustrated and kept insisting that I didn't understand and couldn't possibly help him. Every time I tried to defend myself, his attack escalated. Finally, Chris stood up abruptly and said, "Doctor, I paid your receptionist for a double session. I've only been here fifteen minutes, but this session is over. I'm going to walk out that door right now and you're never going to see me again. But you can keep the money. The money doesn't mean a thing to me."

As he reached for the door, I remembered that I'd written a chapter in *Feeling Good* on how to handle criticism, and it suddenly dawned on me that I wasn't using any of the techniques I'd described. I turned to Chris and said, "I feel sad that you're about to leave, and I realize that I haven't done a very good job of responding to your concerns. I'm wondering if you could do me one small favor before you walk out the door. Could we just take it from the top one more time?"

He paused and said, "Sure. I'll give you that. I was just trying to tell you that you're too young to be my doctor."

I replied, "Chris, you're absolutely right. I am quite young. I've only been in practice for four years, and I can imagine how disappointing it must be to have come so far, and to have been so excited about a promising new approach, only to have your hopes dashed the moment you meet your new psychiatrist. But it's even worse than that. When you tried to tell me I was too young, I got defensive instead of acknowledging how you felt. That was pretty amateurish, and I wouldn't be surprised if you were feeling really frustrated and annoyed with me right now. I know that's how I'd feel if I were in your shoes. I have tremendous respect for you and feel badly that I've let you down. When you walk out that door, there's just one thing I hope you'll remember."

Chris seemed to soften just a little bit and asked, "What's that? What am I supposed to remember?"

I said, "Please remember that you were right, and I was wrong."

Chris slowly sank back into his chair, looked directly into my eyes, and said, "Doctor, no shrink has *ever* talked to me like that before. *You're* my man. *You're* the guy I want to work with!" This was the start of a rewarding and extremely successful course of therapy together.

What had happened? When Chris criticized me and said I was too young, I felt hurt and tried to defend myself. I wanted to prove that he was wrong. But I actually proved that he was right because I didn't respond to his concerns with empathy or compassion, which is exactly the kind of error that a young therapist might make. When I finally agreed that I *was* too young and showed genuine concern for his feelings, I proved that I really *wasn't* too young, because I was listening and validating his feelings. That was what he'd been yearning to hear.

When I acknowledged how disappointed, frustrated, and annoyed Chris felt, he saw that I finally understood what he'd been trying to say and how he felt inside. The tension dissolved almost immediately, and we were suddenly on the same team. And when I said, "I have tremendous respect for you and feel badly that I've let you down," it was music to his ears because I sounded human and vulnerable, instead of arrogant and defensive. Even though we were both feeling frustrated and annoyed, I conveyed the spirit of respect. Chris had been feeling demoralized and was hoping to connect with someone who cared about him.

The Five Secrets of Effective Communication
Listening Skills
1. **The Disarming Technique (DT).** You find some truth in what the other person is saying, even if it seems totally unreasonable or unfair.
2. **Empathy.** You put yourself in the other person's shoes and try to see the world through his or her eyes. • **Thought Empathy (TE).** You paraphrase the other person's words. • **Feeling Empathy (FE).** You acknowledge how the other person is probably feeling, based on what he or she said.
3. **Inquiry (IN).** You ask gentle, probing questions to learn more about how the other person is thinking and feeling.
Self-Expression Skills
4. **"I Feel" Statements (IF).** You use "I Feel" Statements, such as, "I feel upset," rather than "You" Statements, such as, "You're wrong!" or "You're making me furious!"
5. **Stroking (ST).** You find something genuinely positive to say to the other person, even in the heat of battle. You convey an attitude of respect, even though you may feel very angry with the other person.

Copyright © 1991 by David D. Burns, M.D. Revised 1992.

When I responded to Chris, I was using the Five Secrets of Effective Communication:

As you can see, they build on the same listening and self-expression skills we've been using to distinguish good versus bad communication. Learning to use these techniques effectively will require hard work and practice because they're radically different from the ways most of us react to the people we're not getting along with.

In the next few chapters, I'll show you how to use the Five Secrets to resolve practically any kind of relationship problem. These techniques can be incredibly powerful, but they're not gimmicks or magic formulas you can use to manipulate people. If you don't speak from the heart and convey genuine compassion and respect, they won't be effective. If you use these techniques skillfully, they can transform your relationships.

In the next five chapters, I'm going to show you how to use each of the Five Secrets, one by one. I'll give you lots of examples of how they work, along with exercises that will help you master these techniques. This will be much like a karate class, where you practice various moves, one by one, until they become second nature. Then I'll show you how to integrate the Five Secrets so you can use them effectively to deal with virtually any relationship problem.

Chapter 13

The Disarming Technique

The Disarming Technique is the most powerful communication technique of all. When you use the Disarming Technique, you find genuine truth in what the other person is saying, even if it seems totally unreasonable or unfair. If you do this skillfully, you'll put the lie to the criticism, and it won't be true any more. You saw an example of this paradox in the last chapter. The moment I genuinely agreed with Chris, he suddenly concluded that I was *not* too young to be his doctor.

The Law of Opposites

I call this phenomenon the Law of Opposites. When you try to defend yourself from a criticism that seems totally irrational or unfair, you'll instantly prove that the criticism is completely valid. This is a paradox. In contrast, if you genuinely agree with a criticism that seems totally untrue or unfair, you'll instantly prove that the criticism is wrong, and the other person will suddenly see you in an entirely different light. This is also a paradox.

For example, I'm sure you recall reading about Hannah and

her husband, Hal. When Hal said, "You never listen!" Hannah said nothing and ignored him. She felt that his criticism was so ridiculous that it wasn't even worthy of a response. Paradoxically, she proved that Hal was right because she was ignoring him. Once again, she wasn't listening.

How could Hannah have responded when Hal said, "You never listen"? Put yourself in her shoes and try to write a more effective response that incorporates the Disarming Technique. Remember, when you disarm the other person, you agree that his criticism is valid. You acknowledge the truth in what he's saying. Don't worry about coming up with something elegant or perfect. Just jot something down on a separate piece of paper before you continue reading. That will be good enough. When you're done, I'll share my thinking with you.

Step 5. Revised Response

If Hannah wanted to try the Disarming Technique, she might say something like this:

> You're right, Hal. It's embarrassing to admit it, but I realize that I haven't been a very good listener. You've been trying to tell me that for a long time and I've been ignoring you. You must be feeling so frustrated with me. Can we talk about it?

The moment Hannah admits that she *hasn't* been listening, and that she's been shutting him out, she shows that she *is* listening. And it's exactly what Hal has been yearning to hear for the past thirty-five years. We all want to feel validated when we're upset. This creates the possibility for communication and intimacy.

You can be creative when you complete Step 5 of the Relationship Journal. There isn't any one "correct" answer or way to respond. You'll need to find the words and the language that works for you.

When Pride Gets in the Way

The effects of the Disarming Technique can be astonishing, but it's also the most difficult technique to learn. There are several reasons for this. First, pride gets in the way. It hurts to admit that you're wrong or that you've fallen short in someone else's eyes. It's even more painful if you care about the person who's criticizing you and you sense that they're right. Nobody wants to feel like a failure. We don't want to hear that we've been a bad father or mother, or that we've hurt someone we love, because it feels so shameful. Shame is one of the biggest barriers to intimacy.

For the past several years, I've had the opportunity to work with my daughter, Signe. She's been my editor in chief and has helped me edit several books, including this one. I was very excited when Signe agreed to work with me, because I've always had tremendous respect for her writing skills and was looking forward to the chance to spend more time with her.

When we first began working together, Signe would drive down from San Francisco several days each week and we'd start editing around ten thirty in the morning. By midafternoon our brains would be frazzled, so we'd take a break and sit on the back deck and talk. My wife and I had just adopted two wonderful little kittens, Happy and Popcorn. Signe and I would bring the kittens out on the porch and watch them jump and try to catch flies while we shot the breeze. I treasured these chats. Life seemed good.

One afternoon, we were talking about the past and Signe got choked up. I asked what was bothering her, and she said, "Dad, this isn't easy for me to say, but if you want to know the truth, you weren't always the kind of father I needed when I was a teenager."

That really hurt, and I felt a tremendous sense of shame and sadness. I felt like a lightning bolt had suddenly struck my heart. It was terribly painful to hear those words. She went on to explain that she felt that I was too achievement-oriented when she was growing up, and that she felt a lot of academic pressure when what she really wanted was more TLC and support.

I had an overwhelming urge to defend myself and point out what a *good* father I'd been and how no father is perfect, but I knew that would be a big mistake. Instead, I said that I felt devastated to hear that I'd failed her like that. I told her that I loved her dearly, and hugged her. She hugged me back and cried. That moment brought us so much closer. In fact, if I look back on my entire life, I would say that that was one of the most rewarding and meaningful experiences I've ever had.

Since that day, our work together has been incredibly rewarding. We've been a fabulous team and have hopefully done some excellent work. We've also had tremendous fun, and I get to find out about all the things that are going on in Signe's life while we're working together. But there was a price to pay for this reward—it didn't feel very good when it was time for my pride to die.

When Fear Gets in the Way

Fear and mistrust can also make it hard to disarm someone who's criticizing you or mad at you. You may think that something terrible will happen if you find truth in what the other person is saying, so you defend yourself. You're afraid that her attack will escalate out of control and she'll start bombarding you with every negative feeling in the book, so you insist that she's wrong.

In fact, it often works the other way around. When you're afraid to acknowledge the truth in what the other person is saying, her negative feelings *will* escalate, and she'll usually attack you more intensely. If, on the other hand, you agree that she's right, and find some truth in her criticisms, it takes the wind out of her sails and you end up on the same team.

When Signe criticized me, I felt devastated. I was afraid to agree that I wasn't supportive enough when she was growing up because I felt so ashamed. I thought something awful would happen if I agreed that I'd let her down. Would she stop loving me? But the moment I agreed with her and showed her how I felt, we suddenly felt closer than ever before, and that experience opened the door to a far more loving relationship.

The Disarming Technique is also effective in business negotiations, but fear can be just as big a barrier as it is in your relationships with friends and loved ones. A man named Pedro brought his entire family to my clinic in Philadelphia after reading my first book, *Feeling Good*. He said that he was so excited that he wanted his whole family to be treated with the cognitive therapy techniques he'd been reading about in *Feeling Good*. He'd brought his wife and four children all the way from Venezuela to participate in our intensive therapy program. This meant that every family member would receive one or more sessions every day so we could try to condense months or even years of therapy into just a few weeks.

At my clinic, patients paid for their sessions at the time the service was delivered. Because six members of Pedro's family were receiving treatment, I asked if he could pay for the sessions his family had received at the end of each day. Pedro protested and said he wanted me to bill him once a week instead.

I explained that we'd tried that approach in the past but it hadn't been satisfactory. Pedro explained that he was a businessman with far more knowledge about such things than I had, and he insisted that I bill him once a week. I felt pretty strongly about it, and soon we were locked in a power struggle over how and when he'd pay his bill.

Pedro was a large, intimidating man who was used to getting his way, so we couldn't resolve our differences. At the end of the session, I felt frustrated and exhausted because we were still on opposite sides of the fence. Pedro had another session scheduled later in the day, and I found myself dreading it.

Between sessions, I thought about what had happened, and it dawned on me that I'd gotten so caught up in the heat of battle that I'd completely forgotten to use the Five Secrets of Effective Communication. When Pedro sat down for his next session several hours later, I was determined not to repeat my errors. I said, "Pedro, I felt really bad after our session this morning because I realized that I was wasting precious time arguing with you about money. That must have felt insulting. You were absolutely right when you said that you have way more business experience than I do. In addition, you've made a tremendous sacrifice coming all the way from Venezuela with your family so we could work together. I can imagine that you're pretty disappointed and frustrated with me. I feel like I've really let you down, and I owe you an apology."

Pedro looked stunned. He pulled out his chequebook, wrote out a cheque, and handed it to me. When I glanced at it, I realized that he'd written a cheque for twenty sessions in advance. It was the only time in my entire career that I ever got paid in advance!

Why was my statement so effective? Pedro was a warmhearted and generous person, but he was used to being in charge. His forceful personality was his greatest strength, because it had led to considerable success in business, but it was also his greatest weakness, because he was overly controlling and lonely. He didn't feel close to his colleagues, wife, or children. When I fell into the trap of arguing about who was right, it felt like we were on competing teams. Pride was on the line, and we were both determined not to lose. But when I found truth in Pedro's point of view and acknowledged how he was feeling, he gave me far more than I'd asked for.

Now you may have the question, "Well, what if he *still* hadn't paid?" Sometimes you have to set limits and be assertive in a negotiation, and you won't always get what you want, no matter how skillful you are. However, you'll nearly always end up with much more if you use the Disarming Technique and treat the other person with respect.

When Truth Gets in the Way

Perhaps more than any other technique or concept in this book, the Disarming Technique has changed my life. I use it every day of my life, and it rarely lets me down. But it's very tough to learn because of a little voice in your head that says, "I *shouldn't have to* agree with him because there *isn't* any truth in what he's saying. I'm *right* and he's *wrong*!" If you listen to that voice and give in to the urge to defend yourself, you'll nearly always get embroiled in conflict.

I always try to remind myself that when someone is criticizing me, he's trying to tell me something important, and that, on some level, he's *always* right. My job is to listen carefully so I can hear the valid part of what he's trying to say, rather than dwelling on the part that seems distorted or unfair. If you do this skillfully, you can work miracles in your interactions with other people.

However, you have to see that the criticism really is true and acknowledge that truth in a friendly way, conveying humility and self-respect. I'm convinced that there's *always* a great deal of truth in any criticism, but if you can't see the truth in what the other person is saying, or if you're so hurt and angry that you don't want to acknowledge that truth, the Disarming Technique won't produce the desired result.

A man named Jeremy recently told me, "There's *no way* I could agree with my wife when she says I'm stubborn. That's rubbish!" When Jeremy claims that he's *not* stubborn, he sounds pretty stubborn. This is a good example of the Law of Opposites: when you insist that the other person is wrong, you'll nearly always prove that he or she is right. In contrast, when you agree with the criticism, you'll put the lie to it, and the other person will suddenly see you in an entirely different light. But this can be difficult because your own view of the situation may cloud your mind so much that you think there's *no way* you could agree with the other person.

A woman named Raina described the difficulty she had when she was first trying to use the Disarming Technique during arguments with her husband, Milt. She explained:

> When I started to work with you, it was very important to me to prove that Milt's criticisms weren't true because his criticisms were exaggerated and filled with distortions, like All-or-Nothing Thinking. It was passionately important to me to try to make him admit that he was wrong. And I'd wait to turn the knife and escalate things, but I'd end up feeling even more miserable. The need to prove him wrong would make everything a hundred times worse, or a thousand times worse. And I still slip up at times.
>
> For example, we had a big fight two days ago. Now that our kids have grown up, we've decided to move to a smaller house. Milt decided that if we renovate the living room and kitchen, we could get a better price for our house. I agreed, but we started arguing about the renovations.
>
> In the middle of the discussion, Milt experienced some

floaters and flashes in his right eye. They're usually totally benign, but on rare occasions they can indicate a tear in the retina, so you need to have the problem checked out. He had the same symptoms several days ago, but the optician said everything was fine. This morning, he woke up with more floaters in his eye, and he was freaking out. He was very anxious and wasn't listening to me, so I got bitchy and kept interrupting him. I got mad and did every anti–David Burns thing in the book.

This is how their argument went:

Milt: You're *always* so bitchy with me. I see how sweet and wonderful you are with your friends, and with strangers, and yet you seem to save all the bitchiness for me. Why don't you just treat me the way you treat your friend Sarah?

Raina: That's not fair! I'm *not* always bitchy to you.

Milt: Yes you are. You're *always* bitchy. When we built the house, it was the exact same thing. We *always* fought.

Raina: That's not true. We *didn't* always fight. In fact, the builders told us they'd never seen a couple who were so easy to get along with, and who supported each other so much in making decisions. And we built our house in five months. That's almost a record.

Milt: Here I am going back to work tomorrow with these floaters, with a big cobweb in front of my eye. This is not the time to be so bitchy and awful to me. I'm going through something horrible and it's the last day of my holiday. You have no appreciation for what it's like or how I feel. I was looking forward to doing some fun projects together, and you certainly know how to ruin it every time. And don't tell me this is your day off, too. You have free time all the time. I don't ever have free time! And I have to stand here with this big cobweb in my eye, and face going back to work tomorrow and be on my own, without my partner there, doing surgery all alone with this big cobweb in my eye, and having to be on call this weekend, and this is what you're doing to me? You don't know what it's like to have my job, and to be under this kind of pressure, and now my vision is going, and you don't even care!

Raina: I *do* know what it's like and I *do* care. I've often told you I'd love to come with you to work and follow you around, and see what it's like.

Milt: So what do you want to do, go into the operating room and watch me cut into somebody? And then you can throw up? What you should really be saying is, "Wow, that's tough," or "Boy, that must be so frustrating or scary to do." Can't you give me a little support?

You can see how Raina defends herself at every juncture. Instead of disarming Milt, she tells him that he's wrong. But every time she insists that he's wrong, he gets angrier and more convinced that he's right. That's because Raina *is* acting bitchy, which is exactly what he's complaining about.

Raina explained how she turned the situation around:

I finally swallowed my pride and said, "You know, Milt, you're right. I *have* been acting like a bitch, and you have every right to be pissed off. It's embarrassing to admit that. I can imagine that the floaters in your eye are incredibly anxiety provoking. I haven't been giving you any support, and this is your last day of holiday. I feel terrible right now."

Then he suddenly said, "You're right, too. I've been acting like a jerk, and I really love you." I was shocked by how quickly the Disarming Technique turned everything around. The moment I admitted that Milt was right, he suddenly lowered his defenses and owned up to his role in the problem. That was the end of the fight, and we had a wonderful day together.

I've learned that it's not really so important to prove that he's wrong, because what he's saying probably isn't even completely true to him. He's just being mean and angry and trying to hurt me because he feels hurt and frustrated. It helps to remind myself that I matter a great deal to Milt, and that he loves me and wants to be in a relationship with me.

It's all about moving on and letting go of the need for retaliation or the need to be right. When I started going to you, we had horrible fights, and Milt would stay mad for a long time. When he walked into the house, I thought, "He's an asshole. Why should *I* have to do all the work? It's unfair!" Now I tell myself, "This is really frustrating right now, but I love him, and I've got some tools that work if I'm willing to pick them up and use them."

Sometimes it feels unfair, because it seems like I'm the only one who's working, I'm the only one who's using the Five Secrets of Effective Communication. It's the same with my friends. I ask myself, "When are *they* going to use these techniques?" But they don't know how to use these techniques, so I'm always the one who has to make the effort to be enlightened.

Am I always enlightened? Do I always behave the David Burns way? No! The other day, it backfired because I got sucked into my need to prove him wrong. But now I know that I have a choice. You have to ask yourself, "Do you love this person in spite of all his faults?" When you say yes, then you decide that you're willing to do the work.

It isn't always easy. In fact, it's incredibly hard at times because I have to say no to that little voice in my brain that eggs me on. Is it worth it? Well, here's the benefit: Milt and I have been married almost thirty-five years. Now we fight very seldom, and we're madly in love with each other. And when we do argue, it doesn't last. Our lives have been incredibly enriched.

Let's practice the Disarming Technique again. You may recall Nan from chapter 9. When her daughter said, "You're putting my husband down," Nan replied, "I feel like I'm working hard to have a good relationship with him." This was a conversation stopper because Nan was implying that Jill's criticism had no merit.

Put yourself in Nan's shoes and see if you can come up with a more effective response. You may be afraid that you're going to get this "wrong." If your Revised Response sounds lame, that's okay. I wasn't very good at this at first, either. Sometimes I *still* sound lame. But if you work at it, you'll improve. Give it a try now. Imagine that your daughter just said, "You're putting my husband down." What will you say to her? Write out your response on a separate piece of paper. Remember to use the Disarming Technique. That means finding some truth in what your daughter said.

Step 5. Revised Response
Nan could say:

> Jill, it really hurts to hear you say that because I think you're right. I have been critical of Frank. It isn't easy to admit it, but I realize that I haven't done a very good job of getting to know him. I've been sensing some tension in the air, and it upsets me because I love you so much. I want to know more about how you and Frank have been feeling.

Your response was probably different from mine, and that's okay. We all have different styles and personalities. If your response didn't sound natural or genuine, you can revise it to make it more effective. I often have to edit my Revised Responses on the Relationship Journal several times before I come up with something that I like.

Sometimes, the most effective responses require feeling some pain. It may not be easy for Nan to admit that there's truth in what Jill is saying. Love comes at a price. As a parent, I know this very well. If Nan is willing to swallow her pride, she'll be able to develop a much closer relationship with her daughter. She'll have to decide if she's willing to pay the price.

You might ask, "Well, what if Nan can't honestly say, 'I haven't done a very good job of getting to know him'? What if she thinks she *has* been doing a good job?" In this case, Nan could modify her response. She might say, "This really comes as a surprise because I thought I had a great relationship with Frank. I like him a lot and I've never sensed any tension between us. But if you feel like I'm putting him down, or if he feels that way, then I definitely must have said or done something that hurt his feelings. That's upsetting for me to think about because I don't want to hurt either of you. I love you both a great deal. Can you tell me more about what happened?"

Once again, Nan is finding some truth in her daughter's statement, but she's being honest and genuine at the same time. She's not faking it. The facts aren't nearly as important as your tone of voice. If you sound false or manipulative, other people will see right through you.

When I was developing the Five Secrets of Effective Communication, the Disarming Technique was the toughest one for me to learn. It will probably be challenging for you as well. Sometimes it was hard for me to figure out how the criticisms of patients, colleagues, or family members could possibly be valid. In order to get better at it, I used to write down the most absurd, impossible criticisms I could imagine someone saying to me. Then I'd try to find some truth in them. This exercise was invaluable. It was like a game, and I got pretty good at it after a while.

Overleaf, you'll find several harsh criticisms. See if you can find a way to agree with each of them, using the Disarming Technique. Put your responses in the right-hand column. When you're done, you can review my answers on page 113.

You can also write down the worst imaginable criticisms you might ever hear from your spouse, family members, friends, or colleagues. You can make the criticisms as extreme and irrational as you want. Make sure you include criticisms that would be upsetting to you. Then try to find some truth in each criticism. This exercise can be an eye-opener.

Here are some tips that may make it easier for you to learn the Disarming Technique. First, try to transform vague, global criticisms into specifics. For example, imagine that a friend suddenly says, "You're an idiot!" You may feel upset and have the urge to defend yourself. Instead, you can say something along these lines: "I feel bad that my comment upset you, and I wish I hadn't put it that way. Can you tell me more about how you're feeling?" Notice that you're transforming a global and rather meaningless criticism—"You're an idiot!"—into a meaningful dialogue about something you said that upset your friend. This response invites collaboration, and you won't look like an idiot any more.

Disarming Technique Exercise

Instructions: Try to come up with an effective response to each criticism using the Disarming Technique. In the blank boxes at the bottom, write down a few criticisms you think you might hear from other people, and put your responses to them in the right-hand column.

Harsh Criticisms	Disarming Responses
I hate you! You're a total jerk! You're a loser!	
You're mean.	
You're selfish. All you care about is yourself.	

Second, remember that you don't have to agree with the criticism in a literal way when you use the Disarming Technique. Instead, you can agree with the *spirit* of what the other person is saying. In addition, make sure that your response won't hurt the other person's feelings. I always try to respond tactfully and convey respect in the heat of battle.

For example, let's say that someone says, "You don't *really* like me!" Therapists hear this criticism all the time from angry patients, but you might also hear it from a child or friend you're not getting along with. Here's a bad example of the Disarming Technique: "You're right. I *don't* like you, and I don't think anyone else can stand you, either! In fact, your own mother probably doesn't like you." Although this may sound like the Disarming Technique, it's really just a way of being mean. Here's a better response:

Disarming Technique Exercise: Answers	
Harsh Criticisms	Disarming Responses
I hate you! You're a total jerk! You're a loser!	"It sounds like you're furious with me, and I realize I didn't handle things very well. I did screw up and I'm embarrassed about it. Can you tell me more about how you're feeling?"
You're mean.	"I think my comment hurt your feelings, and I feel bad about that because I really care about you. Can we talk about it?"
You're selfish. All you care about is yourself.	"You're right. I haven't taken your feelings into account, and you have every right to be mad at me. This is hard for me to hear. Are there other things I've done or said that also seemed selfish or uncaring?"

Wow, it really hurts to hear you say that, but I agree with you. There's some tension in the air, and it feels awkward. I've been frustrated, too. Let's talk this out. Your friendship means a lot to me. Can you tell me what I did or said that turned you off?

This response disarms the critic without running the risk of making her feel put down or rejected. It also transforms a global criticism—"You don't *really* like me"—into something specific. You're admitting that the two of you haven't been getting along very well lately and that you haven't been as supportive as you might be. Paradoxically, the other person will suddenly feel that you *do* care.

Earlier, when we were talking about the toxic effects of blame, I mentioned that although the ideas and techniques in this book are based on research, many of these concepts also have philosophical and spiritual roots.

A former priest who attended one of my Intimacy Workshops shared an insight he'd had when I demonstrated the Disarming Technique. He explained that after he left the priesthood, he went back to university and got a doctoral degree in ancient languages. In one of his classes, he learned that the Christian concept of "confession of sin" is actually based on a mistranslation of a word in the Aramaic language. He said the correct translation is not "to confess" but rather "to agree with." He didn't give this idea too much thought until he attended my workshop and it dawned on him that the Christian concept of confession is very similar to my Disarming Technique. That's because when you agree with the critic, instead of defending yourself, you are actually "confessing" your sin. And the moment you do this, you'll be forgiven. This notion is not unique to Christianity but is embedded in practically every religious tradition.

The Buddhists talk about "the great death," which is the death of the ego, or the self. If you sincerely agree with a critic, it often feels like you're dying. In fact, your pride and sense of "self" may both have to die, but if you disarm the critic skillfully and with an open heart, you'll be reborn at the same moment that you die. In other words, your "death" and "rebirth" are actually the same thing—they're just different ways of describing the same experience. You might even say that when you disarm someone you've been fighting with, you'll both die and be reborn together, because the antagonism, mistrust, and frustration that were plaguing you will be instantly transformed into warmth, love, and respect.

Chapter 14

Thought and Feeling Empathy

Practically every prominent therapist, dating all the way back to Freud, has emphasized the importance of empathy. In chapter 9, I emphasized empathy as well—it's one of the three key ingredients of good communication. But is it really so important? Or is it just a touchy-feely concept for encounter groups? What is empathy? And will it really make a difference in our lives?

Most of us believe that we *are* reasonably empathic. We're convinced that we have a pretty good idea about how other people think and feel and how they feel about us. For example, you probably think you know how your colleagues, friends, and family members feel and how they feel about you. And you may also think that they know how you feel. So if we already know how other people feel, why make such a big deal about empathy?

Our perceptions about how other people feel and how they feel about us can be off base. In fact, they nearly always are. This is even true of therapists, who are presumably experts in human relationships. We *think* we know how other people feel, but we don't.

I've recently completed a study of therapist accuracy at the Stanford University Hospital, California. In this study, eight research therapists spent several hours interviewing recently admitted psychiatric patients about the problems and feelings they were struggling with. Seventy patients participated in the study. At the end of each interview, each patient completed several brief but highly accurate assessment tests that measure feelings such as depression, anxiety, and anger, indicating how he or she was feeling "right now, at this moment." Each patient also rated the warmth and compassion of the research therapist who conducted the interview. At the same time, the researchers completed the same questionnaires, but were instructed to guess the patient's answers.

The researchers knew that their accuracy was being tested, so they were trying hard to get it right and were concentrating on what the patients said during the interviews. How accurate were these researchers? One way of assessing accuracy is with a statistical measure called the correlation coefficient. That's a complex term, but the concept is simple. A correlation coefficient can range between 0 and 1.* A value of 1 would mean that the therapists' perceptions of how the patients felt were perfectly accurate. A value of 0 would mean that there was no relationship whatsoever between the patients' feelings and the therapists' perceptions. This would be the worst possible result.

Can you guess the results? Nearly all of the correlations were close to zero. This meant that the researchers' perceptions of how the patients felt were almost completely unrelated to how the patients actually felt. We could just as well have asked taxi drivers who'd never met these patients to guess how the patients were feeling, and their guesses would have been almost as good as the therapists' estimates! The low correlations were especially surprising in light of the fact that the researchers had just spent two or three hours talking to the patients about their feelings. They *thought* they knew, but their perceptions were far less accurate than they thought.

I don't mean to criticize my colleagues. The researchers in the study were extremely skillful and compassionate, some of the best

---

* Technically, a correlation coefficient can vary between –1 and +1. Negative correlations mean that high scores on one variable are associated with low scores on another variable.

I've ever seen. We *all* have this problem. We *think* we know how other people feel and how they feel about us, but we don't. This includes loved ones, friends, neighbors, colleagues, and customers.

This problem isn't limited to medical or psychiatric settings. A colleague recently told me about a fascinating study of several hundred children who were asked to rate how depressed or angry they felt. Their parents, teachers, and counselors were also asked to estimate how the children felt, using the same scales. Once again, there was no meaningful relationship between how the children felt and how their parents, teachers, and counselors thought they felt.

The implications of these studies are mind boggling and may help explain why people are so shocked when they learn on the evening news that the boy next door just murdered his parents or walked into the local school with a shotgun and started blowing people away. People often say, "I had no idea he was feeling like that! He seemed like such a *nice* boy."

The bottom line is this: your thoughts about how other people feel and how they feel about you are probably far less accurate than you think and may not be accurate at all. That's one reason why empathy is such an important skill. It makes no difference if you're dealing with a personal conflict with a family member or friend, or a business problem such as a disagreement with your boss or customer—accurate knowledge of how the other person is thinking and feeling will be invaluable.

How can you develop empathy skills? First, we've got to define terms. What's the definition of empathy? I'd say that I'm empathizing with you if:

1. I understand what you're thinking so accurately that you'll be able to say, "You got it right. That's *exactly* what I'm thinking." I call this Thought Empathy.
2. I also understand how you're feeling inside, so that you'll be able to say, "Yes, that's *exactly* how I feel." I call this Feeling Empathy.
3. I convey my understanding with warmth and respect so you won't have to feel ashamed or put down.

Thought Empathy

Let's examine these three aspects of empathy in more detail. Thought Empathy means that you repeat what the other person said to you so he'll see that you got the message. You concentrate on what he is saying so you can summarize it accurately, almost like a court reporter who listens carefully and records every word.

Thought Empathy may seem simple, but it can be hard to master, especially during a conflict. When we're under attack, most of us feel panicky or upset. There's a tendency to concentrate on what you're going to say next so you can defend yourself. But when you do this, you might lose track of what the other person is saying, so you end up responding to the wrong thing altogether. This annoys the other person because he will see that you weren't listening.

If, in contrast, you accurately paraphrase what the other person said, he'll see that you *were* listening and that you "got it." Thought Empathy usually reduces the tension, particularly if your tone of voice is respectful. In addition, when you concentrate on what the other person is saying and repeat it out loud, you'll buy some time to figure out what to say next.

Using Thought Empathy skillfully means changing your focus from your own thoughts and feelings to what the other person is saying. You could say that Thought Empathy is an "other-centered" communication technique, as opposed to the "self-centered" approach that so many people seem to rely on.

The following expressions will give you an idea about the kinds of things you can say when you're using Thought Empathy:

- "What you seem to be saying is that . . ."
- "Tell me if I got this right. You just said that . . ."
- "If I heard you right, it sounds like you think that . . ."
- "Let me see if I understand you, because you just said three things that sounded important. First, you said that . . . Second, you expressed concern about . . . And third, you mentioned your feelings about . . . Did I get that right?"

Anything along these lines will do. Remember to paraphrase what the other person said in a tone of voice that sounds respectful, relaxed, and curious. Notice that in the last example, I ended with a question: "Did I get that right?" This allows the other person to let you know if your assessment of what he or she is thinking is correct.

Here's an example. Suppose you've been arguing with your friend Caroline because you think the guy she's been dating is bad for her, but she's infatuated with him and just doesn't want to hear it. Suddenly, she says:

> You're totally wrong about Lance. In the first place, he really loves me and I know that he'd *never* date anyone behind my back. He'd *never* cheat on me. And when he got arrested for shoplifting yesterday, I know that it was a big mistake. The store security thought he was someone else. Lance is the most honest person I know.

Using Thought Empathy, you could say:

> Caroline, it sounds like I've got the wrong idea about Lance, and I'm feeling bad right now because I said some things that were upsetting to you. You're telling me that Lance really loves you and wouldn't ever cheat on you. In addition, you're convinced that he wasn't really shoplifting, and that he's basically an honest guy. Did I get that right?

Thought Empathy is relatively easy to learn because all you have to do is repeat what the other person said in a respectful tone of voice. You don't have to agree that what they said is right, and you definitely won't want to argue and insist they're wrong. Sincerity and genuineness will be vitally important. If you simply regurgitate the other person's words in a formulaic way, you'll sound like a parrot. Here's the type of problem I'm referring to:

Wife: You're pissing me off!

Husband (who just learned about Thought Empathy): I hear you saying that I'm pissing you off.

Wife: What the hell are you doing? You sound like a parrot!

Husband: You seem to be saying that I sound like a parrot and you're not sure what I'm doing.

Wife: For crying out loud, stop repeating everything I say! This is driving me nuts!

Husband: I hear you saying that you want me to stop repeating what you say because it's driving you nuts.

This fellow sounds incredibly mechanical. He's using Thought Empathy to put up a wall. He's not really listening, but simply deflecting what his wife is saying, and it's annoying. Here's a more effective response:

Wife: You're pissing me off!

Husband: Wow, I can see that you're really mad at me. I'm feeling pretty anxious right now because I'm not sure what I did or said that was upsetting to you. Can you tell me more about how you're feeling?

As you can see, this husband is sharing his feelings at the same time that he's empathizing with his wife. When he says, "Wow," he's expressing genuine surprise. He also admits that he feels anxious and isn't quite sure what happened. These statements make him sound human and vulnerable. He no longer sounds like a parrot because he's responding from the heart and asking for more information. At the end, he asks an open-ended question. This shows that he's concerned and willing to listen. When you empathize, a flexible, curious mind and a loving, compassionate heart will be the keys to your success.

Feeling Empathy

Thought Empathy is extremely helpful, but it usually won't be enough. You'll also have to use Feeling Empathy and acknowledge the other person's feelings. During a conflict, the other person will probably be upset. She may be feeling hurt, insulted, frustrated, or annoyed with you. If you don't acknowledge her feelings, they'll escalate and may spiral out of control. That's because she wants you to see where she's coming from emotionally as well. We all want that. When people realize that you're taking their feelings into account, they won't be so likely to get defensive or to act out their feelings. They'll also be more receptive and willing to listen to how you're feeling.

Feeling Empathy means that you acknowledge how the other person is probably feeling, given what he just said to you. How do you do this? When you paraphrase what the other person said, ask yourself, "How is he likely to be feeling, given the way he's thinking about the situation?" For example, if someone tells you that you're a jerk, it doesn't take a rocket scientist to figure out that he's probably ticked off. And if your best friend says that her brother was just diagnosed with leukemia, she may be feeling shocked, sad, frightened, and overwhelmed with grief.

When you use Feeling Empathy, you can say something like this: "Yolanda, given what you just said, I can imagine that you might be feeling X, Y, or Z. Am I reading you right?" X, Y, and Z refer to Feeling Words from the list on page 78. If you finish with a question, it will give the other person the chance to correct anything you got wrong and tell you more about how she is feeling.

Imagine that you said this to me: "Dr. Burns, my father gets mad at me every time I try to talk to him. He's so critical. I can't do anything right." Here's how I might respond, using Thought and Feeling Empathy:

I'm sad to hear that. It sounds like your father gets really critical when you try to talk to him. That must feel horrible. It can be devastating when someone you love criticizes you and you feel like you can't do anything right. I can imagine that you might be feeling hurt or put down. Or maybe you're feeling mad or scared. Tell me how you feel when he does that to you.

Notice that I've repeated what you said to me (Thought Empathy), acknowledged how you might be feeling (Feeling Empathy), and finished with a question. It's important to finish with a question so the other person will feel encouraged to open up and tell you more about the problem. In addition, he or she can tell you if you got it right. Often, you'll discover that your perception of how the other person is thinking or feeling is somewhat off base.

When you're using Feeling Empathy, try to put yourself in the other person's shoes and think about the kinds of feelings he or she is probably having. Let's say that your twelve-year-old daughter, Janine, wants to stay out until one a.m. at a party with her friends on Saturday night, but you tell her that she can't stay out that late. Suddenly, she blurts out, "All my friends can stay out until one o'clock. It's no big deal. You don't care about me! All you want to do is boss me around."

How do you think Janine might be feeling, given what she just said to you? Take a look at the Feeling Words on page 78 and select at least three or four words before you continue reading.

Janine definitely sounds angry, frustrated, and upset. She's probably feeling sad and disappointed as well. She might also be feeling embarrassed and humiliated, because she'll have to leave the party before any of her friends. Perhaps she's afraid that her friends will think less of her because she has an early curfew. And when she says that you don't care or understand, she sounds hurt and rejected.

Now play the part of Janine's mother. How will you respond? Write out what you'd say to her on a separate piece of paper. Try to use Thought and Feeling Empathy—paraphrase what she just said, acknowledge how she might be feeling, and ask if you got it right. Please do this exercise on paper before you continue reading.

Step 5. Revised Response
Here's one approach:

Janine, I can see that you're upset and I feel bad because I hate to let you down. I'd love to let you stay out later, but

---

I'm really concerned because of the kids from your school who were hurt in that horrible drink-driving accident a few weeks ago, and I could never forgive myself if something happened to you. At the same time, if all your friends can stay out until one o'clock, it must feel unfair that you can't. Can you tell me more about how you're feeling? I wouldn't be a bit surprised if you're feeling really frustrated and ticked off at me right now.

In this response, you're putting yourself into Janine's shoes and acknowledging how she's probably feeling. You're also finding some truth in what she said and encouraging her to tell you more. In addition, you're sharing your own feelings in a loving way. This response will probably make it easier for Janine to open up so you can have a meaningful dialogue without engaging in a power struggle. This doesn't mean that you'll have to give in to her demands. Ultimately, you'll have the right to make that decision, but the medicine will go down a lot more easily if you listen skillfully and talk about the problem in a loving way, without shutting her out of the dialogue.

Keep in mind that this is not a pure science. There's no way you can know exactly how other people are thinking or feeling until you ask them. That's why you'll almost always want to combine Thought and Feeling Empathy with Inquiry, the third listening skill listed on page 98. When you use Inquiry, you ask the other person if you got it right or if he can tell you more about how he's thinking and feeling. In fact, I've used Inquiry in nearly all of the examples in this chapter. We'll talk more about Inquiry in the next chapter.

It's also important to remember that when you're using Feeling Empathy, the words you select should always be influenced by the context. If your wife is upset because you forgot your anniversary, you can acknowledge that she probably feels hurt and angry. But if your boss criticizes your performance at work, you probably don't want to say, "It sounds like you feel hurt and angry." Your boss would think you were a nut! Instead, you can use words that are more appropriate for a business environment.

Suppose that you slaved over a proposal, but weren't sure you were on the right track. After reviewing it, your boss tells you that it isn't up to speed. You might say:

I'm sorry to hear that you were disappointed with the proposal, but I'm not surprised. When I was writing it, I felt like it wasn't coming together in the way I wanted it to. If you can tell me about some of the problems you spotted, I'd be happy to revise it and try to make it better.

This response sounds professional. You're acknowledging that your boss was disappointed, which is appropriate. You're also using the Disarming Technique along with Thought and Feeling Empathy, and asking for more information. Your boss will probably be pleased because you sound like a team player and you're expressing respect for his expertise.

You may recall reading about Harriet, the woman who was convinced that her husband, Jerry, couldn't handle negative feelings. When Jerry said, "I feel hurt and blamed when you judge me," Harriet responded by saying, "It seems like anytime I disagree with you or say anything negative, you get upset. I feel like I have to be super careful about what I say, and sometimes I feel like I have to keep quiet just to keep the peace. But I don't want false peace."

Harriet's response was not effective because she sounded moralistic. Furthermore, Jerry had just tried to express his feelings, and Harriet punished him. In addition, she failed to express her own feelings, the exact thing she was blaming Jerry for. Once again, we can see that she's creating the exact problem that she's complaining about, but she's not aware of it.

Put yourself in Harriet's shoes and see if you can come up with a more effective response to Jerry, using Thought and Feeling Empathy. Ask yourself how Jerry is likely to be feeling, given the fact that he just said, "I feel hurt and blamed when you judge me." Review the Feeling Words list on page 78 and ask yourself how Jerry's probably feeling. Write down your response on a separate piece of paper before you continue reading.

Step 5. Revised Response

Here's one approach:

> Jerry, you say that you feel hurt and blamed, and I feel terrible because I think I have been judgmental. I wouldn't be surprised if you're feeling frustrated and annoyed with me, too. Sometimes it seems like we're walking on eggshells when we talk, and I also end up feeling shut out, lonely, and frustrated. It bothers me a lot, because I love you so much. Can you tell me more about how I've been judging you, and how that makes you feel?

Harriet acknowledges his feelings, shares her own, and invites him to open up. This will allow them to connect on a deeper emotional level instead of constantly bickering about who's right and who's wrong, or who's to blame for the problem.

Listening vs. Helping

When you're using Thought and Feeling Empathy, try to remember that your goal is not to "help" the other person or solve the problem that's bothering him, but simply to show that you genuinely want to understand how he feels. Most of the time, a little understanding is all he really wants and needs. There's a time to solve problems, but it's definitely not when the other person is upset. Skillful listening has to come first. This requires discipline and determination.

I made the foolish mistake of "helping" rather than listening during a recent lecture. It was embarrassing. After my book *When Panic Attacks* came out, I had the chance to give a talk and sign autographs at a local bookstore. During the Q&A period, a woman in the front row excitedly raised her hand. I was hoping for a question about anxiety, because that was the focus of my talk, but her question was on an unrelated topic. She said, "Dr. Burns, my daughter won't *ever* listen to me. I try to tell her what to do, but she just won't listen. Why is she so stubborn? How can I make her listen to me when I know that what I'm saying is right? I've tried *everything* but *nothing* works!" She sounded irate. It seemed clear that she was involved in a gigantic power struggle with her daughter.

I said that sometimes when we try too hard to get other people to do what we want them to do, it backfires. Often, the solution involves just the opposite—learning to empathize so you can really listen and understand where the other person is coming from. This means trying to see the world through her eyes, instead of trying to control her or get her to listen to you.

The woman defiantly announced, "Doctor, you're way off base. I'm an *excellent* listener, but it just won't work with my daughter. What should I do? Nothing will work with her!" I hate to admit it, but I felt like saying, "If you want to know the truth, it seems obvious that you're trying to control your daughter and that your listening skills stink! In fact, you're not even listening to me right now." Fortunately, I bit my tongue and didn't say that.

This woman was convinced that she was a great listener, but it didn't look like that. But I made the same error! I tried to tell her what to do, rather than acknowledging all the frustration and heartbreak she was experiencing with her daughter. All she really wanted at that moment was a little bit of understanding. She wanted someone to agree that she was right. She needed to vent and wasn't ready to examine her own role in the conflict with her daughter, much less try a new and radically different approach.

When I examine my own interactions with people, as well as the problems my students and patients describe, I'm always surprised at how seductive and irresistible these relationship traps can be. And they seem to spread like a virus, so we all get infected. This woman was annoyed because her daughter wouldn't listen to her, but she wasn't listening to her daughter. I was annoyed that she wasn't listening to me, but I wasn't listening to her.

Although this chapter is about practical communication techniques, we're really discussing a spiritual theme. Empathy is closely related to the concepts of compassion and acceptance. It involves getting out of our own heads and egos and instead trying to comprehend the thoughts, feelings, and suffering of another person.

Kindness, humility, consideration, and (dare I say) love itself, along with an earnest desire to see and comprehend the other person's point of view, are all vitally important components of empathy.

It's not easy to be purely receptive and compassionate. You have to surrender your own agenda and forget about your *self* so you can focus entirely on the other person's thoughts, feelings, and values. And you have to do this with the spirit of acceptance and respect, rather than judgment or blame.

I sometimes think of empathy as the "zero technique." Instead of promoting your own thoughts, needs, and feelings, you zero in on where the other person is coming from. You become totally receptive, so in a sense, you give that person nothing. You become a zero. But paradoxically, you are giving him or her something priceless.

Chapter 15

Inquiry: "Did I Get That Right?"

In the last chapter, we talked about the vital importance of empathy. Accurate understanding of how the other person is thinking and feeling is equally important in personal and business settings, including sales. The biggest mistake most of us make is promoting our own ideas and pushing our own agendas without really listening. This strategy is doomed to failure because the other person will simply shut down.

But how can you develop accurate understanding? Ask! You might have noticed in the last chapter that I ended almost every example of Thought and Feeling Empathy with a question. This technique is called Inquiry.

Inquiry is one of the most useful communication techniques and perhaps the easiest to master—although there are a few mistakes people nearly always make when they're first learning to use Inquiry. When you use Inquiry, you ask gentle, probing questions to learn more about what the other person is thinking and feeling. Your goal is to open the other person up like a book instead of shutting him or her down or letting the conversation die. In the last chapter, we talked about the fact that you can never be sure that you understand how someone else is thinking and feeling. Inquiry gives the other person the chance to tell you. It shows that you have a genuine interest in how he or she is thinking and feeling.

Inquiry walks hand in hand with Empathy. When you empathize, you try to grasp exactly how the other person is thinking and feeling. When you use Inquiry, you invite the other person to tell you more about what's going on inside. You show a curiosity, an eagerness to learn about how the other person sees the situation, and how he really feels. You're also giving him the chance to let you know if you got it right, and if you're really tuning in to what he's trying to say.

You can use Inquiry in a variety of ways. First, you can ask more about how the other person is thinking and feeling. Here are some examples:

- "Could you tell me more about that? I'm really interested in what you just said about . . ."
- "How do you see the situation?"
- "I'd like to hear more about how you were feeling when . . ."
- "Tell me more about what happened, and how you felt."

Second, you can ask if your perceptions of the other person's thoughts and feelings are valid:

- "It sounds like you're feeling lonely and upset, and maybe even a little angry with me. Am I reading you right?"
- "It seems like you're really discouraged and overwhelmed right now. Is that how you're feeling?"

Third, you can use open-ended questions to prompt the other person to tell you more:

- "I'd like to hear more about that."
- "What you're saying sounds important. Can you tell me more about how you're thinking about this problem?"

Fourth, you can use open-ended questions for brainstorming and problem solving:

- "What are your ideas about this?"
- "Have you thought about how we might approach this problem differently?"
- "What do you think would be helpful?"

Inquiry will be most effective if you ask questions in a friendly and nonconfrontational way. A question can sound sarcastic or respectful, depending on your attitude and tone of voice. The other person has to sense that you're genuinely interested in his feelings and point of view. The spirit of relaxed curiosity will set him at ease. If you sound demanding, hurt, or defensive, the other person won't be very eager to open up to you. Your body language will be just as important as the words you use. If your arms are folded defiantly across your chest and you're scowling, the other person will notice and feel put off.

In chapter 11, you read about a man named Barry who was convinced that his partner, Richard, was too controlling. When he was parking the car at the cinema, Richard said, "Why didn't you park over there instead of driving around the car park three times?" Barry responded, "I wanted to get a really good parking place." The bickering continued because Barry didn't acknowledge Richard's feelings or express his own feelings. What could he have said instead?

Here's what Barry and I came up with:

You're right, Richard. I could have parked over there, and that would have saved time. At the same time, I'm feeling a bit put down right now because there's a sharp edge in your voice, and it seems like you're annoyed with me. Can we talk about it?

In this response, Barry accepts Richard's criticism while bringing the hidden hostility out into the open in a direct but gentle way. He asks if Richard is annoyed and respectfully expresses his own feelings. This is a skillful example of Inquiry.

At first, this type of direct communication may be uncomfortable for them because they're both used to avoiding conflict. If they begin to talk about their feelings more openly, they'll have the chance to experience real closeness for the first time in years.

Premature Problem Solving

One of the most common Inquiry errors is to ask the person who's upset how you can fix the problem. Problem solving is effective in a business environment but may not work when you're talking to a friend or family member who feels upset. Most of the time, the other person just needs to vent. If you jump in and offer to help the other person solve the problem that's bugging her, she'll probably get annoyed. That's because premature problem solving prevents the other person from expressing feelings such as hurt or anger. It's also patronizing because it puts the other person in a one-down position, as if she has a problem and you're the expert who's going to solve it for her.

Problem solving isn't always a mistake, but timing is important. If you jump in and try to solve the problem before the other person has had the chance to vent, or when the tensions are high, your attempts will fail because the other person needs the chance to express his or her feelings. However, if you listen to and validate what the other person is saying, and encourage him or her to open up, there often won't be any need to solve the "real" problem. Often, the real problem is simply the fact that you weren't listening.

A cabinetmaker named Dean said this to me during one of our therapy sessions: "Doctor, my wife feels like you're not helping me. She thinks I'm not making any real progress."

Suppose I responded by saying, "Dean, what do you think I could do that would be more helpful to you?" This may sound like a skillful example of Inquiry, but it's not. Can you see any problems with this response?

It's not going to be effective for several reasons. First, Dean probably doesn't have any idea what would be more helpful to him. After all, he's coming to me for help, and I'm supposed to be the expert. Second, I haven't asked about how he feels, or how his wife feels. Maybe he thinks he's making excellent progress, but his wife is frustrated and upset with him about something. Or maybe he feels that the therapy isn't going very well, but he's afraid of hurting my feelings, so he tells me that his wife is unhappy with the treatment. In addition, I haven't asked about the problems that his wife is concerned about. What does she mean when she says he isn't making progress? Is he struggling with low self-esteem? A drinking problem? A marital conflict? Perhaps there's an important problem that we should be focusing on.

Put yourself in my shoes and see if you can come up with a more effective response. Write down your response on a separate piece of paper before you continue reading. Feel free to use any of the communication techniques you've been learning about, such as the Disarming Technique and Thought and Feeling Empathy, but make sure you include Inquiry.

Step 5. Revised Response
Here's a response that might work:

> Dean, I'm surprised to hear that because I thought we were making excellent progress, but I might be misreading the situation, and I'm really glad you told me how your wife has been feeling. Can you tell me a bit more about what she said, and how you've been feeling as well? If we've gotten off track, this could help us get pointed in the right direction.

This statement conveys respect and reframes the problem as an opportunity to talk things over and get the therapy moving forward.

The three skills you've learned so far—the Disarming Technique, Thought and Feeling Empathy, and Inquiry—can help you become a great listener, but good communication requires more than just listening skills. The other person's thoughts and feelings are definitely important, but so are yours. If you want other people to listen and respect your point of view, you'll need to combine skillful listening (Empathy) with effective self-expression (Assertiveness) in the spirit of acceptance and caring (Respect). If any of these three components is missing, your efforts probably won't be effective. Now I'm going to show you how to talk so that people will listen to you.

Chapter 16

"I Feel" Statements

We've already discussed the fact that skillful listening requires a certain amount of self-disclosure so you'll sound natural and real. However, you can't just bombard the other person with your own point of view and expect some good to come out of it. That's the mistake that the assertiveness training movement made: focusing excessively on the importance of asserting your own wants, needs, and feelings in a kind of self-centered way. Assertiveness sounds great on paper, but it doesn't always work in real-world situations. You've probably noticed that often, when you try to express your own feelings or point of view, the other person simply will not listen. For example, your spouse may get defensive and insist that you don't know what you're talking about.

How can you express your feelings so that people *will* listen? "I Feel" Statements can be very helpful. If you review the Five Secrets of Effective Communication on page 98, you'll see that when you use "I Feel" Statements, you express your own thoughts and feelings openly and directly, using words that clearly describe your emotions. For example, you might say, "I'm feeling frustrated," or "I'm upset."

This is different from saying, "You're wrong," or "You're making me upset." These are classic examples of "You" Statements. "You" Statements place blame and put people on the defensive. In contrast, when you use "I Feel" Statements, you're simply informing people about how you think and feel, and you're maintaining ownership of those feelings.

I don't like to reduce things to simple formulas because formulaic statements don't sound genuine; however, a formula can point you in the right direction, as long as you don't apply the formula too literally or mechanically. The formula for an "I Feel" Statement is similar to the approach I described for Feeling Empathy, except that you talk about your own feelings. You can say, "I feel X, Y, or Z," where X, Y, and Z refer to Feeling Words from the chart on page 78. Here are some specific examples of "I Feel" Statements:

- I'm upset right now.
- I'm feeling hurt and put down.
- I feel sad and concerned to hear that.
- I'm really lonely.
- I'm frustrated.
- I'm embarrassed, but I have to admit that you're right.
- To tell you the truth, I'm feeling ticked off right now.

As you can see, "I Feel" Statements are pretty straightforward, but they can get tricky in real-world settings. Suppose a friend tells you, "You're so stubborn! You always have to be right!" Which of the following is an "I Feel" Statement?

- I feel like you're acting like a jerk.
- I feel like you're wrong! I'm *not* being stubborn, and I don't always have to be right.
- I feel like you're judging me.
- I feel like you're making me mad.
- I'm feeling a bit awkward right now.

Think about it for a moment before you continue reading.

The first four responses may sound like "I Feel" Statements, because they all start with "I feel . . . ,") but they're not. They're "You" Statements. They all involve unflattering descriptions of the other person's behavior rather than descriptions of how you're feeling. In the first response, you're labeling the other person as a jerk. The second response is a defensive counterattack. In the third example, you're accusing the other person of judging you, and the fourth response sounds like an accusation and will put the other person on the defensive. The final response, "I'm feeling a bit awkward right now," is an "I Feel" Statement because you're expressing your feelings openly without attacking the other person.

Of course, when someone criticizes you, you'll have to respond with more than just an "I Feel" Statement or your response will fall flat. The Disarming Technique, Thought and Feeling Empathy, and Inquiry can be invaluable. When you use an "I Feel" Statement, remember that your feelings may seem threatening or upsetting to other people, so they may get defensive. This reaction is a good indicator that you came on too strong, or that the other person is feeling especially vulnerable and fragile and isn't ready to listen. You'll have to switch gears immediately. Stop trying to express your feelings and use the three listening skills again: the Disarming Technique, Thought and Feeling Empathy, and Inquiry. Once the other person feels relaxed and begins to trust you again, you can try to express your feelings in a gentle manner.

I always try to soften my "I Feel" Statements, especially if the other person seems to be upset. Stroking, which we'll discuss in depth in the next chapter, is the sugar that makes the medicine go down. Stroking means expressing positive regard for the person you're at odds with. For example, you could say, "I really want to talk this out because I like you a lot, and your friendship means a great deal to me." It can also be helpful to convey humility whenever there's tension in the air.

Do you recall Jed and his wife, Marjorie? When Jed came home from work, Marjorie said, "I'm mad. You got drunk on the way home from work again. You choose alcohol over me. You'll probably sit on the sofa in a stupor and channel-surf all night long. You stink, too, and it pisses me off."

Then Jed said, "I might as well get drunk. You're about as warm and cuddly as an ice cube. *Nothing* turns you on!"

Jed felt hurt, but he attacked his wife instead of sharing his feelings with her. Can you think of a more effective response that incorporates an "I Feel" Statement? You can use any of the Five Secrets of Effective Communication on page 98, but make sure you include at least one "I Feel" Statement. Write down your response on a separate piece of paper before you continue reading.

Step 5. Revised Response
Jed could say:

> You're right, I did drink too much on the way home from work, and you have every right to feel ticked off. I've been feeling frustrated and rejected, and I've been avoiding you instead of talking it out. I feel like we're drifting apart, and it hurts because I don't want to lose you. Right now, I'm feeling hurt and put down. It sounds like you've been feeling hurt and angry and rejected, too. Can we talk about it? This is hard for me, but I want to know more about how you've been feeling.

Jed's Revised Response will give Marjorie the chance to connect more openly and talk about her feelings. You may think that the Revised Response I suggested sounds too sweet, or that it's not the way real people talk to each other. If so, you can revise it to make it sound more natural. There's no single correct way to share your feelings. When you do Step 5 of the Relationship Journal, you can edit your responses as often as you like until you're comfortable with them.

Learning to communicate skillfully is an art. It's a lot like learning to play a musical instrument. You could think of the Five Secrets of Effective Communication as the keys on a piano. Anyone can sit down and pound on the keys, but it won't sound very good. If you practice and work at it, your skills will improve and you'll learn how to make more beautiful music.

Although nearly everyone would agree that it's important to express your feelings openly and directly, most people resist using "I Feel" Statements during actual conflicts with other people. There are many reasons for this. You may feel that it would be inappropriate to share your feelings, or that you'd sound silly or overly personal.

This is a genuine concern, and the comments I made in the chapter on empathy also pertain here. The way you express your feelings will vary in different settings. In a business setting, you can use low-key, professional words when you express your feelings. For example, if you're not getting along with a colleague, you might say that you're feeling uncomfortable or awkward, rather than saying that you feel hurt, resentful, or angry. In contrast, if you're talking to your spouse, son, or daughter, you can be more open and spontaneous.

Some people resist using "I Feel" Statements because of a mind-set called Mind Reading: you may tell yourself that if someone really loves you and cares about you, he should know what you want and how you feel without your having to tell him. This belief has a certain romantic appeal, and lots of people seem to buy into it. It also gives you a good excuse for not telling people how you're thinking and feeling.

I once treated a woman named Mina who complained of sexual difficulties. Mina explained that for more than twenty years, she'd been unable to achieve orgasm during intercourse. Her husband, Abe, felt that it was his fault. He was five feet five and had never been very good at sports when he was growing up, and he felt that he wasn't macho enough to excite his wife. To compensate for this, he took up bodybuilding and worked at it with enormous dedication. Over the years, he'd become extremely strong and muscular, and had actually won a number of local bodybuilding competitions in his age and weight division. I asked Mina if this had helped their sex life. She said that it had actually made the problem worse.

I asked Mina why she was having so much trouble enjoying sex. Was she brought up in a strict, religious home and perhaps felt guilty about sex? Was her husband's approach to lovemaking unappealing? Mina lowered her eyes and hesitantly confessed that every time they started making love, Abe grabbed her nipples and started squeezing them. She said the longer they made love, the tighter he squeezed, and it was excruciatingly painful. She said he'd gotten so strong that it was like having her nipples in a vice.

I said I could *completely* understand why she was having so much trouble with sex and told her that I might even have a solution for the problem. She perked up and asked what it was.

I asked, "Have you ever considered talking things over with Abe? You could tell him what you like and dislike sexually, and let him know how much it hurts when he squeezes your nipples. You could also show him how you like to be touched. That way, he'd learn how to be a better lover and you'd probably both enjoy sex a whole lot more."

Mina immediately became indignant and said, "I shouldn't have to do that! You'd think that after twenty years, he'd finally get the message!"

Mina didn't want to tell her husband how she was feeling because she thought he should know how she felt, or perhaps because she was afraid of vulnerability and intimacy. In an ideal world, we wouldn't have to tell people what we want or how we feel. They'd be so sensitive that they'd know. Remember that other people can't actually tell how you're thinking and feeling, no matter how much they love you. Direct communication with "I Feel" Statements may seem less romantic than the scenes from a Hollywood movie, but it's more effective than waiting for people to read your mind!

Chapter 17

Stroking: "I—It" vs. "I—Thou" Relationships

S troking is the fifth secret of effective communication. Stroking means that you express positive regard for the other person, no matter how upset you feel. You've seen many examples of this technique already. We're really talking about kindness, caring, and respect. If you want a better relationship with anyone, Stroking is mandatory. You can't put people down and expect them to love you in return. This may seem obvious, but it seems difficult for many people to accept. We all *want* love and respect, but sometimes we don't want to *give* love and respect, especially when we're at odds with someone and we're feeling hurt or angry.

Stroking is based on the work of the twentieth-century theologian Martin Buber, who described two types of human relationships: "I—It" relationships and "I—Thou" relationships. In an "I—It" relationship, you view the other person as an object, an "It" to be manipulated. You treat him like the enemy, and your goal is to attack, defeat, or exploit him. For example, some men view attractive women as sex objects to use and discard. One-night stands are good examples of "I—It" relationships. Con artists and predators view people as objects to hurt and exploit. Those are "I—It" relationships, too.

The competitive mind-set I described earlier is another type of "I—It" relationship, and it's easy to get caught up in it. In sports, competition can be healthy and exhilarating, but if you're not getting along with a friend or colleague, the same mind-set can cause problems. Your thinking may become dominated by the idea that one of you is going to win and the other is going to lose. It goes without saying that you're determined to be the winner, so you want to make sure the other person ends up as the loser.

The "I—It" mind-set is highly seductive because it feels justified. When we're looking down on other people and treating them in a shabby way, we tell ourselves that we're doing the *right* thing and giving other people what they deserve. After all, they really *are* jerks!

"I—Thou" relationships are just the opposite. In an "I—Thou" relationship you choose to treat the other person with dignity and respect. You convey the desire to develop a closer, better relationship, even if you and the other person are feeling frustrated and mad at each other.

The "I—It" and "I—Thou" mind-sets both function as self-fulfilling prophecies. If you look down on people and treat them badly, they'll retaliate and appear just as annoying and hostile as you expected. If, in contrast, you treat people with kindness and respect in spite of your anger, they'll nearly always be far more flexible and responsive to your feelings and point of view. Still, "I—Thou" relationships are pretty unpopular, and I think they've been out of fashion for thousands of years.

People justify "I—It" relationships with all kinds of arguments. They tell me that they just *can't* treat the other person with respect, but what they really mean is, "I don't *want* to," or "I refuse to." You may have a long list of compelling reasons why you shouldn't have to treat your spouse, your sibling, your neighbor, or that irritating colleague with respect.

Some people don't want to use Stroking because they're afraid of sounding fake. This is a valid concern. Most people can see right through a fake. However, you don't have to act false or overly sweet when you use Stroking, and you don't have to deny or suppress your true feelings. Faking it is *not* one of the Five Secrets of Effective Communication!

Suppose that you're ticked off at your husband. You're mad because you've been arguing and going around in circles, and he called you a goddamned bitch. You can express your anger in a direct but respectful way, without sounding false, like this:

> Gregory, I'm feeling so mad and hurt right now that I'm about to burst. In fact, I feel like I want to wring your neck. At the same time, I can see that you're feeling annoyed with me. I really love you, and it bothers me when we fight like this. Let's talk about it. Can you tell me what I've been doing that's been annoying you?

This statement makes it abundantly clear that you're mad. You haven't pulled any punches or faked how you feel, but you've been careful to preserve Gregory's sense of self-esteem. You're not trying to put him down or humiliate him. He probably won't feel the need to battle with you because you've conveyed respect and haven't belittled him or backed him up against the wall.

Resistance to Stroking

When I teach people about Stroking, they often say something along these lines: "Why should I have to treat my sister with respect? She's a hostile bitch. Why doesn't *she* treat *me* with a little respect?" I can identify with that feeling. When you're mad, you probably won't want to express positive regard for the person you're mad at. It seems like it would be infinitely more gratifying to tell her off.

Here are some more things I've heard from people who didn't want to use Stroking:

- "I shouldn't have to be nice to him. He doesn't deserve it."
- "I'm just too angry to be nice to her."
- "I can't think of anything positive to say about him."
- "Why should I be nice to her when she's treated me like this?"

- "I can't think of anything positive to say about him. He really is a jerk."

Ultimately, we all have to choose between "I—It" and "I—Thou" relationships. You certainly don't have to use Stroking, and many people decide not to. However, none of the Five Secrets of Effective Communication will be effective without Stroking. If, in contrast, you decide to convey genuine respect in the heat of battle, your efforts will be far more effective.

Stroking is almost more of a philosophy than a specific technique. It's the spirit and attitude that you bring to the interaction and convey to the other person. There are several ways to use Stroking:

- You can give the other person a genuine compliment. For example, you can comment on some positive quality or trait she has, or something that you really like.
- You can let the other person know that you like, respect, or admire him, and value his friendship even though you're both feeling angry or disagreeing with each other right now.
- You can express your feelings with respectful, noninsulting, nonhurtful language.
- You can convey warmth and caring through your body language, showing that you're interested, open, and receptive, as opposed to frowning, crossing your arms across your chest, and shaking your head in a judgmental way.

You can also frame the other person's motives in a more positive and flattering light. Let's imagine that you and a friend are arguing about religion or politics and going around in circles, and you feel that he's being stubborn or bullheaded. If you say, "You're being unreasonable and you're wrong," he'll feel offended and become even more stubborn. No one enjoys being put down. Furthermore, he's convinced that *you're* the one who's being unreasonable.

Instead of insisting that he's stupid, dogmatic, or mean-spirited, you could tell him that you respect the fact that he's got the courage of his convictions, and that even though your own thinking is different, you want to understand more about his point of view. When he begins to explain himself, you can use the Disarming Technique and find some truth in what he's saying. You can also use Inquiry to draw him out. If you do this in a sincere way, it will have a calming effect and he'll be far more open to your ideas. In fact, he'll probably stop arguing the moment he feels validated and senses that you respect him.

But do you have to stroke people who really *are* jerks? Isn't it better to be honest and let people know what losers and idiots they are?

Several years ago, my beloved dog, Salty, was diagnosed with colon cancer. After much family debate and tears, we decided on surgery to try to remove the tumor, but the surgery was only partly successful. As the cancer spread, the poor guy began having more and more trouble controlling his bowels and bladder, and he started staining our carpets almost every day. We didn't have the heart to keep Salty outside in the cold or limit him to the bathroom area because we loved him so much. So the carpets got worse and worse.

One day, I was at the local pharmacy and noticed that they had large, impressive-looking carpet-cleaning machines for rent. I rented one and enthusiastically loaded it into my car. I had to wedge the carpet cleaner into the tiny compartment behind the front seat. It was so big that it obstructed my view in the rearview mirror. Once I started driving, I realized that I couldn't see behind me at all.

A few blocks down the road, I paused at a stop sign to see if I could arrange the side mirrors a little better. Suddenly, I heard loud shouting and cursing. I leaned out the window and realized that a huge lorry was directly behind me. It had enormous tyres and a big spotlight mounted on the cab. Two beefy young men were leaning out the windows, shaking their fists and shouting at me, using four-letter words and blasting me with their horn.

I felt a chill down my spine. I immediately drove across the intersection and pulled over to the side of the road so they could pass me. They roared past, shouting and making obscene gestures. One of them threw an empty beer can at my car. They were obviously drunk.

I had to follow them because there was only one lane. About half a mile ahead, the road divided into two lanes at a traffic light. The light was red, so I pulled up next to the lorry, on the left.

The young man in the passenger seat leaned out of his window and glared down at me, holding a can of beer in his hand. It seemed like he was about to start cursing again or challenge me to a fight. I thought about the difference between an "I—It" relationship and an "I—Thou" relationship, so I looked up at him and said:

> I wanted to apologize for holding you guys up at the stop sign back there. I rented this carpet cleaner because my dog, Salty, is dying from colon cancer and he's been doing a number on the carpets. As you can see, the carpet cleaner is so big that I couldn't see you in my rearview mirror. Obviously, you guys are in a hurry and I'm really sorry.

He started apologizing profusely. He said that he had a dog, too, and asked if I wanted a beer. He seemed intensely embarrassed. I think they would have come home and helped me clean the carpets if I'd asked them!

So now we can revisit the question, "Why should I have to treat someone with respect if he or she is treating me in a shabby, hostile way?" The answer is that you *don't* have to treat anyone with respect. You can respond to people any way you want. It just depends on the kinds of relationships you want.

The young men were inviting me to do battle. They wanted me to take the bait, and it was tempting because my pride was on the line. I felt like I *had* to stick up for myself and let them know what losers they were. But when I treated them with respect and expressed humility, it instantly transformed our interaction. Paradoxically, this put me in control. If I'd tried to be strong and tough,

I would have been playing their game, and I probably would have lost. I'm not very good at kicking ass any more!

Will the Five Secrets of Effective Communication *always* work like this? Is this some form of magic? Of course not. There's no magic formula that will solve all of life's problems.

Will these methods *usually* work? Yes, but only if you use them skillfully. If you use the Five Secrets in a clumsy, false, or manipulative way, you won't get the results you're looking for. But if you're genuine and convey respect, you can often achieve amazing results.

Here's a useful exercise that will help you develop greater skill and appreciation for this technique. Over the next week, make it a point to give out at least twenty-five compliments. Make sure that you include friends, family members, shop assistants, and even strangers. I do this all the time. For example, I just had to call about one of our bank accounts that had been temporarily frozen because they thought an unauthorized person had tried to gain access to it. It turned out to be an error. The woman from the bank explained the problem and did an excellent job of straightening it out. I was tremendously relieved and told her how grateful I felt for the professional and friendly way she'd handled the problem. She seemed thrilled and grateful. She probably goes through the day and works really hard without hearing many compliments or thanks for the hard work that she does. You'd be amazed at how people, even strangers, will light up when you say something nice to them.

The Power of Admiration, Respect, and Kindness

Sometimes we all have to express negative feelings and tell people something that may upset them. Stroking is invaluable in this situation as well. We all have a deep need to feel admired and respected. If you treat people with kindness and make sure that your comments will never hurt or humiliate them, you can get away with saying just about anything. If you have to criticize someone, but you convey liking or respect at the same time, that person won't be so tempted to get defensive and dismiss your comments or write you off as a jerk. Stroking is actually a form of empowerment because people will be far more receptive and likely to listen to you.

But how can you convey genuine liking and respect if the person you're not getting along with is truly repulsive or disgusting? What if you can't stand someone and feel like you couldn't possibly say anything good about him or her?

Hank was one of the most unappealing individuals I've ever met. It's embarrassing to admit it, because he was my patient, but that's how I felt. Hank was a beefy, twenty-three-year-old tough guy who was referred to me by his parents. He worked as a construction worker and he lived with his parents. They were concerned that he was depressed, lonely, and drinking too much. He was a loner who didn't have any real friends.

When Hank showed up for his first session, I was taken aback. He looked totally disheveled and reeked of urine. To make matters worse, when he left the office, the chair he was sitting on smelled of urine. The rest of my patients that day hinted that the office had a strong smell, and I was worried that they might think that *I* was the one who smelled like urine. It took a week for the smell to clear, and then Hank returned for his next session, just as disheveled and smelly as he'd been the week before. This went on for several weeks, and my office smelled like an outhouse.

As if that weren't enough, Hank talked about things that I found disgusting. For example, he'd laugh and tell me how much fun it would be if he and I could hang out together, get drunk, and take advantage of women. He never did any of his psychotherapy homework between sessions, and there was no improvement in his symptoms.

I feel it's important to be honest and open with my patients to the greatest extent possible. When there's tension in the air, and I ignore it, things always get worse. But how could I possibly tell Hank that he smelled like piss and I couldn't stand being around him? The prospect seemed awkward, to say the least, so I procrastinated, hoping that the situation would improve on its own. But it didn't. Hank showed up faithfully for every session, smelling like a toilet with a mouth to match.

I struggled to muster up the courage to discuss the problem with Hank. But what could I possibly say that wouldn't hurt his feelings or cause him to drop out of therapy? After feeling anxious for several weeks, I finally bit the bullet and forced myself to say this to Hank:

> Hank, there's something that I need to tell you. This is hard for me to say, because I definitely don't want to hurt your feelings, but I feel the need to clear the air, so I'm going to give it a try. Let me apologize ahead of time if I don't say this quite right. I don't know how often you bathe, or if you're even aware that you sometimes have a strong odor. It even stays on the furniture after you leave, and some of my patients have complained about it. It's bothered me, too.
>
> In addition, when you say how much fun it would be for us to go out and take advantage of women, I'm not sure if you've considered how I might feel about that. In fact, I find the topic pretty upsetting. I've also noticed that you're not doing any of the psychotherapy homework assignments, and I'm concerned that we're not making the kind of progress you came here for.
>
> But then I got to thinking about this, and something really intriguing popped into my mind. Here you are, struggling with feelings of loneliness, and I like you, but I feel pushed away and dread our sessions. Do you see what I mean? I got excited when I thought about it like that, because it seemed important. I don't even know if you're aware that you've been pushing me away, or if you want to be doing that.
>
> I want to emphasize that I respect you and appreciate the chance to work with you, and I'm convinced that we could do some terrific work together that could change your life. But at the same time, I felt like I needed to tell you how I was feeling so we could clear the air and start to work together as a team.

Hank accepted this message gracefully, and didn't seem at all perturbed. Much to my surprise, he came to his next session cleaned up and looking good. He'd been working hard on his psychotherapy homework for the first time, and had several problems he wanted help with. He confessed that he was sexually frustrated but had never had a date and didn't even know how to talk to women. I began to look forward to our sessions, and our work together became much more productive. I actually became fond of Hank and greatly enjoyed our work together.

What caused the turnaround? When I conveyed my negative feelings in a direct and respectful way, without hostility, Hank felt cared about. I also used Stroking and made it abundantly clear that I had positive regard for him. My comments were genuine and came from the heart—Hank could see that I was not just paying him a false compliment. Most people saw him as a disgusting social outcast and a loser, so he was just playing the role that everyone expected him to play. When I expressed my feelings in a kind way, he could see that I wasn't going to judge or reject him, but I wasn't going to be false or hide my feelings, either. We all have a deep need for acceptance. Hank was no exception.

Chapter 18

Putting It All Together: Solutions to Common Relationship Problems

Now that you've learned a little about the Five Secrets of Effective Communication, we're going to use these techniques to solve a variety of common relationship problems most of us run into almost every day. Perhaps you have a friend who complains endlessly but won't ever listen to your helpful advice. Or a colleague with a big ego. Or a husband who's stubborn and lazy and won't help out around the house. Or a family member who always has to have her way. Or a jealous sister who's relentlessly critical of you. You'll discover that the Five Secrets of Effective Communication can be extraordinarily helpful in all of these situations, but certain techniques will be especially important when dealing with specific kinds of problems.

However, there aren't any simple formulas or gimmicks that will solve all of your relationship problems, and the specifics will vary from situation to situation. If you use the Relationship Journal, you'll have a powerful, flexible, and systematic method for analyzing and resolving practically any conflict with anyone. Always start out with one specific interaction that didn't work out. Write down one thing the other person said to you, and exactly what you said next. The rest will naturally flow from that example.

I've included partially filled-out Relationship Journals for many of the problems in this chapter, and we'll complete them together while you're reading. When we do Step 5, I'll ask you to write out a more effective response, using the Five Secrets of Effective Communication. After each sentence you write down, indicate what technique or techniques you used in parentheses, using the abbreviations on page 98. For example, you can put (DT) at the end of the sentence if you used the Disarming Technique in that sentence, or (FE) if you used Feeling Empathy. Feel free to use more than one technique per sentence. When you're done with each exercise, I'll share my thinking with you and tell you what I might have said if I'd been in that situation.

I encourage you to do the written exercises while you're reading. The practice will be invaluable when you work on your own relationship problems.

How to Cope with a Complainer

There are several mistakes people nearly always make when dealing with someone who complains a lot: they give advice or try to help or cheer the complainer up. These strategies are doomed to fail. The complainer will just keep complaining. Do you know why? People who complain aren't usually asking for advice, help, or cheerful affirmations. They're not asking you to solve the problem they're complaining about. Most of the time, they just want you to listen. They want you to understand what they're saying, accept how they feel, and agree that there's some truth in their complaints. They also want to know that someone cares about them. That's why the Disarming Technique, Thought and Feeling Empathy, and Stroking are so important when you're dealing with someone who complains. These techniques work like magic. If you use them skillfully, the complaining will stop almost instantly because the complainer will feel like somebody is finally listening. But it takes discipline to learn to respond like this!

A woman named Tracey told me that she was estranged from her elderly father, and that all her siblings were in the same boat.

He'd alienated everyone and had been alone for years. Tracey called him on Father's Day out of a sense of obligation. When she asked how he was doing, he said, "Getting older." Tracey felt guilty and defensive, but playfully responded, "Aren't we all?" Her father responded, "But some of us are dying."

Tracey felt angry because she knew he was actually in pretty good health. She explained that this was how their conversations always went and was a perfect example of why she avoided him. She hated feeling anxious and guilty and getting sucked in by his incessant complaining every time they interacted.

Let's examine their interaction. When Tracey asked her father how he was doing, he said, "Getting older." She replied, "Aren't we all?" Would you say that Tracey's response was an example of good communication or bad communication?

It's easy to see that Tracey's response was an example of bad communication: she didn't acknowledge how her father was feeling, she didn't express her own feelings, and she didn't convey respect. The consequences of her response are also obvious. Her comment triggered another complaint because she didn't listen. She blew her father off, so he upped the ante by saying, "But some of us are dying."

Can you think of a more effective response, using the Five Secrets of Effective Communication on page 98? What could Tracey say when her father says, "Getting older"? Write down your revised response on a separate piece of paper before you continue reading. Remember to put the names of the techniques you used in parentheses, using the abbreviations on page 98, at the end of each sentence.

Step 5. Revised Response

Here's what Tracey came up with when she did Step 5 of her Relationship Journal.

> Dad, you're right. (DT) You *are* getting older, and I'm sure it's no fun to feel that way. (TE; DT; FE) It upsets me to hear that you're not feeling well. (IF; ST) Have you been having problems with your health? (IN) Have you been having a hard time lately? (IN)

Then, whatever he says next, Tracey can respond along similar lines, making sure to include the Disarming Technique. For example, let's assume that he says, "Oh, my arthritis is acting up again but the doctors never listen. If you're old and poor, all they seem to care about is getting you out of the office as fast as they can." What could Tracey say next?

Here's one approach:

Dad, I can see why you're feeling unhappy. (FE; DT) Arthritis can be awfully painful, and the doctors can be pretty darn insensitive, especially when you're old and poor. (TE; DT; FE) It's frustrating when the doctor rushes you out of the office without taking the time to help you. (FE; DT) You have every right to be upset. (DT; FE)

Many of us are afraid that if we find truth in what the complainer says, it will open the floodgates for more complaining. In fact, the opposite happens. If you use the Disarming Technique skillfully, the complainer will nearly always stop complaining because he or she will feel that you're listening.

I often demonstrate this phenomenon in workshops with a role-playing exercise. I ask a volunteer to play the role of a complainer and to voice all kinds of complaints, such as "Nobody loves me," or "Life sucks." After each complaint, I simply find some truth in what the complainer just said. If you try this exercise with a friend, you'll discover that it takes the wind out of her sails and she loses all desire to keep complaining. It works like magic.

Here's an example:

Complainer: Nobody loves me!
You: You're right, you don't get nearly as much love as you deserve. (DT; ST)
Complainer: My husband spends more time surfing the Internet than hanging out with me. I think he's going to porn sites.
You: You could be right about that, too. (DT) Lots of men get addicted to online porn sites and ignore their wives. (DT) That must be upsetting. (FE)

Complainer: My hemorrhoids hurt.

You: How dreadful! (FE) Hemorrhoids can be a pain in the ass! (DT)

Complainer: I've tried various creams, but they don't help.

You: They're not nearly as good as they're cracked up to be. (DT)

Try this exercise with a friend. It's a real eye-opener. When you're playing the role of the complainer, you'll find that it's practically impossible to keep complaining if the other person uses the Disarming Technique skillfully and genuinely agrees with you.

This approach may involve a drastic change in the way you communicate and think about people who complain. Complainers seem to be making demands on you, so you may feel resentful, frustrated, guilty, and panicky. Then you try to help them, cheer them up or give them some advice, hoping they'll shut up and stop complaining. But this never works. In fact, you're making demands on them as well. You want them to listen to your good advice and stop being so relentlessly negative. This is what keeps the battle alive. You're enmeshed in a power struggle, and you both feel frustrated because neither of you is getting what you want.

The moment you understand that complainers usually aren't looking for advice or asking for help, the solution becomes simple. Most of the time, they just want you to listen, care about them, and find some truth in their complaints. If you do this, 99 percent of the time the complaining will stop. This may come as a surprise. You may feel like you've given the complainer nothing, but you've actually given him exactly what he wanted all along—to feel validated and cared about.

How to Deal with a Big Ego

People with big egos are extremely difficult to get along with. They can be demanding, fragile, self-centered, and hostile. They brag about themselves and put other people down. Mental health professionals sometimes refer to people with these personality traits as narcissists. Narcissistic individuals have several characteristics:

- They crave flattery.
- They feel superior to other people.
- They're easily wounded and can't tolerate criticism, disloyalty, or disrespect.
- They're incredibly demanding and exploit others for their own purposes.
- They're usually charming and charismatic, and know how to lure you into their web.

If you know the secret of interacting with narcissists, they can actually be the easiest people of all to get along with. In fact, you can get them eating out of your hand almost instantly—if you know the secret. How do you do it? All of the Five Secrets of Effective Communication can be helpful when dealing with a narcissist, but Stroking is the key. Narcissists are absolutely vulnerable to it because they crave adulation and will instantly come under your spell.

You can nearly always come up with a genuine compliment. We all have good qualities—along with the bad—and narcissists are often very talented or successful. It's usually easy to find something positive to say about them.

I recently conducted an Intimacy Workshop for a group of mental health professionals, and I ran into problems with a psychologist in the audience named Reggie who appeared to have fairly strong narcissistic tendencies. He seemed to be competing with me for attention and for the control of the group. After each segment, during the Q&A period, Reggie would raise his hand so enthusiastically that I felt obligated to call on him. Then, instead of asking a question, he'd comment on some error I'd made during the previous segment. For example, he'd say things like, "You completely overlooked the most important problem of all, which is shame. You simply *cannot* work with people with troubled relationships unless you deal with the problem of shame. But you didn't even talk about shame!"

I realized that there was no point in doing battle with Reggie and decided to try to practice what I was preaching. I responded to him with generous doses of Stroking and Disarming every time he criticized me. For example, I said, "Reggie, you're absolutely right. Shame probably is one of the greatest barriers to intimacy. I'm glad that you brought that up and I definitely should have mentioned it in the last segment. Any theory of interpersonal conflict that doesn't highlight the toxic role of shame is missing an important point."

Reggie would begrudgingly quiet down until the next Q&A period, when he'd do the exact same thing. It was clear that he wanted everyone to admire him and think of him as the real expert in the room. So I just kept Stroking and Disarming, Stroking and Disarming, every time he attacked me. I tried to play the role of his ally and not his adversary, but he never let his guard down.

At the end of the workshop, I invited the attendees to comment on what they'd learned and what the workshop meant to them professionally and personally. One by one, people stood and described what they'd experienced and learned during the workshop. Many gave moving testimonials with tears in their eyes.

I saw Reggie's hand wagging enthusiastically again. I thought, "Oh, no, now he's going to throw cold water on everything one more time." My heart sank as I called on him.

Reggie stood up and said nothing for nearly a minute. He appeared to be struggling to compose himself. The room was dead silent. He finally said this in a soft voice:

Some of you may have felt like I was grandstanding during the workshop. This is really hard for me to say, but I've been struggling with narcissism my entire life. I always feel like I have to be right, and I act like I'm superior to other people. I end up in fights with practically everyone. I market myself as a relationship expert, but I've been divorced three times. If you want to know the truth, I'm a pretty lonely guy, but I've always been too ashamed to admit it. And I want Dr. Burns to know, and all the rest of you to know, that this was the best workshop I've *ever* attended. I can't thank you enough. This experience has changed my life.

Tears were streaming down his cheeks as he spoke. After the workshop, Reggie approached me and asked if I might have a few minutes to talk. I wasn't in a hurry so we shot the breeze for nearly an hour. The conversation was extremely rewarding. Sometimes your greatest adversary turns out to be your greatest ally in disguise.

Let's practice. One of my neighbors occasionally runs into a woman called Melinda who gets under her skin. Melinda's husband and daughter made enormous amounts of money during the Internet boom of the 1990s. My neighbor finds Melinda extremely irritating and dreads seeing her because Melinda constantly brags about herself and her family and never expresses any interest in anyone else. She explained, "Melinda is impossible to deal with. She just won't stop bragging. It's always, 'me, me, me.' If my husband made one million dollars, she has to remind me that her husband just made twenty million dollars. It's sickening and it drives me batty. I don't know how to deal with that woman. I'd love to avoid her, but we're members of the same volunteer group, and we always get together for everyone's birthday. So I have to interact with her."

Imagine that you run into Melinda and you feel obligated to ask how things are going. She says:

Oh, everything is going great, as usual! Knock on wood! Chad just graduated first in his class at Harvard, but then, *all* of my children were first in their classes, so it wasn't *that* big of a surprise, if you know what I mean. And of course, I'm so pleased with my daughter, Betsy, for having created that startup company that just sold for two billion dollars. Oh my goodness! She just doesn't know *what* to do with all the money. Did you hear that she's going to be on the cover of *Time* magazine next week? And of course, our littlest one, Wayne, just qualified for the Olympics. Oh, by the way, how is your son doing at—where was it he was applying to? Was it the local college? Isn't he the one who did really well in the Scouts?

How would you respond to Melinda? Think about it for a moment before you continue reading. Although all Five Secrets can help, remember that Stroking will be the most effective technique when dealing with a narcissist. Put your answer on a separate piece of paper before you continue reading. Remember to put the names of the techniques you used in parentheses after each sentence, using the abbreviations on page 98.

Step 5. Revised Response

There are two different approaches that might work and your choice will depend on what you're looking for in the relationship. If you don't have any desire to form a friendly, close relationship with Melinda, a response along these lines will probably be sufficient:

> You know, Melinda, I'm not a bit surprised that your kids are so incredibly talented and successful. (ST) After all, they got some pretty terrific genes, wouldn't you agree? (ST; IN) You have every right to be proud of them. (ST)

If you said this, Melinda would be delighted. She'd think that you were *wonderful* because you'd be giving her the adulation that she so desperately craves.

This approach may strike you as dishonest or superficial. You're right about that, and I'll gladly illustrate a radically different approach in a moment. However, I don't think that we have to be deadly serious and open with everyone, and I don't think it makes sense to try to get close to everyone. In most cases, when I sense that someone is incredibly narcissistic, and preoccupied with herself, I simply use Stroking and don't try to pursue a close relationship with her. This usually works well, and saves me a great deal of frustration and resentment.

If, on the other hand, you do want to develop a more meaningful relationship with Melinda, then you could respond more along these lines:

> Melinda, I'm always amazed to hear how much you and everyone in your family has accomplished. (ST) You're a truly

remarkable human being, and I'm definitely not in your league. (ST; IF) But there's one thing that's been bothering me, and I wanted to share it with you in the spirit of friendship. (ST; IF)

Sometimes I feel like I haven't done a very good job of getting to know you. (IF) In fact, sometimes it almost feels like we're involved in some kind of competition about whose husband is making the most money, or whose children are the smartest, and that type of thing. (IF) It bothers me, and I'm wondering if you've noticed that as well? (IF; IN) I'm probably to blame for this. (DT) Maybe I've been trying to impress you, because you've accomplished so much. (ST; IF) If so, I owe you an apology. (ST) Have you noticed how awkward it feels? (IN)

In this response, you share your feelings and allow yourself to be vulnerable instead of trying to compete and win. You're also capitalizing on the generous use of Stroking. If you make Melinda feel special, it will be far easier for her to lower her defenses and open up. There's no guarantee this strategy will work, but it's definitely worth a try. You may be surprised to discover that she's actually feeling lonely and empty behind the façade, or that she sometimes feels insecure at times, just like the rest of us.

If Melinda still puts up a wall, you'll know that you've taken the high ground. You've conveyed respect and invited her to develop a friendlier and more meaningful relationship. She'll have to decide whether to accept the invitation.

So now you know the secret of dealing with a narcissist. That's pretty much all there is to it. Stroking is easy and remarkably effective. But there's also a downside to this approach. You may have to drastically lower your expectations about your relationship with someone who's narcissistic, because he or she may never develop the capacity to love you or express a genuine interest in you. If you keep hoping for more, you may set yourself up for endless feelings of disappointment.

If this idea seems sad, remember that there are two sides to every coin. If you lower your expectations about a narcissist and stop trying to get blood from a stone, you can spend your time and energy with people who *will* give you what you want and need.

Dealing with Someone Who's Lazy and Stubborn

Here's a complaint I often hear: "My husband never helps out around the house. Why is he so lazy and stubborn?" This problem is so common as to sound like a cliché, but it's a huge issue for many couples. The wife tells me, "He can rebuild a carburetor but can't figure out how to work the vacuum cleaner!" The variations on this theme are endless.

A couple of years ago, I treated an attractive businesswoman named Jewell who was confused about whether to get engaged to her boyfriend, Rasheed. After she sorted out her options, she decided to break up with Rasheed and felt a tremendous sense of relief. Six months later, they began dating again. Jewell decided that he really was "the one" for her, and they got married.

Two years later, Jewell contacted me again. She was seven months pregnant with her first child and felt concerned about her marriage. Although she didn't think they had any serious marital problems, she'd been getting more and more annoyed with Rasheed. One of her complaints was that Rasheed seemed stubborn and uncooperative whenever she asked him to help out around the house. Here's how she explained the problem:

> I love Rasheed, but lately I've been angry with him. Truth is, I know I'm very lucky and he's a great guy, but I don't always get what I really need from him. I get so mad that I just shut down and we stop communicating. Some days I wake up and feel like I'm a husband abuser. I ruined the whole day yesterday just because I was annoyed by the fact that he didn't want to cook the potatoes my way. I was so frustrated that I had to take a shower. Why do I let one stupid small annoyance ruin our relationship for an entire day?

When Rasheed was preparing the potatoes, she gently suggested that it might be a good idea to use the food processor. When she came back into the kitchen ten minutes later, Rasheed hadn't even taken the food processor out of the cabinet. She mentioned it again but he ignored her. When she came back to check on him again ten minutes later and saw the food processor sitting on the counter, she said, "I see that you *finally* got the food processor out!" Rasheed replied, "Don't be so pushy! Leave me alone!" Then Jewell asked, "Does it bother you when I suggest things that may make life a bit easier?" Rasheed replied, "Just focus on what *you're* doing and *I'll* do the potatoes." Jewell stormed off in a huff.

Jewell was also concerned because Rasheed wasn't as affectionate as she wanted him to be. For example, whenever she asked him to put his hand on her belly so he could feel the baby kick, he seemed reluctant. She told me:

I've been feeling annoyed because Rasheed doesn't take more than a passing interest in the ultrasound photos. Last night, the baby was kicking up a storm. I was lying on the sofa dying to have him feel the baby so I said, 'Oh, you have to feel this.' He put his hand on my belly super lightly and then quickly pulled it away saying, 'Oh I felt it!' Then he went right back to watching TV.

I *know* the baby didn't move during the two seconds his hand was there. It bugs me because he never grabs me and puts his arms around me and feels my belly. Other men come up to me on the street and do it, but not my Rasheed. He's always been at arm's reach when it comes to close physical contact. I should have listened to my mom when she warned me that people don't change!

Many of us go into marriage with an exciting, romantic idea of what our spouse is going to be like. When you discover that your spouse isn't the way you expected him to be, you have a choice. You can try to change him, or you can accept him the way he is. We've already seen that trying to change someone never works, but accepting him feels like settling for second best. You may think you couldn't possibly be happy or fulfilled until your spouse changes, but the harder you try to change him, the more he digs in his heels and resists. Then you both end up feeling frustrated and disappointed.

I asked Jewell if she thought she might have a tendency to be a little bit on the controlling side, and whether this might be fueling the fire. She said, "You're right. I am *totally* controlling, but I've noticed that when I try to relinquish the reins with Rasheed, things just don't get done, *period!* This really irks me because I end up doing almost everything myself. I feel like I'm training him to think that I'll always take care of everything."

Notice how Jewell's fears operate as a self-fulfilling prophecy. She thinks that Rasheed is stubborn and she's afraid that he won't do his share, so she hounds him and constantly checks up on him. This irritates him and kills his motivation to help out, so he does nothing. He gets mad, but doesn't express his feelings. Instead, he punishes her by ignoring her and "forgetting" to do the things that she keeps telling him to do. As a result, Jewell ends up having to do all the chores herself. This rewards his passive-aggressive behavior. In fact, she's created a powerful behavioral reinforcement program that practically guarantees that he won't help out or take her needs into account. Of course, this is the first principle of CIT—we create the exact relationship problems that we complain about, but we're not aware of this, so we blame the other person and feel like victims.

Jewell tells herself that Rasheed *shouldn't* be so stubborn, lazy, and unaffectionate, so she desperately tries to change him, but she keeps running into a wall of resistance. She has another option. If she's willing to focus on *her* role in the problem, and changing herself, she'll have a much better chance of getting what she wants.

I suggested that we could begin by focusing on one specific moment when Jewell and Rasheed weren't getting along. What was one thing that Rasheed said, and what did she say next? Jewell decided to use the food processor example. When Rasheed said, "Don't be so pushy! Leave me alone!" she replied, "Does it bother you when I try to suggest things that may make life a bit easier?" Jewell recorded these statements as Steps 1 and 2 on a Relationship Journal.

Now let's do Step 3. Take a look at the EAR Checklist on page 73 and ask yourself whether Jewell's response is an example of good communication or bad communication. It shouldn't be difficult to figure this one out. First, Jewell didn't empathize or listen to Rasheed. He probably felt hounded and annoyed, but she didn't acknowledge any of his feelings or try to find some truth in what he was saying. Jewell clearly didn't express her own feelings, either. She felt frustrated and hurt, but instead of telling Rasheed how she felt, she implied that he was some kind of idiot for ignoring her helpful suggestions. Finally, she definitely didn't convey any warmth or respect. Instead, she put him down by asking a sarcastic question. It was a bit of a shock for Jewell to discover that she was zero for three on the EAR Checklist.

Next, I asked Jewell to think about the consequences of her statement. How will her response affect Rasheed? Will it make the situation better or worse? Think about it for a moment before you continue reading.

Once again, the analysis was pretty straightforward. Jewell has been feeling frustrated because Rasheed ignores her, doesn't help out, and pushes her away whenever she tries to get close. She wants him to open up emotionally and feel more excited about her and their baby. But when Rasheed tried to tell her how he was feeling, she put him down and implied that he was being stubborn. As a result, Rasheed will feel irritated and even less motivated to help her, cuddle with her, or share his feelings with her. He won't want to do any of the things she asks either, because he's ticked off and has a great deal of bottled-up resentment.

Jewel wanted to know why her husband was so lazy, stubborn, and unaffectionate. Now she knows the answer. It's because she forces him to be that way. You can clearly see the exact same pattern in any interaction between them. She nags, and he withdraws or "forgets" to do his part to help out around the house. The exchange we analyzed was typical of how they interact with each other every single day.

It can be tremendously painful to discover that you've been causing the problem that you've been complaining about. If you have the courage to examine the impact of your own behavior on someone you're not getting along with, it can be very empowering. When Jewell realized that she was pushing Rasheed away and that he was dutifully playing the very role that she'd scripted for him, she began to cry.

Jewell's vulnerability can be an asset. If she's willing to share her tears with Rasheed and to talk about the conflict in a kind and respectful way, without any hint of blame or judgment, he'll begin to feel closer to her. She needs to encourage him to express his angry feelings, and she's got to be willing to listen and support him. If she wants to get love, she'll have to give love, not bossiness or bitterness. This means using generous doses of the Disarming Technique, Thought and Feeling Empathy, Inquiry, and Stroking when she responds to Rasheed. She'll also have to share her feelings in a caring and nonjudgmental way, using "I Feel" Statements, rather than putting up a wall and acting bossy or critical when she feels hurt.

What could Jewell have said when Rasheed said, "Don't be so pushy! Leave me alone!" Review the Five Secrets of Effective Communication and write down your Revised Response on a separate piece of paper before you continue reading. Remember to put the names of the techniques you're using in parentheses at the end of each sentence, using the abbreviations on page 98.

Step 5. Revised Response

Jewell could say something like this:

> Rasheed, it's hard for me to hear you say that I'm pushy because I know you're right, and I'm sure it's irritating. (IF; DT; FE) I really love you and want to hear more about how you're feeling. (ST; IN) You're probably feeling really pissed off at me. (FE) At the same time, you just asked me to leave you alone, and I would definitely understand if you feel like you're not in the mood to talk to me right now. (TE; FE; ST)

Paradoxically, the moment that Jewell agrees that she's been pushy, she won't seem pushy any more. When she acknowledges that her behavior is irritating to Rasheed, and that he's justified in feeling that way, he probably won't feel nearly as irritated. However, her attitude and tone of voice will be crucial. The slightest hint of defensiveness or hostility will sabotage her efforts. If she wants Rasheed to open up, kindness and respect will be vitally important. If she puts him down or implies that he's got a problem, he'll shut down again.

So, how do you motivate someone who's stubborn and lazy? You have to examine your own behavior and see if you're subconsciously fueling the fire. Jewell has been telling herself that it's all Rasheed's fault, so she's been trying so hard to change him. She tells him what to do and constantly reminds him of all the things he hasn't done. But nothing seems to work. In fact, the harder she tries, the worse the problem becomes.

Instead of trying to "solve" this problem, she can focus on how he feels and share her feelings with him. There are strong emotions right under the surface that they're both ignoring. These feelings are eating away at both of them, but they're avoiding their feelings. They can't solve the problem because they're not connecting emotionally. There's no intimacy, just a constant battle for control. Once Jewell and Rasheed air out their feelings and begin to feel close again, most of the "real" problems will naturally disappear. They won't need to deal with them. But if there's a problem they still need to solve, it will be vastly easier if they're working together as a loving team.

How to Deal with a Control Freak

Do you know someone who's a control freak? It could be your boss, spouse, or sibling. They want to call all the shots and won't take your ideas or feelings into account. If you don't do everything their way, they get very huffy.

A woman named Terry told me that her older sister, Margot, was extremely controlling. Terry was frustrated and annoyed with the way Margot was taking care of their elderly mother, who was disabled and becoming increasingly demented. Terry was upset because Margot wasn't including her in the decision-making process.

Terry explained, "Margot's doing the brunt of the work setting up a home care program for Mom, but I think that she's got the wrong idea. Margot's spending more than ten thousand dollars a month hiring people to care for Mom at home, but Mom's estate can't last forever if Margot keeps spending at such a high rate. I think that Mom should be in a nursing home."

Terry wanted to know what to do. I asked Terry for a specific example of the conflict. Could she describe one thing that Margot had said to her, and exactly what she said next?

Terry said that over the weekend, she and Margot had been talking about their mother's failing health, and Margot said, "I'm so disappointed in you because you haven't supported my decisions." Terry replied, "You're making all the decisions unilaterally and not consulting with me." I asked Terry to record these two statements as Steps 1 and 2 on a Relationship Journal.

Let's do Step 3. Would you say that Terry's response was an example of good communication or bad communication? Did she listen, express her own feelings openly, and convey caring or respect?

Terry failed on all three counts. First, she ignored Margot's feelings. Margot sounded disappointed and implied that she needed more support. Margot might have been feeling frustrated, lonely, and overwhelmed as well. Terry didn't express her own feelings either. She was also feeling frustrated and left out, but criticized Margot instead of opening up. And she certainly didn't convey any love or respect. Her response sounded judgmental and critical.

Now let's do Step 4 of the Relationship Journal. What are the consequences of Terry's response? Will her response make the problem better or worse?

When Margot tried to tell Terry that she felt a lack of support and didn't think they were working together as a team, Terry didn't listen or acknowledge the obvious truth in what Margot had just said. Instead, she blamed Margot for the lack of teamwork. Margot and Terry seem to be asking for the same thing—more teamwork. But instead of acknowledging this, Terry criticized Margot. This will trigger more fighting and mistrust. Margot won't ask Terry to share in the decisions if Terry puts her down whenever she tries to talk things over with her.

Terry was convinced that the lack of teamwork resulted from Margot's controlling tendencies. When Terry suddenly realized that she was pushing Margot away and sabotaging any possibility for teamwork or closeness, she said she felt ashamed. It was a shocking revelation because she'd been so convinced that the problem was her sister's fault.

Now we're ready for Step 5. How could Terry respond when Margot said, "I'm so disappointed in you because you haven't supported my decisions"? Any of the Five Secrets of Effective Communication could be helpful, but the Disarming Technique and Stroking will be especially important, along with skillful use of Feeling Empathy and "I Feel" Statements. Write your Revised Response on a separate piece of paper before you continue reading. Remember to put the names of the techniques you're using in parentheses at the end of each sentence, using the abbreviations on page 98.

Step 5. Revised Response

Here's the Revised Response that Terry came up with when she did Step 5 of the Relationship Journal:

> Gosh, Margot, it sounds like we've both been feeling the same way. (IF; DT) You say that you're disappointed in me because I haven't supported your decisions. (TE; FE) I feel bad about that and realize that you've been carrying the entire burden on your shoulders. (IF; DT; FE) You're probably feeling overwhelmed and frustrated with me for not helping you more. (FE) I love you and want to work with you. (IF; ST) Tell me how you've been feeling and what your ideas are about Mom. (IN)

In this response, Terry is admitting that she hasn't given Margot the support she needs. It's hard to admit that you've failed someone you care about, but the sadness you feel and express can sometimes be the springboard to greater intimacy and trust.

Sometimes when you think you're at odds with someone, the conflict is an illusion. You get so upset that you don't notice that you're both feeling the same way and asking for the same thing. You may even express yourself so forcefully that you create a battle instead of a dialogue. It's easy to get trapped by the labels we use. The moment you think of someone as a control freak, you'll instantly get involved in a power struggle with that person. You'll both start fighting for control and end up in a battle that no one can win.

The solution I'm proposing is a little different. Instead of blaming, fighting, making demands, or assertively sticking up for yourself, you can listen skillfully, share your feelings in a kind way, and convey genuine caring and respect. This will nearly always lead to trust, teamwork, and collaboration.

Dealing with Someone Who's Jealous

An interior decorator named Liz told me that her sister, Katrina, had always been jealous of her. When they were growing up, Katrina had a severe weight problem that she never overcame, and she resented the fact that Liz was smart, thin, and popular. Liz often tried to talk to Katrina and desperately wanted a better relationship with her, but said that Katrina always rebuffed her.

I asked Liz for an example of one thing that Katrina had said to her, and what she said next. A day earlier, Liz had been talking to Katrina about their relationship, and Katrina said, "We have nothing in common." Liz replied, "I long to be close to you," and tried to hug Katrina, who pushed her away. Liz felt hurt and snapped, "You're so jealous! Get real!"

Would you say that Liz's response was an example of good communication or bad communication? On the surface, Liz's response sounds loving, but if we examine her statement more closely with the EAR Checklist on page 73, we may come to a different conclusion.

Did Liz empathize with Katrina? Katrina has felt jealous and resentful of Liz since they were kids, and she probably still feels lonely and inadequate. Katrina was probably feeling hurt and mad at Liz as well, but Liz didn't acknowledge any of Katrina's feelings. That's why Katrina pushed her away.

Liz didn't express her own feelings in a direct and respectful manner, either. When Katrina said, "We have nothing in common," Liz felt wounded, rejected, hurt, and sad, but she kept her feelings hidden. Instead, she said, "I want to be close to you." When she said this, she was actually lying, because she wasn't really feeling any "longing" at that moment. She was feeling pissed off! Instead of sharing her feelings, Liz acted out her anger and put Katrina down, causing Katrina to push her away. Then Liz accused Katrina of being jealous and told her to "get real." This certainly didn't convey genuine love or respect. Her first statement sounded false, and her second statement was hostile.

Liz scored zero for three on the EAR Checklist. Now let's do Step 4. What are the consequences of Liz's response to her sister? How will her statements affect Katrina? This is a no-brainer. Here's how Liz sized up her response: "Katrina will see me as an adversary and conclude that we still have nothing in common."

Put yourself in Liz's shoes and see if you can come up with a more effective response, using the Five Secrets of Effective Communication. What could you have responded to Katrina's statement, "We have nothing in common"? Write down your Revised Response on a separate piece of paper.

Step 5. Revised Response
Here's what Liz and I came up with:

> Katrina, it really hurts to hear you say that we have nothing in common, but I agree with you. (IF; TE; DT) Our relationship hasn't been so great over the years, and it really bothers me. (DT; IF) It seems like you're pretty mad at me right now. (FE) I know that a lot of the problem has been my fault, but for a long time, I didn't realize it, so I kept blaming you. (DT) I want you to know that I love you and feel sad that we've never been

close. (ST; IF) Would you be willing to give our relationship another chance and tell me how you've been feeling? (IN)

When Katrina said, "We have nothing in common," it seemed like she was trying to close the door on her sister for good, but there's another way to think about this comment. Sometimes people put up a wall and act prickly to protect themselves from being hurt and disappointed. Liz could think about Katrina's rebuff as a golden opportunity to get close to her sister. This will involve validating Katrina's feelings, encouraging her to open up, and letting her know that she loves her. Liz will have to share her own feelings in an open and respectful way as well.

Your assumptions and beliefs about an interaction will have an almost instantaneous impact on what happens next. If you tell yourself that the other person is your enemy, you'll immediately be at war. But if you think about the conflict as an opportunity to develop greater understanding and love, your "adversary" will begin to see you as an ally. This is one of the fundamental principles of CIT—we create our own interpersonal reality at every moment of every day, but don't realize that we have so much power.

Reconciliation with Katrina will take much more than one skillful response from Liz. If Katrina begins to open up, it will be crucial for Liz to respond nondefensively. Katrina undoubtedly has a long list of criticisms, hurt feelings, and injustices to unload. If Liz listens and continues to validate Katrina's complaints in a respectful and loving way, the odds are high that Katrina will lower her guard and begin to see her sister in a far more positive light.

How to Cope with Criticism

Criticism is probably the most common relationship problem of all, and if you want to learn how to handle criticism skillfully, the Disarming Technique will be the most important tool. If you use it skillfully, you can put the lie to practically any criticism almost instantly. However, this can be difficult because it hurts so much when someone puts you down. In addition, criticisms often seem wrong, unfair, or mean-spirited, so we tend to get indignant and defensive. Of course, this makes things worse.

During one of my Intimacy Workshops, a college English professor named Sylvia described a long-standing conflict with her sister, Joan. Sylvia explained, "I'm the only one in our family who completed college and graduate school, and my relationship with Joan has always been rocky. Ever since we were little, she's accused me of acting superior and looking down on her. But that's not fair. How can I get her to see that she's wrong about me?"

Trying to prove that someone's "wrong" about you can be an uphill battle, especially when she's upset and she's had negative feelings about you for a long time. Furthermore, the other person won't be able to see that she's wrong until you agree that she's right. I'm not talking about a manipulation or a trick with words. You have to see that her criticisms of you really *are* valid. This isn't always easy, because we're often blind to the way our behavior affects the people around us.

I asked Sylvia if she thought there might be a grain of truth in Joan's criticisms. She insisted that she'd *never* acted superior or projected a holier-than-thou attitude toward her sister. I asked if she could give me an example of what happened when the two of them tried to talk. What was one thing that Joan had said to her, and what did she say next? Sylvia told me that the previous week, Joan had said, "You think you're better than the whole family!" Sylvia responded, "You have *no idea* what my experience is!"

Now let's do Step 3. Would you say Sylvia's response was an example of good communication or bad communication? Did Sylvia empathize and acknowledge how her sister was feeling? Did she express her own feelings openly, using "I Feel" Statements? Did she convey caring or respect? Review the communication chart on page 73 and think about it for a moment before you continue reading.

Step 3. Good Communication vs. Bad Communication
Here's how Sylvia evaluated her response:

My response was bad communication because I didn't acknowledge Joan's feelings or try to find any truth in her criticism. Instead, I defended myself. I didn't share my own feelings, either. I felt hurt, sad, and angry but didn't tell Joan how I felt. Instead, I implied that she was stupid and didn't know what she was talking about. This certainly didn't convey any caring or respect.

Now let's do Step 4. Think about the consequences of Sylvia's response. What will Joan think and feel when Sylvia says, "You have *no idea* what my experience is"?

Sylvia seems to be telling Joan that she's wrong. But this was exactly what Joan has been complaining about. Sylvia's comment sounds like a put-down. She could just as easily have said, "You're an idiot! You don't know what you're talking about!" Joan will be even more convinced that her sister thinks she's better than the whole family.

Sylvia was convinced that Joan couldn't *possibly* be right. I pointed out that this was exactly what Joan was claiming—that Sylvia really *did* feel superior. Sylvia conveyed this condescending message in her response to her sister.

Sylvia's original question was, "How can I show my sister that she's wrong about me?" It was painful for Sylvia to discover that her sister *wasn't* wrong about her. She really *had* been treating Joan disrespectfully and looking down on her.

Now, put yourself in Sylvia's shoes and see if you can come up with a more effective response. Remember, Joan has just said, "You think you're better than the whole family!" You can use any of the Five Secrets of Effective Communication on page 98, but the Disarming Technique will be the key. Joan won't see that she's *wrong* about Sylvia until Sylvia agrees that what she's saying is absolutely *right*. This will require courage, love, and humility. Write down your Revised Response on a separate piece of paper before you continue reading.

Step 5. Revised Response

Here's the Revised Response that Sylvia and I came up with:

You're right, Joan, I think I *have* acted holier-than-thou at times. (DT; TE) It hurts me tremendously to hear you say this, because I realize that I've let you down and I don't think I've ever let you know how much I love you. (IF; DT; ST) You're probably so disappointed in me. (FE) It wouldn't surprise me if you're feeling hurt and mad at me, too. (FE) Let's talk about it. (IN) Can you tell me about some of the things I've done or said that have turned you off? (IN)

This response demonstrates the Law of Opposites that we talked about in chapter 13. When Sylvia admits that Joan's criticism is right, the criticism no longer seems valid because Sylvia sounds humble, remorseful, and loving. This isn't the way that people who feel "superior" communicate! If Sylvia speaks from the heart, her sister's perception of her will change, and they'll have the chance to repair their relationship.

Part Four

Making the Five Secrets Work for You

Chapter 19

Mastering the Five Secrets

I f you want to use the Five Secrets of Effective Communication in your daily life, four things will be necessary:

1. You'll need to study these methods and agree that they make sense on an intellectual level.
2. You'll need humility. It isn't easy to discover that you've been contributing to the problem you've been complaining about, and it's not much fun to admit that there's truth in someone's criticism. If you check-in your ego at the door, it will be a whole lot easier.
3. You'll need a strong desire to develop a more loving or satisfying relationship with the other person. If you don't want a better relationship with the person you're not getting along with, none of these techniques will be effective.
4. You'll need patience, persistence, and practice.

When I first started learning these techniques, I worked with the Relationship Journal every evening to analyze and modify my interactions with patients, colleagues, and family members. The first four steps were often painful, especially when I examined the impact of my behavior on other people. When I did Step 5, my Revised Responses were pretty lame at first. But before long, my skills improved.

Mastering the Five Secrets of Effective Communication is a lot like learning to play tennis. At first, it feels awkward and your shots may not go where you want them to go. But if you practice, you'll get better and better over time.

Now these techniques have become second nature. I use them every day in my clinical work, teaching, and personal life. I can't claim that I'm 100 percent consistent, and there are times when I completely forget to use them. But I do use them most of the time, and they work amazingly well. For me, they've been truly life changing. I'm convinced that they can change your life as well.

This would be a good time for you to complete Step 5 of the Relationship Journal you were working on earlier (page 68). Ask yourself what you could have said to the other person that would have been more effective, using the Five Secrets of Effective Communication. Put your Revised Response on page 68 now. Remember to identify the communication techniques you're using in parentheses after each sentence you write down, using the two-letter abbreviations listed on page 98. Identifying the techniques you're using will speed up your learning considerably.

There isn't any simple formula for how or when to use which technique. Sometimes you'll use the Disarming Technique first and acknowledge that the other person's statement is absolutely valid. Sometimes you'll use Thought Empathy and summarize what the other person just said to you, so he or she will see that you really listened. Sometimes you'll use Feeling Empathy, and acknowledge how he or she feels. And sometimes you might just respond with a brief "I Feel" Statement, like, "Wow, I'm feeling blown away right now. (IF)" There's plenty of room for creativity and individuality.

If your Revised Response doesn't sound genuine or natural, it won't be effective. Sometimes a Revised Response will seem solid at first, but when you look at what you wrote down a few hours later, you might discover that it sounds stilted, lame, false, hostile, or defensive. You can revise it to make it better. Coming up with good responses requires lots of practice. When I first began working with the Relationship Journal, I often had to revise my responses five or ten times before I came up with one that I really liked. Complete Step 5 of your Relationship Journal now. When you're done, you can continue.

The reading can be helpful, but if you want to learn to use these techniques in real time, the written exercises will be necessary. I'd recommend working with the Relationship Journal for ten or fifteen minutes every day. (Remember that you can photocopy extras from the blank copies in Your Intimacy Toolkit on page 260.) However, you don't have to complete all five steps at one sitting. You can do the first three or four steps today and finish tomorrow. Sleeping on it helps. You may suddenly see something you couldn't see at first. It may take many tries before you come up with a really good Revised Response when you do Step 5, but the effort will pay off. If you stick with it, your understanding will increase dramatically.

Chapter 20

Using the Five Secrets in Real Time: The Intimacy Exercise

Once you've completed Step 5 and you're satisfied with your Revised Response, you may wonder whether you'll be able to use the Five Secrets of Effective Communication skillfully in real-life situations. If you're like everyone else, you'll get so caught up in your feelings and usual knee-jerk reactions that you'll forget to use these techniques at first. And if you do try to use them, you'll probably make errors that you're not aware of, so the techniques may backfire. For many people, the hardest part is giving up the urge to defend yourself from criticism.

Don't lose hope! I've developed a powerful and fun role-playing technique that will help you learn to respond skillfully to any conflict or problem in real time. It's called the Intimacy Exercise. In my seminars at Stanford and workshops around the United States, the Intimacy Exercise has been very popular and helpful.

To do this exercise, you'll need a practice partner. Preferably, it won't be the person you're having trouble getting along with, but someone who's helping you develop improved communication skills. It could be a friend, family member, or colleague. By the way, she'll benefit from the exercise as much as you will.

Here's how it works: Ask your practice partner to play the role of the person you're not getting along with (your Adversary). Tell her to attack you in the same way that the person you're not getting along with ordinarily attacks you. Hand your practice partner one of your Relationship Journals and ask her to read Step 1 out loud with gusto. For example, she might say, "All you care about is yourself," or "You're *so* demanding," or "I'm right and you're wrong." Your job will be to respond as effectively as you can, using the Five Secrets of Effective Communication. Make sure you both have a copy of the list of the Five Secrets on page 262 so you can refer to it during the role-playing.

After you respond to your partner's attack, *stop* the role-playing. Don't continue arguing back and forth. Limit your interaction to one attack from your practice partner and one response. This is vitally important. Now ask your partner to give you three specific kinds of feedback about how you did, using the instructions overleaf.

First, your partner will give you a grade between an A and an F so you can see how well you did overall. When you do this exercise for the first time, your practice partner will almost definitely give you a grade below an A. Even mental health professionals get poor grades at first. Bs, Cs, and Ds are common. The grade is crucial because it will show you exactly where you stand right away. For example, if you get a B, it means that you did reasonably well, but there's room for improvement.

After you've received your letter grade, ask your partner to tell you what you did right and what you did wrong. What worked, and what didn't work? Ask your partner to comment on what you said as well as your body language. Did you look open, receptive, and interested? Or did you shrug, turn away, frown, or raise your eyebrows?

Finally, ask your practice partner to tell you how skillfully you used the Five Secrets of Effective Communication. Everyone makes errors at first. You may forget to use the Five Secrets of Effective Communication altogether, or you may leave out a technique that would have been helpful. For example, your partner

Adversary's Instructions

1. **Attack your partner.** Read one of the statements from Step 1 of your partner's Relationship Journal with gusto. Your partner will respond as effectively as possible, using the Five Secrets of Effective Communication. Now *stop* the role-playing and proceed to Step 2. Resist the urge to keep criticizing or dialoguing.

2. **Grade your partner.** Grade your partner's response overall. Did she get an A, B, C, or D? At first, your partner will probably get a B, a C, or even lower. The grade will be invaluable because your partner will see exactly how well she did.

3. **General feedback.** Tell your partner what worked and what didn't work for you. Did she sound false or genuine? Will her response lead to greater warmth, trust, and openness, or to more antagonism? Did she open the doors of communication and trust, or put up a wall and push you away? Comment on her words and body language.

4. **Specific feedback.** How effectively did your partner use the Five Secrets of Effective Communication? Provide specific feedback about how she used each technique:
   - **The Disarming Technique.** Did she find genuine truth in what you said or get defensive?
   - **Thought and Feeling Empathy.** Did she accurately summarize what you said and acknowledge your negative feelings, such as anger, frustration, or sadness?
   - **Inquiry.** Did she encourage you to open up?
   - **"I Feel" Statements.** Did she express her feelings directly and openly using "I Feel" Statements?
   - **Stroking.** Did she convey genuine warmth and respect?

may point out that you didn't paraphrase what she said or that you forgot to acknowledge her anger. Perhaps you didn't find the truth in what she was trying to tell you.

If you received a grade that's below an A—and I can guarantee that this *will* happen—do a role reversal. Now, you'll play the role of the Adversary and your practice partner will play your role. You can attack her with the same statement that she attacked you with, and she will try to model a more effective response. Then you can give her the three kinds of feedback described previously.

- Give her a grade between A and F.
- Tell her how effective her response was. What worked and what didn't work?
- Tell her how skillfully she used (or failed to use) the Five Secrets of Effective Communication.

You'll learn a tremendous amount in the Adversary's role. For example, you'll see firsthand just how irritating it can be when the other person responds defensively or forgets to acknowledge your feelings. You'll also see how annoying it can be when you express sad feelings, such as discouragement, guilt, or worthlessness, and the other person tries to cheer you up instead of empathizing and encouraging you to open up. It can be reassuring to see that it's equally hard for other people to respond effectively in conflict situations. These are skills that we all need to learn and master.

Repeat the exercise until you can respond effectively to almost anything the Adversary fires at you. You probably won't get to this level the first time you practice, but your understanding and skills will increase tremendously every time you work with the Intimacy Exercise. Many of my colleagues and patients have told me that this exercise changed their lives.

Here's an important tip lots of people overlook: remember to work with only *one* criticism and *one* response. Don't talk on and on endlessly when you do the role-playing. After the Adversary attacks you, and you've responded, *stop*. Now your practice partner will critique your response. If you ignore this instruction and continue the dialogue, things will spiral out of control, leaving you both feeling confused and demoralized. One attack and one response is all you need.

When you do the Intimacy Exercise, you'll be doing exactly what you did when you completed Step 5 of the Relationship Journal, but this time, you'll be speaking rather than writing. You'll discover that the role-playing can feel very real and quite intimidating. That's why it's so helpful.

Pinpointing Your Blind Spot

When you do the role-playing, you may discover that there's one technique that you consistently have trouble with. You may use that technique in a clumsy way or completely forget to use it. For example, lots of people have trouble with the Disarming Technique at first. They sound defensive and can't find the truth in the Adversary's criticism. Others have trouble with Thought Empathy or Feeling Empathy. They get so caught up in their own emotions that they can't remember what the other person just said, or they forget to acknowledge how the other person might be feeling. Many people don't use Inquiry skillfully. Instead, they apologize or look for a way to fix the problem. Others have trouble with "I Feel" Statements—they sweep their feelings under the carpet and end up looking fake. And if you're feeling hurt or angry, you may forget to use Stroking, so there's no warmth or spark of kindness in your responses.

Once you've identified the technique you're having trouble with, you can master it by asking your practice partner to attack you repeatedly with short zingers, such as "You're a loser." Your job will be to respond with the technique you're having the most trouble with. For example, if you're having trouble with "I Feel" Statements, all you have to do is say something like, "I'm feeling X and Y." X and Y refer to Feeling Words from the chart on page 78. Hold the chart in your hand while you practice so you can refer to it. For example, you might respond by saying, "I'm feeling hurt and put down right now."

Then your partner will attack you again, and you can respond with another "I Feel" Statement. Do this over and over again. After a few minutes, you'll discover that you've developed expertise in the technique that seemed so difficult for you to master. You'll also find that you won't get so anxious and confused in the midst of a real argument with someone you're not getting along with, because the practice will immunize you to a certain extent. You'll learn to be calm in the heat of battle.

Once you're getting consistently high marks on the Intimacy Exercise, you'll be ready to use the Five Secrets of Effective Communication in real-life situations. The first time you try, you may luck out and get a terrific response from the other person. If this happens, it's great, because you'll see right away just how powerful these techniques can be.

If the techniques don't seem to work in real-life interactions, don't give up. The odds are overwhelming that you didn't use them skillfully. This is very common. Just go back to the basics. Fill out the Relationship Journal and focus on the precise moment when the techniques didn't work. Write down what the other person said (Step 1) and what you said next (Step 2). When you do Steps 3 and 4, it will be pretty obvious why your statement didn't work and why the conflict escalated. When you do Step 5, you can generate a more effective response. Learning these techniques is hard for everyone at first. If it were easy to listen, share your feelings openly, and convey respect, the world would be a very different kind of place.

Chapter 21

Intimacy Training for Couples: The One-Minute Drill

If the person you're at odds with is someone close to you, such as your spouse or partner, and you both want to improve the quality of your relationship, the One-Minute Drill can give you a terrific boost. This fun, easy exercise will allow you to improve your communication skills almost immediately in a nonthreatening, supportive atmosphere. You'll learn how to express your feelings effectively and how to listen far more skillfully.

The most important difference between the Intimacy Exercise and the One-Minute Drill will be this: when you do the Intimacy Exercise, your practice partner will be a colleague, friend, or family member who's volunteered to help you practice, but is not the person you're having trouble with. When you do the One-Minute Drill, your partner will be the person you're not getting along with.

Here's how the One-Minute Drill works. One of you will be the Talker while the other is the Listener. The Talker can say anything he or she wants for approximately thirty seconds. When the Talker finishes, the listener will summarize what the Talker just said, as well as how the Talker was feeling inside, as accurately as possible. The Talker now gives the Listener a grade between 0 percent and 100 percent to indicate how accurate the summary was.

If the grade is below 95 percent, the Talker will point out what the Listener missed or got wrong.

Once the Listener summarizes the part that he or she got wrong, the Talker will give the Listener a new grade, which will usually be higher. Do this until the Listener's grade is at least 95 percent. Then you can do a role reversal—the Talker becomes the Listener, and vice versa. The Talker can continue with the same topic or move on to something entirely new.

Any two people can use the One-Minute Drill. You could be married, living together, or working together. You could practice with your son or daughter. The exercise simply requires two cooperative individuals who are committed to improving their relationship. If one person is in a hostile or vindictive mood, or secretly wants out of the relationship, this exercise probably won't help.

Set aside fifteen minutes for the One-Minute Drill. Select a quiet room and make sure there are no interruptions or distractions. Turn off the TV, radio, or stereo, and close the door to ensure privacy. You should not be intoxicated, eating, or working on other projects while you do this exercise.

You and your partner can sit in chairs facing each other. Decide who will be the Talker first and who will be the Listener. It makes no difference which role you're in first, because you'll do a role reversal in a few minutes.

Talker Instructions

When you're the Talker, your job will be to express your thoughts and feelings. You can discuss problems you've had a hard time talking about. This is your chance to say anything you want, but remember to limit yourself to about thirty seconds without rambling on and on. Thirty seconds of emotionally charged information will be sufficiently challenging for your partner.

Because your partner will be listening attentively, you won't need to express yourself in an overly powerful or harsh way. You can express your feelings in strong, clear, direct language, but you won't need to shout, exaggerate, or put your partner down. For example, you might say:

> When I come home from work, I feel tired and I need some quiet time. But you nag me or tell me I'm supposed to spend time with the kids. This makes me feel frustrated and ticked off. I work hard and I'm exhausted at the end of the day. I feel like I deserve a little time to unwind and relax, not listen to more demands.
>
> Here's another thing that bugs me. I feel like you're always trying to control me and tell me what to do, but when I try to tell you how controlling you are, you act innocent and insist that everything's my fault. This infuriates me. Sometimes I wish that you'd admit, just once, that you're not so perfect. You have just as many faults as I do.

When you're done, your partner will try to summarize exactly what you said and how you were probably feeling inside. In the preceding example, the Listener might say:

> You just told me that you feel exhausted when you come home at night because you've been working hard all day. When I tell you I want you to spend time with the kids, you feel frustrated and ticked off because you're tired and you need time to unwind. You see me as very demanding, and you're probably feeling like I don't appreciate you.

When your partner has finished summarizing what you said, tell him or her how accurate it was on a scale from 0 percent to 100 percent. If your rating is below 95 percent, tell your partner what he or she missed. In this example, the Listener's summary was decent, but she missed a few things. Therefore, the Talker might say something like this:

> I'll give you a seventy-five percent on that. You got most of what I said but missed the part about being defensive when I try to tell you how controlling you are. Whenever I criticize

you, it seems like you always get defensive and blame me for the problem. You act like you're perfect and never admit that you're at fault. That bugs me. Just once, I wish that you'd admit that you're wrong.

Now, as the Listener, you can summarize that part. If your rating jumps to 95 percent or better, you'll be ready for a role reversal.

Listener Instructions

While your partner talks for thirty seconds, sit and listen respectfully without interrupting. Look into your partner's eyes to convey a receptive attitude. Avoid grimacing or using negative body language. Try not to appear judgmental or defensive. Don't slouch down in the chair or fold your arms defiantly across your chest, because this conveys antagonism. Don't roll your eyes toward the ceiling, or shake your head back and forth, as if to say, "You're full of it."

Your job is not to agree or disagree with your partner. Instead, try to understand exactly what he or she is saying. Then ask yourself how your partner might be feeling, given what he or she is saying. If you like, you can take a few notes. This can help a great deal because you'll be able to jot down the main points and won't have to struggle when you try to remember what your partner just said, but don't bury your head in your notes. Look up at him or her from time to time. After your partner has finished talking, summarize what he or she said as accurately as possible. Try to mention all the key points, and then comment on how he or she is likely to be feeling.

When you're the Listener, try to see the world through your partner's eyes. Don't make judgments about who's right and who's wrong. Don't attack your partner for the way he or she feels. Instead, try to grasp where your partner is coming from. Summarize exactly what your partner said so that he or she will see that you listened and got the message. Remember to acknowledge how your partner might be feeling, given what he or she said.

If your partner gives you a grade of 95 percent or better, it's time for a role reversal. If your grade is lower than 95 percent, ask your partner to tell you what you missed or got wrong. Listen attentively while he or she speaks. Then paraphrase your partner's words again. Continue this process until your score is 95 percent or better.

When you've both had at least one turn as Talker and one turn as Listener, you've completed the exercise. You can either stop or continue for another round. If you decide to continue, you can talk about the same topic or another problem. It makes no difference.

The first time you try to summarize what your partner said, you may get a low score. This is normal. Don't worry about that, because you'll get up to speed quickly. Once you've tried this exercise a few times, you'll find that you can nearly always get ratings of 95 percent or better on the first or second try.

Is this technique guaranteed to work? No. When you're the Talker, you can make statements that are so hurtful and cutting that they'll sabotage your partner's chances for success. It will be clear that your goal is to attack or humiliate rather than share your feelings in a respectful way.

When you're the Listener, you can also sabotage the exercise by paraphrasing your partner's statements in a sarcastic, whiny, or condescending way that communicates the message, "Screw you! I don't care how you feel! Our problems are all your fault."

These techniques are simply tools. To use them successfully, humility and goodwill are required. A surgeon can use a scalpel to save someone's life, but a murderer could use the same scalpel to slit someone's throat. Your success will depend on the way you use these tools, and your motivation will have a great impact on your success. If you don't *want* to get close to someone, then there are no tools or techniques in the world that will lead to greater intimacy or trust.

If you and your partner want to try the One-Minute Drill, you can make two copies of the Brief Instructions on pages 264–265. You and your partner can refer to these instructions the first couple of times you try the exercise. After you've practiced once or twice, you won't need the written instructions anymore.

Part Five

Common Traps—and How to Avoid Them

Chapter 22

"Help! The Five Secrets Didn't Work!"

If you use the Five Secrets of Effective Communication skillfully, they'll rarely fail. But when you first try to use them, you may stumble and fall a few times, and the person you're interacting with may get more upset. You may be tempted to conclude that the techniques didn't work. Telling yourself that the Five Secrets didn't work is a lot like blaming the tennis racket when you hit the ball into the net. The real problem will nearly always be that you didn't use them skillfully.

I've had thousands of therapy sessions with men and women with troubled relationships, and thousands of mental health professionals have attended my psychotherapy workshops throughout the United States and Canada. These experiences have shown me that there are a number of predictable errors that people nearly always make when they're learning how to use the Five Secrets. In fact, I think it's fair to say that *every* person I've ever trained has made the same kinds of errors at first. If you're aware of these traps, you can save yourself a few stubbed toes later on.

Common Disarming Errors

Some people have a complete misunderstanding of how the Five Secrets actually work. For example, a woman named Mildred told me that she'd tried to use the Disarming Technique with her husband, Brad, but it hadn't worked at all. She said she *knew* it wasn't going to work because he was impossible to get along with. Mildred explained that after one of our therapy sessions, she went home and prepared Brad's favorite meal as a surprise when he came home from work. She slaved in the kitchen for hours and even placed candles on the dinner table. She put on a sexy dress, dimmed the lights, and lit the candles just before he walked through the front door.

When Brad saw all the elaborate dinner preparations, he seemed baffled and asked Mildred what the special occasion was. She said, "I just thought you deserved a nice reward for all your hard work today."

After they started to eat, Mildred asked how he liked the meal. Brad said he thought the meal was great. Then she asked, "Is there anything that isn't just right?" He said he loved everything, but thought the pork might be just a tad on the dry side. Mildred felt hurt and snapped, "Well, if you don't like the pork, you can stick it up your frigging ass!"

I told Mildred I could see why the Disarming Technique hadn't been quite as effective as she'd hoped! Mildred's intentions were good, but she didn't really understand the Disarming Technique. She thought it meant being nice to the person you weren't getting along with. Of course, there's nothing wrong with being thoughtful or doing loving things for someone you care about, but that's not the Disarming Technique. When you disarm a critic, you find truth in what he or she said, even if the criticism seems irrational or unfair.

There are several other errors to watch out for when you're learning how to use the Disarming Technique:

1. **Failing to find any truth in what the other person is saying.** This is extremely common. Often, your own ideas are so different, or your own view of the situation clouds your mind

to such a great extent, that you can't really see things through the other person's eyes. Sometimes the criticism seems so threatening or shameful that you feel an overwhelming urge to defend yourself. If you give in to this urge, you'll nearly always convince the other person that his or her criticism is absolutely valid, and the argument will intensify.

2. **Agreeing in a patronizing way.** This is also common and it's extremely irritating. For example, when you're criticized, you might say, "Well, I can see how you might *feel* like that," or "I can see how it might *seem* that way from your perspective." These are just subtle ways of saying, "You're wrong!"

3. **Agreeing in a superficial way, without really grasping where the other person is coming from.** When you do this, you're giving the other person the brush-off, like a salesperson who's trying to manipulate a customer in order to make a sale.

4. **"Yes-butting" the other person.** An example would be, "I can see what you're saying, but . . ." The word *but* always shows that you're defending yourself. As a general rule, stay off your "butt."

Common Thought and Feeling Empathy Errors

You'll recall that Thought Empathy involves paraphrasing what the other person just said, and Feeling Empathy involves acknowledging how he's probably feeling, given what he said. Although this might seem fairly simple, there are several roadblocks you might encounter.

1. **Using Thought and Feeling Empathy in a stereotyped or dismissive way.** For example, you might use the same catchphrases over and over, such as "What you seem to be saying is . . ." For example, if someone says, "I'm ticked off," you might respond, "What you seem to be saying is that you're ticked off." Then he or she might say, "That's what I said, you stupid jerk." You might respond, "What I hear you saying is that I'm a stupid jerk." This will drive the other person up the wall!

2. **Repeating back what the other person said without sharing your own feelings.** As a result, you end up sounding like a parrot. The other person will sense that you're not being real or genuine and will get ticked off, like the husband of one of my patients, who would say, "Stop using that Burns shit on me!"

3. **Missing the point.** Lots of people get so distracted trying to figure out what they're going to say next that they can't paraphrase what the other person just said. This is especially common when the other person is upset or critical of you. You get so anxious and defensive that you don't really comprehend what the other person just said. Then, when you try to paraphrase his or her comments, you say something that misses the point entirely and end up talking at cross-purposes.

4. **Conflict Phobia and Emotophobia.** The most common Feeling Empathy error is failing to use Feeling Words from the chart on page 78 to acknowledge how the other person feels. Anger is the most frequently overlooked emotion, particularly if it's directed at you. I call this mind-set Conflict Phobia, and we'll talk more about it in chapter 24. Lots of people seem to be afraid of acknowledging any negative feelings at all, so they keep things on an overly intellectual level. I call this mind-set Emotophobia, or the fear of negative emotions. You can also call it Emotional Perfectionism, which is the misguided idea that we're supposed to be happy all the time.

5. **Criticizing instead of acknowledging how the other person feels.** For example, you might say, "You're just being picky!" or "You've got no right to feel that way!" Or you might acknowledge the other person's feelings in a judgmental or hostile way by saying, "You sound angry." This will practically force the other person to deny his or her anger because your comment sounds like a put-down or accusation.

6. **Telling people how they feel, rather than suggesting some possibilities.** For example, you might say, "Obviously, you're feeling X, Y, and Z," where X, Y, and Z represent Feeling Words from the list on page 78. This usually backfires because the other person may not be feeling that way, or may resent being told how he or she feels. It works better to ask questions

in a friendly way, suggesting some possibilities: "I can imagine that you might be feeling X, Y, and Z, but I'm not sure. Can you tell me more about how you are feeling?"

Common Inquiry Errors

The idea behind Inquiry is to open people up, using gentle, probing questions. You show that you're interested and invite people to tell you more about how they're thinking and feeling. Once again, this sounds simple, but there are several common Inquiry errors:

1. **Helping and Problem Solving.** When you're criticized, you might be tempted to ask how you can fix the problem or do better. For example, you might say, "What would you like me to do differently?" or "How could we solve this problem?" This sounds well-meaning, but it can be a big mistake. When people are upset, they generally don't want you to jump in and try to fix things. Most of the time, they want you to listen and try to understand how they feel. We'll talk more about this trap in chapter 23.
2. **Asking questions in a stereotyped, formulaic way.** This is like a therapist who always says, "Mmm. Tell me more."
3. **Asking questions in a sarcastic or adversarial manner.** For example, you might say, "What did you expect me to do?" This is not a genuine question, but a disguised way of defending yourself.
4. **Apologizing.** Saying "I'm sorry" is often just a subtle way of shutting the other person up because you don't want to hear about how hurt and angry he or she feels. We'll talk more about this in chapter 25.

Common Errors in the Use of "I Feel" Statements

Nearly everyone agrees on the importance of being assertive and sharing your feelings openly and directly, but several errors and misconceptions may sabotage your efforts:

1. **Criticizing instead of sharing your feelings.** Many people are reluctant to express their feelings with "I Feel" Statements. Instead, they criticize the other person. For example, you might say, "I feel like you're arguing with me," or "Why don't you admit that you're wrong?" or "I feel like you're not listening." These aren't "I Feel" Statements, but descriptions of the other person's behavior. They're also put-downs. There are a number of other common "I Feel" errors:

2. **Talking on and on about yourself because you're trying to impress the other person.** Shy individuals nearly always make this mistake. It's also a common error during job interviews and interviews for university admission. Most people want you to listen to them and express interest in them.

3. **Active and passive aggression.** Instead of sharing their feelings, some people shout, lash out, name call, or put the other person down. This is incredibly tempting when you're feeling angry and frustrated. Although you may feel powerful and self-righteous when you do this, it's not very effective because the person you're putting down will devalue your thinking and write you off as a loony or a loser.

   Some people have the opposite problem—giving the other person the icy treatment and refusing to talk when they're upset, so they punish the other person with silence. Although they're trying hard to hide their hostile feelings, refusing to talk is also a form of aggression. We'll talk more about active and passive aggression in chapter 24.

4. **Disclosure Phobia.** This is probably the most common problem that I run into when I'm teaching people how to use "I Feel" Statements. Some people are afraid to share their feelings because they think they *shouldn't* feel the way they do, or because they don't want to make themselves vulnerable.

   A woman told me that her mother advised her never to reveal how she was feeling because people might use it against her. She was attractive, had a bubbly personality, and had no problem getting dates. She was also a highly successful businesswoman who ran a large construction company. But she was extremely lonely because she couldn't get close to the men she was going out with.

I call this attitude the Disclosure Phobia. People with this mind-set are convinced that something terrible will happen if they let others know how they're really feeling, so they keep their feelings hidden. They refuse to open up and make themselves vulnerable because they think they'll look foolish and other people will look down on them. They tell themselves that they *shouldn't* feel the way they do. The core problem is a lack of trust—they don't trust their own feelings, and don't believe that others could love and accept them as they are.

You may be surprised to learn that most therapists seem to have this problem. They nearly always hide their feelings and often resort to formulaic expressions when there's tension in the air during therapy sessions. For example, they might say, "Tell me more," or "Thank you for sharing," statements that sound pretty artificial. Or they may say nothing and simply reflect back what the patient says, like a mirror. I was trained to respond like this during my psychiatric residency, and my patients found it extremely upsetting. They complained bitterly that I never said anything helpful to them. But my supervisors, who were psychoanalysts, told me that I was doing excellent work. To me, it felt a bit like Alice in Wonderland. I wondered how I could expect them to grow and become more genuine and open when I was acting like such a fake!

A neurologist named Dr. Weiss told me that he was concerned about his relationship with his son, Ralph. He explained that Ralph was a graduate student in biology, studying for his Ph.D., but was living at home to save money. Dr. Weiss loved Ralph but said they'd never really been close. When they were together, they always talked about trivial things, such as sports. Dr. Weiss explained that Ralph never opened up or talked about his feelings, his relationships with the women he was dating, or his dreams for the future.

Dr. Weiss said he felt lonely and wanted a more meaningful relationship with his son. He explained that one of his colleagues had recently had a stroke and his best friend had suddenly dropped dead from a heart attack. He said that he'd just turned fifty-eight and was worried that he might die without ever getting to know his son.

I explained that close relationships depend on being emotionally open. That means opening up, telling people how you feel and asking about how they feel. Dr. Weiss said that this made a lot of sense and asked what he should say to Ralph. I said that it was actually pretty simple. The next time he was talking to Ralph, he could try to open up a bit more. For example, he could tell Ralph that he loved him but sometimes felt lonely because they didn't often talk about anything that was really important to either of them. He could also say that he wanted to get to know Ralph better and find out how he was feeling about his life.

Dr. Weiss seemed shocked. He said that he couldn't *possibly* tell Ralph that he was feeling lonely! He said it would sound weird or unmanly and Ralph would think he was a lunatic. Of course, there might be some truth in his concerns, especially if Dr. Weiss doesn't express himself skillfully, but his fears of opening up went deeper than that. He believed that even the most skillful disclosure of his feelings would be inappropriate.

Sometimes the thing you fear the most is the path to your own enlightenment, but you can't experience enlightenment unless you're willing to confront that fear. It may be hard for Dr. Weiss to open up and share his feelings because he's been stuck in the same familiar groove his entire life. In addition, when you try a new communication technique, you may not be skillful at first. For example, if you express your feelings in an overly self-effacing way, the other person may end up feeling sorry for you. Or you may go overboard and express yourself in an overly aggressive way that will trigger an argument.

The role-playing exercises in chapters 20 and 21 can help you overcome these tendencies. Your practice partner will give you immediate feedback on how you're coming across and model more effective ways of expressing your feelings. This will help you overcome your fears of being vulnerable. After a while, it won't feel nearly as embarrassing or anxiety provoking to share your feelings openly. You'll also see that your practice partner isn't perfect, either, which can be a huge relief. And of course, you'll learn to express your feelings skillfully in real time.

Dr. Weiss practiced with me in the office. He also practiced with his wife at home before he mustered up the courage to approach his son. In fact, he was awkward during the roleplaying because he wasn't used to sharing his feelings. But his awkwardness was an asset, because he appeared genuine and came across in a gentle and caring manner.

When Dr. Weiss talked to Ralph, he was surprised to learn that Ralph had also been feeling lonely and was worried about his career. Although he'd been doing well at school, he'd been struggling with feelings of self-doubt because he didn't know if he was talented enough to pursue a career in research. He also doubted his abilities to teach, because he had public speaking anxiety and tended to freeze up whenever he had to present his findings in classes. Ralph confessed that he'd never shared these feelings with his dad because he felt that he wasn't *supposed* to feel anxious or insecure, and he was afraid that his dad would be disappointed in him and think that *he* was some kind of loony! Dr. Weiss was amazed at how quickly his relationship to his son deepened once he mustered up the courage to confront his fears and open up.

Common Stroking Errors

When you're at odds with someone, a little bit of Stroking can go a long way toward detoxifying the interaction, because all human beings have a deep need to be liked or admired. However, there are several errors that people often make when they're learning how to use Stroking:

1. **Complimenting the other person too much.** If you lay it on too thick, you may come across as needy, desperate, or inferior.

If your compliments sound exaggerated or over the top, the other person may discount your comments and conclude that you're a fake who's trying to manipulate him or her.

2. **Hiding your feelings.** If you're not genuine and open when you compliment the other person, your attempts at Stroking will fall flat. For example, if you're uncomfortable or upset, but you don't acknowledge this, your compliments may sound insincere, like psychobabble.

3. **Praising the other person in a superficial or insincere way.** Some people use Stroking to avoid dealing with conflict and anger. I illustrated this problem with a role-play demonstration during a recent workshop. I asked one therapist to play the role of an angry, difficult patient, and asked the other therapist to try to respond, using the Five Secrets of Effective Communication. The "patient" accused the therapist of being a fake. The therapist replied, "I'm so glad you said that. It's courageous of you to be so open and honest. It must have been hard for you to say that." This irritated the man who played the role of the "patient" because it sounded so condescending. And it wasn't honest, either. The therapist certainly didn't feel "glad" when he was criticized and it wasn't hard for his "patient" to criticize him. In fact, he enjoyed it!

Chapter 23

Helping and Problem Solving

Two common mind-sets called the Helping Addiction and the Problem-Solving Addiction often get in the way of skillful listening. That may sound strange, because we usually think of helping and solving problems as good things to do. We want to help the people we care about, and we want to solve the problems in our relationships. But sometimes helping is the most unhelpful thing you can do.

When Helping Hurts

When I was in Philadelphia, I supervised a clinical psychology student named Jake who had trouble empathizing with his patients. Jake was treating a young woman named Sunny who felt depressed and lonely. Sunny gave Jake poor empathy scores at the end of every therapy session. This was upsetting to Jake, because he was trying hard and was convinced he was doing good work with her. I had the chance to watch a video of one of their therapy sessions so I could try to diagnose the problem.

On the video, Sunny was upset and mad at herself. She said that she felt lonely because she always acted fake in her interactions with people, fearing that if she was genuine and honest with people, they'd reject her. She said that she often lied about herself, exaggerating her accomplishments and trying to portray herself as something different from what she really was. She said that people sometimes caught her in the little white lies and ended up rejecting her, the very result she was trying so desperately to avoid.

I noticed a pattern on the video. Every time Sunny began to describe how she felt, Jake tried to cheer her up. For example, he'd say things like, "Oh, we all tend to act fake at times in social interactions," or "You shouldn't feel that way because you're a *good* person and you have a *great deal* to offer."

Although Jake was trying to be helpful, his "encouraging" comments actually shut Sunny down and prevented her from expressing her feelings. He wasn't being honest, either, because he was feeling frustrated with Sunny and with their lack of progress in the therapy, but he was hiding his feelings and acting chipper and upbeat. Of course, this was the exact problem he was trying to help Sunny with—not being genuine or open with people.

Trying to fix or help someone who's upset usually doesn't work because it can sound patronizing, condescending, and irritating. Sunny needed someone who would listen, encourage her to open up, and validate her feelings *without* trying to cheer her up. Changing this compulsive pattern of "helping" someone in distress sometimes requires more than just training and practice. You may have to give up your own codependent need to fix or help the other person.

Imagine that Sunny is your friend, and she's trying to confide in you. She says, "You know, I nearly always act fake in my interactions with people. Sometimes I even tell little white lies about myself because I feel that people will reject me if they find out how I really feel. But they end up rejecting me anyway." What would you say next?

Write down your ideas on a separate piece of paper before you continue reading. Remember to identify the techniques you used in parentheses after each sentence, using the abbreviations on page 98.

Answer

A response like this might be effective:

> Sunny, what you're telling me sounds very painful. (FE) You say that you often act fake and tell little white lies about yourself to try to impress people, but then you end up getting rejected anyway. (TE) That sounds incredibly frustrating and lonely. (FE) I can imagine that it might be embarrassing or humiliating when that happens. (FE) It's sad for me to hear how you've been struggling in your relationships with people, because I think you have a lot to offer. (FE; ST) Tell me more about what it's been like for you. (IN)

Notice that you're sharing your feelings and encouraging Sunny to open up, rather than trying to fix or help her. Paradoxically, this *will* be helpful. Sunny's incredibly lonely. Listening, without helping, is often the most helpful thing you can do.

The Problem-Solving Trap

Problem solving also gets in the way of intimacy. When you're not getting along with someone, you may try to solve the problem when you should be listening and sharing your feelings. This can be a big mistake.

I recently received a call from an ex-patient I hadn't seen for nearly twenty-five years. It seemed like barely a week or two had passed since Janet and I had last talked. I was so inspired by the work we did together that I wrote a chapter about her in my first book, *Feeling Good*. Since that time, Janet's life had gone exceedingly well. She'd raised her family and had become an internationally renowned author and motivational speaker.

I first met Janet shortly after I opened my practice in Philadelphia. I treated her for depression after her husband had dumped her in order to have an affair with his secretary. Janet was angry and devastated, but pulled out of her depression quickly and soon met a handsome forty-two-year-old divorced minister named Peter. I encouraged Janet to ask him on a date, and they fell madly in love. Janet filed for divorce and married Peter several months later.

When they were engaged, Janet told Peter, "I never want children. I'm a career woman and I'll be a wonderful stepmother." This was perfect for Peter because he'd already raised five children of his own and didn't want any more. He said his fathering days were over.

Seven years later, Janet woke up one morning and said, "I *must* have a baby, and I *must* have one now!" She said, "Peter looked at me like I was crazy. We tried to negotiate and I used all the skills I'd learned in my work as a corporate executive, but we could not solve this problem. It was major to me and major to Peter. By now, he was fifty years old and had no interest whatsoever in being a father again. But I couldn't stop obsessing about a baby."

I invited Janet and Peter to come in for some couples therapy and asked them to talk about the problem while I watched so I could try to diagnose the cause of the impasse. I could see that they were desperately trying to solve the problem but kept running into a wall. There wasn't any solution and there wasn't any way to compromise because they both had intense negative feelings that they weren't expressing or acknowledging.

I pointed out that they didn't have to solve the problem that day, and reminded them that they had an incredibly strong, loving relationship. I encouraged them to put the problem on the shelf and stop trying to solve it. Instead they could focus on listening, supporting each other, and trying to see the problem through each other's eyes, using the Five Secrets of Effective Communication. I told them not to bring the problem down off the shelf until they were both ready.

Janet said that it was the hardest thing she'd ever done, putting the problem on the shelf. But for Peter, it was a relief, because he was under intense pressure. For several weeks, they practiced with the One-Minute Drill I described in chapter 21.

Then, a miracle suddenly occurred. Two weeks later, Peter woke up one morning and said, "Let's take it off the shelf now." He told

Janet that he remembered that she'd compromised on his dream of buying a farm and living in the country, and that was hard for her because of her work in Philadelphia and the long commute. So he said, "Janet, you've supported my dream so much, so how could I not help you conceive your dream?"

Their daughter, Dawn, was born ten months later. Peter said that she turned out to be the greatest gift he ever had. He was excited from the moment she was born, and they've been the best of pals ever since.

Janet explained it this way:

> Dawn absolutely loves the farm. When she was growing up, she and her dad always did a lot of outside work together. Her birth was the most significant thing I've ever done in my life. Nothing else comes close. But it never would have happened if we hadn't stopped trying to solve the problem.
>
> We've used your "put it on the shelf" technique lots of times ever since then—it's been invaluable in our relationship and in my business dealings as well. I've also used it in my personal life, in my interactions with friends. The idea of "putting it on the shelf" just resonated from the time the words came out of your mouth.

You can't use this technique in a vacuum. You have to work hard on listening, acknowledging how the other person was feeling, and sharing your own feelings, without making any demands or trying to find a solution. You stop trying to solve the problem, but you don't stop listening, sharing your feelings, and supporting your partner. Sometimes the attempt to solve the problem *is* the problem, because no one is listening or acknowledging the feelings.

Janet said:

> It was unbelievable. I ended up getting exactly what I wanted. Our whole family uses that technique all the time. Now we're so connected as people. Peter just walked in the door and I almost burst into tears. I'm so thankful for what we've got. Our

relationship is so deep. I feel that he's always reaching for me to make sure I'm okay. After all these years, we still can't bear to be apart. We just want to be together all the time.

The work that we put in early in our relationship, both having come from divorces and very different backgrounds, made a huge difference. I was a little Jewish princess marrying an ex-minister. Your techniques have given us more than words can express. Every day that I can remember we've taken our walks, or sat with a glass of wine before the fire, and I can say that if it ended today, we're the luckiest people in the world.

Chapter 24

Hiding Your Head in the Sand: Conflict Phobia and Anger Phobia

We live in a pretty violent, aggressive society. So it may be surprising that many people have a mind-set I call Anger Phobia, or Conflict Phobia. These terms simply mean that you're afraid of anger or conflict, so you bury your head in the sand when you're not getting along with someone, hoping the negative feelings will go away.

You'll recall that when you use Thought and Feeling Empathy, you paraphrase what the other person said and acknowledge how she's feeling, given what she just said to you. If you do this skillfully, it can reduce the tension in the air. However, there's one feeling that people practically never acknowledge, and that feeling is anger. It seems that most of us will argue and defend ourselves at the drop of a hat, but we almost never acknowledge that the other person may be feeling hurt or angry.

I'm not entirely sure why. Perhaps we're afraid that if we acknowledge the other person's anger, the conflict will mushroom out of control. Of course, the opposite usually happens. When you ignore someone's anger, it escalates. The other person will up the ante because she wants you to acknowledge how she's feeling.

Even mental health professionals have an exceedingly hard time acknowledging anger, even though they've devoted their careers to helping people deal with conflict. Several years ago, I gave a talk for a group of therapists at the Center for Cognitive Therapy at the University of Pennsylvania medical school. I described some of the most common errors therapists make when interacting with challenging, mistrustful patients. I explained that a common but little-known problem is the fact that nearly all therapists have an intense Conflict Phobia and will practically *never* acknowledge a patient's anger, even when the patient is clearly enraged. This is a big mistake, because the patient feels ignored and gets even angrier.

To illustrate this problem, I asked for two volunteers to do an amazing role-playing demonstration. I explained that one of them would play the role of an incredibly angry patient, and the other would play the role of the therapist. The therapist's job would be to listen and acknowledge the patient's anger.

A staff psychologist named William volunteered to play the role of therapist. One of his colleagues, Pam, offered to play the role of the angry patient. I told Pam to tear into William in the most humiliating, ruthless manner possible. I told William to sit and listen while Pam criticized him. When she was done, his job would be to try to respond to Pam as effectively as he could, using his best therapeutic skills.

I emphasized the fact that Pam would probably sound extremely angry, so it would be especially important for him to acknowledge her anger. For example, he might say something like this: "Pam, it seems like you're really upset and maybe even a bit angry with me right now. What you're saying is important and I'd like to hear more about how you're feeling." I warned William that he probably wouldn't be able to acknowledge her anger, no matter how hard he tried, because nearly all therapists are afraid of anger. But I told him to try his best and see if he could prove me wrong, and reminded him that all he really had to do was use the A-word (anger) when he responded.

I explained that I'd done similar demonstrations in hundreds of workshops all across the United States, and that no mental health professional had *ever once* been able to acknowledge a patient's anger. I turned to William and said, "So you have a golden opportunity right now. You can be the first psychologist in the United States to use the A-word. You can make history today! All that being said, I'm certain that you won't be able to do it." William accepted my challenge in the right spirit and said he was *determined* to acknowledge Pam's anger.

They began, and Pam played the role of the "difficult patient" superbly. She ripped into William and told him he was a joke of a therapist. She said that she was thinking of dropping out of therapy because his so-called treatment was a total waste of time and money. She said that he was obviously a male chauvinist and that her marriage was falling apart because of his stupid advice. She pointed out that he wasn't even married and couldn't possibly help her with her problems, and that she felt worse today than she did at the start of the therapy. In fact, she felt worse every time she came to see him.

While she was speaking, William turned bright red and looked like a deer caught in the headlights. I was grateful that I wasn't in his shoes at that moment! When she was done, it was so quiet that you could hear a pin drop. Everyone was staring at William with great expectations, wondering what he was going to say next. Would he remember to acknowledge how angry she was?

A few tense seconds passed and he didn't say a thing. Finally, he leaned forward and said, in a very patronizing voice, "Thank you for sharing. You must be a *very lonely* woman!" After another awkward silence, everyone started laughing.

I asked, "Is that it? Are you done?" He still looked embarrassed but nodded affirmatively.

Then I asked, "Is there one emotion that no therapist in the United States has ever been able to acknowledge?" William hit the side of his head with his hand, because he realized he'd made the exact error I'd predicted. He'd completely failed to acknowledge Pam's anger. Instead, he responded with psychobabble—"Thank you for sharing"—and labeled her as a "lonely woman," which was a put-down.

Why did this happen? Even though it was just a role-playing exercise, Pam's remarks felt so threatening that William got spaced out and completely forgot what he was supposed to do. This can happen to any of us. Fortunately, William had a good sense of humor and said he learned a lot from the exercise. He said it made him aware of how conflict-phobic he was in his clinical work and in his personal life as well. With determination, you can learn to overcome these defensive, knee-jerk reactions, but it takes practice because it seems that defensiveness and conflict avoidance are hardwired into our brains.

Of course, if you acknowledge the other person's anger in a clumsy way, the problem will get worse. Then you'll conclude that it really is foolish to acknowledge anger. For example, suppose your friend Melody seems upset and says, "Dammit! You're not listening! I'm pissed off." Then you might say, "You sound *very angry*," in a patronizing or judgmental tone of voice. Although you're acknowledging Melody's anger, your statement won't be very effective because it sounds like a put-down. Melody will get defensive and angrily insist that she *isn't* angry. Or else she'll say, "Damn right I'm angry!" Then you'll conclude that it really *isn't* a good idea to talk about anger.

A softer way to acknowledge Melody's anger might be to say:

It's hard for me to hear that I haven't done a very good job of listening, but I think you're right, and I'm not surprised that you're feeling pissed off and frustrated with me right now. (IF; DT; FE) Would you be willing to tell me more about some of the things I've missed? (IN) I really want to understand how you've been feeling. (IN)

This response acknowledges Melody's anger and conveys respect. If you validate her anger, she won't feel judged and won't feel the need to deny her feelings. This will make it easier for her to open up. Paradoxically, she'll probably feel less angry because you listened.

Let's practice. For this exercise, let's imagine that you haven't been doing the written exercises while you've been reading. You've been skipping over them. I know this doesn't describe you, and that you've been working hard on the written exercises while you've been reading, but we can pretend. I'll play the role of an annoying author named David, and I say this to you in a hyper-critical tone of voice:

> Over and over I've encouraged you to do the written exercises in this book, but you just seem to skip over them and keep reading. I've also told you that you can't *possibly* learn how to use these techniques in real-life situations unless you do the damn exercises. Weren't you listening? Or did you think what I was saying wasn't important? Huh?

How will you respond? Write down your response on a separate piece of paper. You can use any of the Five Secrets of Effective Communication, but make sure you include Feeling Empathy. Remember to put the names of the techniques you used in parentheses at the end of each sentence, using the abbreviations on page 98.

Answer
Here's an approach that might work:

> Wow, David, I'm feeling a bit on the spot right now. (IF) I love your book, but I'm embarrassed to admit that I have been skipping over the written exercises. (ST; IF; DT) It sounds like you're feeling frustrated, and maybe even a bit angry with me. (FE) I know you've had lots of experience, and I have no doubt that the exercises are important. (ST; DT) Do most of your readers do the exercises? (IN) Are there many who resist? (IN) It must be annoying. (IF)

In this example, you acknowledge how you're feeling and express some admiration for David. His narcissism seems to be wounded, so the skillful use of Stroking and the Disarming Technique will reduce the tension. And when you acknowledge David's frustration and anger, it will be much harder for him to keep belittling you. That's because you've brought the negative feelings out into the open in a gentle way.

Now examine what you wrote down. Did you acknowledge David's anger? Did you share your own feelings in a direct but tactful way? Did you find some truth in David's criticism? Did you convey any admiration or respect in the heat of battle?

If your response wasn't effective, you may need to do a few more written exercises. Write down several mean-spirited criticisms or put-downs you might hear from friends, family members, or colleagues, and then write down how you might respond, using the Five Secrets of Effective Communication. Make sure you acknowledge the other person's anger. Once you've gotten good at writing effective responses on paper, ask a friend to role-play with you. Tell your friend to read the zingers to you, one at a time, and explain that you'll try to acknowledge her anger in a friendly, tactful way. Most people develop vastly improved empathy skills after just a few minutes of practice.

Anger Phobia

We've seen that it can be hard to acknowledge someone else's anger. Anger can also be tough to express. One reason for this is that we tend to view anger and love as mutually exclusive. One of my patients told me that when she was growing up, her parents taught her that if you really love someone, you'll never fight or argue with them, and if you fight and argue, it means you're not really in love. This may be an appealing model of marriage, but it doesn't work very well in the real world.

Carl Jung believed that we all have a shadow, or a dark side, as well as a positive, loving side, and that mental health involves the fusion of these two opposite impulses. However, it isn't easy for us to accept the fact that we might have selfish, hostile motives, so we keep the dark side hidden from conscious awareness. That way, we can feel innocent and won't have to experience any guilt when we're angry with someone.

But the dark side always has a way of coming out, directly or indirectly. In fact, the harder you try to hide or suppress your anger, the stronger it gets.

I want to be crystal clear about this: negative feelings are perfectly normal, and you cannot wish them away, no matter how hard you try. We all get annoyed and frustrated from time to time, and it won't usually do you much good to try to hide or suppress those feelings. Sooner or later, the anger *always* comes bubbling out. Your only real choice is how you express your feelings, and you've got three choices:

- **Active aggression.** You can attack the other person with threats, physical violence, name calling, obscenities, put-downs, or arguments about the "truth." This is the most popular way to express anger, and that's because it feels *good* to attack. We *want* to attack. If you give in to this urge, conflict will be inevitable.
- **Passive aggression.** You can maintain a façade of innocence and express your anger indirectly with sarcasm or jibes. Or you can pretend to treat the other person in a friendly way and get back at him behind his back, by gossiping about him and bad-mouthing him to other people, or punishing him silently with scorn. This is the second-most popular way to express anger.
- **Sharing your anger.** You can share your negative feelings in an open, respectful way that preserves the other person's sense of self-esteem and dignity. This is the least popular option, but by far the most effective.

When you share angry feelings, timing will be important. You'll generally need to use the three listening skills first. People need to have their day in court before they'll be willing to listen to you. This means finding truth in what they're saying (the Disarming Technique), acknowledging how they're thinking and feeling (Thought and Feeling Empathy), and inviting them to tell you more (Inquiry).

Conveying positive regard can be incredibly helpful when you feel hurt, angry, or frustrated. Try not to say anything that would sound like a put-down or make the other person lose face. Don't put the other person on the defensive or say anything that would humiliate him.

Imagine that you have a good friend named Tony, but you're mad at him because he made a totally unexpected cutting comment that hurt your feelings. How would you express your anger in a kind and respectful way? Here's one approach:

Tony, you've always been one of my best friends, but I'm upset and frustrated right now. (ST; IF) Your comment had a sharp edge to it, and I'm feeling put down. (FE; IF) Are you pissed off at me about something? (IN)

Notice that you're expressing your feelings openly and directly without threatening Tony or trying to put him down.

Although it may require some discipline, you can always express your feelings in a tactful way, without using inflammatory, threatening language, but it can be difficult. We all feel the urge to lash out or fight back when we're upset, and this is understandable. This urge probably has a genetic basis. Throughout the course of human history, the most aggressive individuals have had the best chance of reproducing, because they were the strongest and most likely to survive. Power and aggression can be sexually attractive as well. Aggressive urges are programmed into our genes. We can't be blamed for wanting to fight back, any more than a lion can be blamed for wanting to stalk and kill its prey.

However, we can choose whether or not to give in to the urge to inflict pain. If you project hostility, you'll have a battle on your hands. In contrast, if you resist this urge and share your angry feelings in a respectful way, and communicate your desire to develop a better relationship with the person you're at odds with, he or she will be far more likely to listen and treat you with respect.

Even if you express your feelings skillfully, the other person may react defensively and lash out at you. People can be fragile or easily hurt. If the other person gets upset when you express your feelings, back off immediately and switch into the listening mode again using the Disarming Technique, Thought and Feeling Empathy, and Inquiry. When the other person feels relaxed and accepted, you can try to express your feelings again in a tactful manner.

Chapter 25

Apologizing: "Can't I Just Say, 'I'm Sorry'?"

One of the most common questions I hear at my Intimacy Workshop is, "Can't I just say, 'I'm sorry'?" Apologizing isn't inherently good or bad, but most of the time it's a trap that gets in the way of skillful listening. Here's why. When someone is feeling upset and mad at you, you may think that all he or she wants is an apology, so you listen to all the complaints and say, "I'm sorry," expecting the problem to be solved. But what's really happening is that your apology is a way of shutting the other person up because you don't want to hear about how hurt and angry he or she feels. Although apologies can be meaningful, they can also be a not-so-subtle way of avoiding intimacy, as the following case illustrates.

Donald and Victoria came to me for help with their turbulent marriage. Several months after their second child was born, Donald had to move to Seattle for six months because of his work. Victoria stayed at their home in Arizona because their oldest son had asthma, and the dry climate was helpful to him. Shortly after Donald left, Victoria discovered that she was pregnant. However, she didn't want another child and arranged to have an abortion without telling Donald. When he heard the news after the fact, he was devastated. He'd always wanted more children and believed that abortion was wrong. He felt bitter and betrayed because Victoria left him out of the loop entirely. However, they never talked about their feelings. They just swept them under the carpet and carried on as if nothing was wrong.

Shortly after he returned to Arizona, Donald had an affair with a woman who lived several blocks from their home. He actually moved in with her and lived with her for three months. Victoria felt humiliated and made excuses to their children every night, pretending that Daddy had to work late and that's why he wasn't coming home for dinner. Donald's affair eventually soured, and he moved back in with Victoria again. They never talked about their feelings, so there was always tension in the air. They sought therapy several years later to see if they could repair the damage and develop a more loving and trusting relationship.

Instead of talking things over when they were upset, they acted their feelings out indirectly by hurting each other. Donald felt hurt and angry about Victoria's secret abortion, but instead of telling her how he felt, he had an affair. Of course, Victoria was crushed. By the same token, her secret abortion may have been payback for something he'd done to hurt her. When he found out about the abortion, Donald said he felt like he'd been kicked in the stomach. They'd been involved in this pattern of superficial niceness, con-flict avoidance, and hostile retaliation since they first met.

I thought the One-Minute Drill might be helpful, so I explained the exercise and encouraged Victoria to tell Donald how she felt when he had his affair. I asked Donald to sit quietly and listen so he could summarize what she said when she was done. Then we could do a role reversal and he could express his feelings while Victoria listened. That way, they'd both have the chance to share their feelings more openly and directly while their partner was listening.

They agreed that the exercise made a lot of sense. Victoria told Donald how ashamed, hurt, and angry she'd felt during his affair. She said it was absolutely devastating to her, and now it was re-ally hard for her to trust him because she had no way of knowing if he'd do the same thing to her again. She said that those three months were the worst time of her life and that the affair was still eating away at her. She explained that she couldn't get it out of her mind, and she still felt resentful. She said that this made it hard for her to feel any love or respect for him, and she'd lost all interest in sex as well because she felt used and humiliated.

When she spoke, Donald sat and listened. When she was done, I encouraged Donald to summarize what Victoria had just said and acknowledge how she was feeling. Instead, he said that he was *sorry* about the affair but thought it was time for her to stop obsessing about the past so they could move forward with their lives. He said that he was tired of having to apologize over and over and that her constant complaining and criticizing was bringing him down.

This was the last thing Victoria needed to hear. Donald needed to admit that he'd hurt her, acknowledge how angry and betrayed she felt, and show some compassion and remorse. When he mouthed his apology and told Victoria to move forward with her life, he was really conveying this message: "Shut up and stop complaining. I'm tired of listening to you. I don't want to hear about how you feel. In fact, I don't even care about your feelings."

Donald's superficial apology frustrated Victoria and made her resentment more intense. Sometimes an apology is just a form of censorship. You apologize as a way of shutting the other person up because you don't want to hear about all the anger and hurt feelings. Of course, saying "I'm sorry" isn't always dysfunctional. It's dysfunctional only if you apologize when you need to listen and acknowledge how the other person is feeling.

When Victoria said, "Those three months were the worst time of my life. Your affair is still eating away at me. I can't stop thinking about it," Donald could have responded like this:

Victoria, I feel terrible to realize how much I've hurt you. (DT; FE) What I did was selfish and outrageous, and you have every right to feel enraged with me. (DT; FE) I can hardly imagine how humiliated, lonely, and miserable you must have felt. (FE) I offer my most profound apology for hurting you, and I can't imagine how you could ever forgive me. (ST; DT) I want you to know that I'm hurting, too, and I can barely live with myself, because I love you so much. (IF; FE) Can you tell me what it was like for you then, and how you're feeling now? (IN)

This apology would be effective. That's because Donald is not trying to shut Victoria up. He's conveying humility, love, and remorse, and giving his wife the chance to open up. Of course, he will have to speak from the heart and mean what he says. If he's just mouthing the words as a manipulation, it won't be effective.

So now we come back to the question I raised in the chapter title: "Can't I just say, 'I'm sorry'?" The answer is—it all depends. If your apology is a way of avoiding the other person's hurt and angry feelings, then it's just another way of copping out and avoiding intimacy. But if you encourage the other person to share his or her hurt feelings, and you share your own, then your apology can be a vitally important expression of humility and love.

Chapter 26

Submissiveness: "I Must Please You"

S ometimes self-defeating attitudes and beliefs make it hard to use the Five Secrets of Effective Communication effectively. These include Truth, Justice, Conflict Phobia, Submissiveness, the Love and Approval Addictions, Entitlement, Problem Solving, and the Helping Addiction, to name just a few. For example, if you're a crusader for Truth, you may feel an overwhelming need to prove that the person you're arguing with is wrong, instead of listening, validating his or her criticisms, and conveying respect. If you have a Helping Addiction, you may have the compulsive need to help or fix friends and family members who are upset, rather than simply listening, acknowledging how they feel, and encouraging them to tell you more about what's bothering them.

One of the most intriguing things about Self-Defeating Beliefs is that although they tend to be unrealistic, they function as self-fulfilling prophecies, so they appear to be true when they aren't. For example, let's say you have a mistrustful, paranoid mind-set—you feel suspicious and afraid that the people you care about will be disloyal and exploit you. This mind-set betrays a profound lack of self-esteem, because you believe that others could not really love and respect you as you are, and that their only interest in you would be to hurt, betray, or exploit you. As a result, you're always reading malignant motives into what other people say and do.

This mind-set will frustrate and annoy other people for a variety of reasons. First, they'll feel hurt and angry because you're constantly imagining that they want to hurt you. Second, they won't be able to get close to you, because you're always hiding behind an enormous wall of mistrust. As a result, they will have negative feelings about you, and they will talk about you behind your back, telling others what a difficult person you are. In a sense, you actually force people to look down on you, the very result you feared all along.

But you're not aware that you're doing this. You think you've made an important discovery about human nature. In a sense, we're always looking at our own attitudes and expectations reflected in the faces and behaviors of the people we interact with. We're constantly creating our own interpersonal reality, but we don't realize that we're doing this. And if you don't know that this is going on, and you're not consciously aware of the impact of your attitudes and expectations on other people, the same patterns will keep repeating themselves over and over.

How to Identify Self-Defeating Beliefs

A technique called the Downward Arrow Technique can help you pinpoint self-defeating beliefs and expectations that may be sabotaging your relationships with people. Here's how it works. Think about a specific moment when you were in conflict with someone you weren't getting along with, and ask yourself how you were thinking and feeling at that moment. What were you telling yourself? Write your negative thoughts on a piece of paper.

Select any thought that's of interest to you and draw a downward arrow under it. The downward arrow is a form of shorthand. It's a reminder to ask yourself these kinds of questions:

If that thought were true, what would it mean to me? Why would it be upsetting to me?

Then a new negative thought will pop into your mind. Write it down and draw a new downward arrow underneath it. Now ask yourself the same kinds of questions. Repeat this over and over until you've generated a chain of several additional negative thoughts. Now review the list of negative thoughts and ask yourself these three questions about your relationship with the other person:

1. What do these thoughts tell me about the kind of person I am? What's my role in this relationship?
2. What do these thoughts tell me about the kind of person he or she is? What's his or her role in this relationship?
3. What do these thoughts tell me about the kind of relationship we have? What's the script that connects these two roles? What are the rules that we're playing by?

The answers to these questions can be illuminating.

A twenty-eight-year-old psychology graduate student named Denise told me that she needed help with her "codependency" problems. There's no such thing as "codependency." It's just a buzzword, and it means different things to different people. I asked Denise for an example of what she meant. Could she think of a specific time when she was struggling with codependency? When was it? What was going on? Who was she interacting with? How was she thinking and feeling?

Denise said that she often got depressed during the winter months, so she'd typically develop a new romantic interest, and that would tide her over emotionally until spring arrived. When the weather changed, she'd usually feel better emotionally, but she'd start to feel trapped by her relationship. Then she wanted out. She explained that she was completing her Ph.D. in anthropology at the University of Pennsylvania and had to commute back and forth from Harrisburg, where she lived with her partner, Lisa. As a result, she was putting in nearly sixty hours a week studying, going to classes, and commuting, and she was exhausted on weekends.

Earlier in the week, Denise had gotten a phone call from Lisa. Lisa was excited and said that she'd made elaborate plans for the two of them for the weekend. On Saturday morning, she and

Denise were going to drive from Harrisburg to Pittsburgh to visit Lisa's parents, and then they were going to go to a party in Pittsburgh Saturday night. On Sunday morning, they were going to drive to Lancaster to meet friends and attend a folk festival, and on Sunday evening, they were going to drive back to Harrisburg. Denise felt exhausted and overwhelmed by the prospect of all the driving and partying; she just wanted to relax and veg out over the weekend. However, she had a hard time saying no because she felt anxious, guilty, frustrated, resentful, and trapped.

I asked Denise what she was thinking at that moment. What negative thoughts were flowing across her mind? She was telling herself:

1. Lisa doesn't understand me.
2. She has a right to expect my support.
3. I can't breathe or move. This is a no-win situation.
4. I'm being selfish.

Now that we've focused on one moment when Denise was upset, we know exactly what she means by "codependency." She was annoyed with Lisa for being so demanding, but felt guilty because she was telling herself that she *should* support Lisa and do what Lisa wanted her to do.

After Denise wrote down the four negative thoughts, I asked her which one was the most upsetting to her. She said it was the fourth thought, "I'm being selfish." I told her to draw a downward arrow under this thought, and asked, "If that were true, what would it say about you? Why would it be upsetting to you?"

Denise said, "That would mean I'm not giving anything to other people." I asked her to write that down, and repeated the same question. Here's the chain of thoughts we generated:

4. I'm being selfish.
   "If that were true, what would it say about you? Why would it be upsetting to you?"

5. That would mean I'm not giving anything to other people.

"If that were true, what would that mean to you? Why would it be upsetting to you?"

6. That would mean I had nothing to offer.
   "Let's assume that you really did have nothing to offer. What would that mean to you?"

7. Then nobody would like me.
   "And then what? Let's assume that nobody likes you because you have nothing to offer. Why would that be upsetting? What would happen next?"

8. I'd be all alone.
   "And then? What would happen if you were all alone?"

↓

9. That would mean I was a bad, rotten human being.

Now review the negative thoughts we generated and ask yourself these three questions about how Denise thinks about intimate relationships:

- How does Denise think about the role she's playing in her relationship with Lisa?
- What's Denise's view of Lisa's role in their relationship?
- How does she understand the nature of a loving relationship? Or, to put it differently, what's the rule, or script, that connects Denise's role with Lisa's role?

. Let's focus on the first question: What's Denise's role in their relationship? Think about it for a moment before you continue reading.

The Role Denise Plays

Denise seems to be telling herself that she needs her partner's love to feel happy and worthwhile. She also seems to believe that she has to earn her partner's love by constantly giving, giving, giving. I call this mind-set Submissiveness. Submissive individuals tell

---

themselves that they must make their partners happy, even at the expense of their own needs and feelings, and even if they make themselves miserable in the process.

Denise was extremely surprised by this insight. Although she was intelligent and interested in psychology, she said she'd never realized that so much of her self-esteem was tied up in the idea that she had to give, give, give in order to earn her partner's love. She said that she'd been aware that she based her self-esteem on her intelligence and accomplishments, but hadn't realized that she also felt that she had to earn her self-esteem by constantly giving to other people. I asked Denise what this implied about her view of herself. She paused and said, "I guess I must think that I'm really kind of worthless."

Now let's think about Lisa's role in the relationship. If Denise is playing the role of a worthless person who has to earn her partner's love by constantly giving, giving, giving, what's her understanding of Lisa's role? Think about it for a moment before you continue reading.

The Role Lisa Plays

Here's how Denise put it: "I must think that Lisa's very demanding. And I must think that she'll reject me if I don't cater to her every whim. This makes it seem like Lisa is very self-centered and that I have to please her all the time or else I'll get rejected."

Now ask yourself this question: If Denise's role is to constantly give, give, give, and Lisa's role is to constantly take, take, take, then what's Denise's understanding of what it means to be in a loving relationship? What game are they playing? What's the rule that connects these two roles? Think about it for a moment before you continue reading.

Denise's View of Loving Relationships

Here's how Denise answered this question: "I must see love as a kind of slavery."

Now we can see why Denise is always getting trapped in intimate relationships, and why, sooner or later, she always wants out. She doesn't experience loving relationships as a source of support or joy because she sees herself as an inferior, worthless human being who constantly has to earn her partner's love by catering to her every whim. Denise said that these insights were like a revelation to her.

Denise said she felt immensely relieved by these insights and didn't think she needed any additional sessions, so we met on only that one occasion. I had the chance to speak with her a year later when she called to thank me and provide me with some follow-up data. She said that the work we did with the Downward Arrow Technique had made a tremendous impact on her. After the session, she decided to break up with Lisa; she subsequently developed a far more balanced and rewarding relationship with a new partner and no longer felt trapped or had any urge to break up. Although understanding alone is rarely enough, Denise said that the insight she gained gave her the courage to move forward with her life.

Are You a People Pleaser?

There's nothing wrong with wanting approval, working hard to do outstanding work, or placing a high value on warm, loving relationships with other people. And there's absolutely nothing wrong with wanting to please the people we care about. In fact, these values are probably programmed into our genes. These mind-sets become dysfunctional only when we hang on to them too rigidly or base our self-esteem on them.

For example, let's say I'm terrified of disapproval and wilt under criticism. Then if you point out something in the book that doesn't seem valid, I'll get defensive and start arguing with you because my self-esteem is on the line. You'll get annoyed because I'm not listening, and we'll end up in an unpleasant, adversarial interaction. Then I'll conclude that disapproval really is terrible and horrible. Although my fear of criticism is self-defeating and unrealistic, I'll be convinced that my fears are valid and real. That's one of the reasons why it can be hard to change these entrenched patterns.

Another reason is that Self-Defeating Beliefs tend to work in the short run, so we get addicted to them. For example, let's say that you have the Submissiveness and Dependency beliefs, like Denise. You constantly cater to everyone else's needs and feelings. For a while, this works very well because other people like the fact that you're always doing things for them and trying to make them happy. You don't make waves in your relationships because you fear rejection. But in the long run, you may start to notice that everyone's using you, and nobody's trying to meet your needs or make you happy. So you end up feeling used, burned out, or trapped, just like Denise.

One day, you realize what's been happening and decide that it's time for a change. You tell yourself that you need to be more assertive and stick up for yourself, so you jump to the opposite pattern. You begin to express yourself in a more demanding or aggressive manner. You stop blaming yourself for the problems in your relationship and start blaming your partner. But this doesn't work very well, either, because that style alienates people and creates arguments, so you give up and go back to your old pattern of suppressing your feelings and trying to please everyone else.

Is Assertiveness Training the Answer?

I got a taste of this myself when I was just starting out in clinical practice and one of my patients told me about a popular assertiveness training book that had been helpful to her. The book was titled *When I Say No, I Feel Guilty*, by Manuel J. Smith. I picked up a copy at the local bookstore because I knew I had a tendency to be overly "nice" and thought some assertiveness might be useful to me as well. I skimmed the book for several days on the train when I was commuting back and forth to work.

One of the methods that the author recommended was called the Broken Record Technique. The idea behind the technique was simple: when you're arguing with someone who refuses to see your point of view, all you have to do is agree with what he or she is saying in a general sort of way and then repeat yourself, like a broken record. For example, you might say, "I hear what you're saying, but . . . ," or "You've got a good point, but . . ." You do this over and over until the other person finally agrees with you or gives in to your demands. I thought, "How cool. If this works, it'll be worth its weight in gold!"

I had a perfect opportunity to try the Broken Record Technique. I'd just purchased a new set of windscreen wipers for our old Fiat at the local petrol station, but when I tried to install them the next day, I discovered that they'd sold me the wrong type. I drove back to the station and found an attendant. I explained that I'd purchased the windscreen wipers the day before, but when I got home, I discovered that they'd sold me the wrong type and I wanted to exchange them.

The attendant said that only the manager was allowed to do exchanges, so I'd have to come back the next morning when he was in. Using the Broken Record Technique, I said, "I hear you saying that the manager won't be in until tomorrow, but I want you to exchange the wipers now because you sold me the wrong type. It might rain this afternoon and I need the car."

He seemed taken aback and repeated what he'd said, but with a bit more emphasis. Our conversation went like this:

Petrol station attendant: I told you that I *can't* exchange the wipers now because the manager isn't in. I'm busy with customers right now and you'll have to come back in the morning when the manager is in.

David: I hear you saying that you're busy with customers and that the manager won't be in until tomorrow morning, but I want you to exchange the wipers now because it might rain this afternoon.

Petrol station attendant: I already told you that I'm not allowed to do that. You'll have to come back in the morning.

David: You're right, you already told me that you're not allowed to do exchanges, and that I'll have to come back in the morning, but I need the wipers now. I'm not going to wait until morning. This was your mistake, and I want you to exchange them now.

Petrol station attendant: What the hell? I told you that I'm busy and that only the manager can exchange the wipers! You'll have to come back in the morning. I can't help you!

David: I hear you saying what the hell and that you're busy and want me to come back in the morning, but I'm going to have to insist that you exchange the wipers right now. I paid for new wipers and I deserve new wipers.

At this point, he threw his hands up in disgust and walked toward a new customer who'd just come in. I followed right behind him and said, "I can see that you're ignoring me and that you're about to wait on that other customer, but I'm not going to leave until you give me the right windscreen wipers."

He stopped, turned, and stared at me with a menacing look. It suddenly dawned on me that he was a whole lot bigger than I was. He growled, "If you keep this up, I'm going to grab that wrench and break your goddamned kneecaps! Get the hell out of here!"

I couldn't recall what technique you were supposed to use when threatened with a wrench, so I said, "Mmm. You say that you're about to hit me with a wrench. I think I'll come back tomorrow morning when the manager is here. What a good idea!" Thus ended my brief love affair with assertiveness training.

It isn't difficult to see why the Broken Record Technique didn't work. If you use the EAR Checklist, it will jump right out at you. I didn't listen or acknowledge the truth in what the petrol station attendant was saying. I didn't express my feelings very skillfully, either. And I certainly didn't convey any respect. Instead, I sounded demanding, self-centered, and silly!

Essentially, I'd jumped from one self-defeating pattern, Submissiveness, to the opposite, Demandingness. This is a common mistake. When people try to change, they often jump back and forth between two equally self-defeating patterns. For example, you may switch from putting yourself down to putting your partner down, or from constantly blaming yourself to blaming your partner. Then you may give up and conclude that *nothing* will work. As a general rule, you can't solve relationship problems by becoming the opposite of the way you are.

CIT represents a different dimension entirely. Remember the three ingredients of good communication: Empathy, Assertiveness, and Respect. The philosophy behind this approach is:

- Your needs and feelings are important.
- My needs and feelings are important.
- We both deserve to be treated with dignity and respect.

Chapter 27

Resistance Revisited: "Why Should *I* Have to Do All the Work?"

Some people have trouble using the Five Secrets of Effective Communication because they don't really understand them, or because Self-Defeating Beliefs get in the way. However, there's another, deeper reason why people have trouble learning these techniques. They don't *want* to use them. They tell me that they *shouldn't have* to listen, share their feelings openly, or treat the other person with caring and respect.

Here are the kinds of things I often hear:

- "Why should *I* have to do all the work? That's unfair! When is my wife going to do her part?"
- "Why should I have to take all the blame? It *really is* my husband's fault!"
- "Why should I try to find some truth in what she's saying? She's completely wrong, and that's a fact!"
- "I'm not going to share my feelings. I'd look like a wimp! I don't go for that touchy-feely stuff."
- "If I agreed with him, I'd look weak. I'm not going to be a doormat and let him walk all over me! I'm going to stick up for myself!"

- "She'll *never* change! I've already tried everything and nothing works."
- "He's a jerk! I've got nothing good to say about him. Why should I have to treat him with respect?"
- "She's got *no right* to feel that way!"

These feelings can be intense. Sometimes you just want to let the person you're mad at know what a loser she is. If you're angrily embroiled in a battle that you're determined to win, it won't do any good for me to show you how distorted and illogical your thoughts are, or how ineffective and self-defeating your communication skills are. You just won't want to hear it. And if you're preoccupied with casting blame or putting the other person down, I probably won't be able to sell you on the joys of intimacy, because you have a different goal in mind. And even if you do want a more loving relationship, there may be a little voice in your mind that says, "Why should *I* have to do all the work when this is all *his* fault?"

I understand these feelings very well. I sometimes have to struggle with my own resistance to the Five Secrets on occasion. Of course, you *don't* have to use any of these techniques, and you don't have to work hard or assume all the responsibility for making your relationship better. Ultimately, you may have to ask yourself the same question I raised at the beginning of this book: "What do I want more? The rewards of the battle or the rewards of a loving, friendly relationship with the person I'm at odds with?"

Do you remember Raina? She's the woman we talked about in chapter 13 who had so much trouble finding the truth in her husband's relentless criticisms. Years later, I had the chance to ask her how things had worked out for her. Here's what she told me:

When you and I first started working together, there was always this little voice in my mind that told me that I shouldn't have to do all the work to make my marriage better. I'll always remember one moment that made a huge impression on me. Milt and I had been doing well, but we'd slipped back into our old patterns and started arguing again. Milt said, "There's nothing wrong with me. It's all your issues, your behavior, your problem. You ought to go back to see David Burns."

I tearfully called you to make an appointment. By the time I saw you, I was a little better, and you suggested that we could do some role-playing. I was playing Milt's role, and you played my role, showing me a different way to respond. In the middle I said, "I don't know why I'm doing this. It takes two people. He has a role in this as well. I'm the only one who's working. This isn't fair or just!"

You said, "Well, you're absolutely right, Raina. You *don't* have to do this at all. You can just continue doing whatever you're doing. Probably things will change or get worse. You may feel even more stressed and unhappy, but you're absolutely right, you *don't* have to do anything."

I said, "Let's continue!" We continued to role-play, and I learned the most important thing of all—that you can ONLY change yourself, you're only in control of yourself. You can't make someone else want to change or do anything you want them to do. The only thing you can do is change yourself.

But a miraculous thing happens when you initiate changes in your own behavior—you become a catalyst for change in the other person, and suddenly things get better. It leaves you with an empowered feeling and you can deal with all the anger and hurt feelings. You can start to look at the problem from the other person's perspective and hear what he has to say. And when you do, he suddenly develops an interest in *your* feelings, and *your* perspective.

There's one other thing that helps me—it makes no difference whose feelings are right or wrong. But if you want to turn things to your advantage, and you want to feel close to the man you love, you have to ignore your own truth for a moment and look at it from his perspective. That's when the magic happens.

Part Six

Advanced Techniques

Chapter 28

Changing the Focus: Is There an Elephant in the Room?

In the next three chapters, I'm going to teach you about three advanced communication techniques called Changing the Focus, Positive Reframing, and Multiple-Choice Empathy. Changing the Focus is useful when there's tension or hostility in the air and you and the other person are in an adversarial relationship. Positive Reframing can help you transform almost any type of hostile relationship failure into one of warmth, trust, and intimacy. You can use Multiple-Choice Empathy when you're trying to talk to a friend or family member who refuses to talk to you, or someone who doesn't know quite how to express what he or she is feeling.

When you're not getting along with someone, there's nearly always tension in the air, but you and the other person may ignore the tension or pretend it isn't there. It's almost like there's an elephant in the room, but everyone dances around it. When you Change the Focus, you point to the elephant and say, "Do you see what I see?" You bring the conflict to conscious awareness in a kindly way so you can talk about it, rather than arguing about who's right and who's wrong. If you use this technique skillfully, you can quickly put an end to almost any type of game playing or awkward, uncomfortable interaction.

A man named Mel was playing a doubles tennis match for his local tennis team, but he was assigned to a new partner named Fred. Mel was uneasy because Fred had a significantly higher ranking and seemed quiet and grouchy during the first set. Mel didn't think it was his fault, because he'd seen Fred playing on another occasion, and he was equally quiet and grouchy on that occasion. Still, Fred's sour attitude put Mel on edge, and they lost the first set, six games to four. Mel said that the tension made the match extremely uncomfortable, and he made a lot of unforced errors.

Mel decided to try Changing the Focus, so between sets, he said, "Fred, I guess you got stuck with me for this match. I really wish I could play as well as you do." Fred immediately replied, "Oh, it's not you. I apologize. Sometimes I get kind of quiet and grumpy." This broke the ice, and they both began to relax. They won the second set, six games to two, and went on to win the tournament.

Mel brought the tension to conscious awareness in a gentle way without putting his new partner on the defensive. When you acknowledge the tension instead of pretending it isn't there, it has a way of melting away.

Changing the Focus can be especially helpful when you and the other person aren't talking about your feelings or listening to each other. It's also helpful when you're:

- arguing and going around in circles.
- feeling bored with each other.
- being competitive instead of working together as a team.
- feeling abused or taken advantage of.

Let's Practice Changing the Focus

A chemistry graduate student named Marla told me about a conflict with her friend Elaine. One evening, they were hanging out together shooting the breeze. Elaine opened a special bottle of wine she'd just purchased and poured two glasses. After Marla tasted it, Elaine said, "Do you like the wine?" Marla felt anxious because she thought it tasted bitter. However, she knew that

Elaine had far more knowledge about wine and didn't want to say anything that would hurt Elaine's feelings, so she replied, "It's okay," in a noncommittal way.

Elaine seemed annoyed and repeated her question in a more demanding tone of voice: "Do you like it, yes or no?!"

Marla felt extremely anxious and didn't know what to say, so she simply repeated, "It's okay." At this point, things went downhill. Elaine got mad and poured the entire bottle of wine down the sink, and their evening was ruined. Marla asked me what she could have said that would have worked better.

Let's examine this interaction. Elaine sounded annoyed and asked a rather demanding question: "Do you like it, yes or no?" Marla responded by saying, "It's okay." Do you think Marla's response was an example of good communication or bad communication?

Marla's response was clearly an example of bad communication for three reasons. First, she didn't empathize. Elaine seemed upset and wanted to know what Marla thought about the wine. Perhaps she'd paid a lot for this special bottle and was feeling disappointed that it didn't meet her standards. Or perhaps she was annoyed because Marla was being evasive, and this set her on edge. Regardless, Marla didn't try to acknowledge how Elaine was feeling.

Marla didn't express her own feelings, either. She felt confused, taken aback, and put on the spot when Elaine kept pushing her to say whether she liked the wine. She also felt anxious and cornered but simply repeated her previous statement, "It's okay." This didn't sound respectful, because she was evasive when Marla was asking how she felt about the wine.

Now let's examine the consequences of Marla's response. Why did Elaine get so upset when Marla said, "It's okay," for the second time? Here's how Marla assessed the impact of her statement on her Relationship Journal:

Step 4. Consequences

Elaine may think I'm dishonest or impossible to please because I didn't give her a straightforward answer, so she upped the ante in order to get a response from me. When I didn't comment on the tension in the air, she felt free to act out her angry feelings.

My vagueness and passivity actually triggered her hostility. She probably went out of her way to buy this special bottle of wine, and I seemed totally indifferent to her efforts to please me.

Marla was trying to avoid the conflict because she felt so anxious and intimidated. Paradoxically, her evasiveness caused Elaine to escalate her demands in an attempt to get a reaction from Marla. Elaine probably felt hurt and disappointed, but neither of them was talking about their feelings. Instead, they were acting them out. This is a perfect opportunity for Changing the Focus.

Put yourself in Marla's shoes, and see if you can come up with a more effective response. You can use any of the Five Secrets of Effective Communication, but make sure you include Changing the Focus. When you use this technique, you focus on the tension in the room and talk about how the two of you are relating to each other, rather than the content of the argument. You read between the lines, so to speak. You stop dancing and talk about the kind of dance the two of you are doing. Ask yourself how the other person is feeling, and how you're feeling. Share your thoughts with the other person in a kindly way and ask how he or she is experiencing the interaction. Put your response on a separate piece of paper before you continue reading:

Answer

Here's what Marla came up with:

> Elaine, I'm feeling put on the spot right now and I think you might be feeling frustrated with me, especially because you were thoughtful and picked out this special bottle of wine for us. I'm thinking that the wine may be a bit sharp, but I don't have nearly your expertise in wine, and I'd be eager to hear what you think about it.

In the first sentence, Marla brings the conflict to conscious awareness by commenting on the tension in the room in a gentle, nonconfrontational manner. She's focusing on the conflict, and how they're both feeling, rather than whether the wine is spoiled. This involves a combination of "I Feel" Statements and Feeling

Empathy. In addition, Marla is using Stroking. She's letting Elaine know that she appreciates her thoughtfulness and admires her expertise in wine. She ends with Inquiry so Elaine will have the chance to open up as well.

Changing the Focus is powerful and may seem simple, but it's hard to master. When we're not getting along with someone, many of us try to ignore the hostility, hoping it will go away. But the negative feelings usually won't simply go away, so the conflict continues, with all the actors dutifully playing their old familiar roles. Marla was playing a meek, innocent role, and Elaine was in a dominant, scolding role. These roles are what we mean when we talk about people's "personalities." But there isn't any fixed set of attributes that are indelibly imprinted on your identity, and you're not obligated to keep playing the same role forever.

When you Change the Focus, you call attention to the fact that you're both feeling awkward or frustrated, and that there's tension in the air. You stop arguing or competing and point instead to the river of emotion that's flowing just under the surface. If you do this in a friendly, respectful way, so the other person doesn't feel judged or put down, you'll find it much easier to connect like allies instead of adversaries. The moment you comment on the game that's being played, the game will tend to disappear.

Changing the Focus has been extremely helpful in my personal life and in my clinical work as well. I once treated a psychologist named Ruthanne who was having difficulties with test anxiety. She was trying to prepare for her licensure examination but was so nervous that she couldn't concentrate. Whenever she tried to study and review the material, she bombarded herself with illogical negative messages like, "I just know I'm going to flunk the test," and "They'll ask about everything I *don't* know, and nothing that I *do* know," and "It's unfair!" These thoughts weren't especially realistic because Ruthanne was an outstanding student and had never flunked a test in her entire life. In addition, these thoughts were triggering the intense anxiety that was bugging Ruthanne.

However, every time I encouraged Ruthanne to challenge those thoughts and replace them with thoughts that were more positive and realistic, she fought me tooth and nail. She'd *yes-but* me and insist that I didn't understand, and we'd end up in an unproductive debate about whether her negative thoughts were realistic. Finally, I decided to Change the Focus. I said, "Ruthanne, I'm feeling awkward because it seems like we often end up debating with each other during sessions. Have you noticed that as well? You're really smart. In fact, you're one of my favorite people to argue with because you're so smart. But I'm concerned because I'd prefer to be working together with you on the same team. That way, I can help you overcome your anxiety about the test. Does this make sense?"

Notice that I wasn't complaining or blaming Ruthanne for the impasse. I was just saying, "Hey, this is what seems to be going on. How do you see it?" Ruthanne agreed that our debates had been uncomfortable for her as well. I suggested that we could give each other a signal whenever we noticed that we were falling into the same trap again. Either of us could raise our hand in the air. That meant, "Hey, we seem to be arguing again. Let's get back on track and work together." We used this technique several times and it worked well.

We also explored why Ruthanne might have been resisting my efforts to help her. Although she'd been intensely anxious, she was afraid to give up her anxiety for fear that she'd get so complacent that she wouldn't study at all. Then she might flunk the exam. However, she admitted that she'd been so paralyzed by fear that she hadn't studied for one minute in the previous five weeks.

Once she realized this, Ruthanne had a change of heart, and we worked together to challenge the irrational thoughts that were making her so anxious. She began to feel more confident and said she actually enjoyed reviewing the material. She passed the licensure exam with flying colors six weeks later. The solution to our problem was not so much figuring out who was right and who was wrong, but bringing the conflict to conscious awareness in a friendly way that didn't seem insulting or shameful to either of us.

Chapter 29

Positive Reframing: Opening the Door to Intimacy—and Success

When you're annoyed with someone, you'll probably see that person in a bad light and attribute negative motives to him or her. You may tell yourself that the other person is being selfish, lazy, or mean. These labels will polarize the interaction and function as self-fulfilling prophecies. For example, if you tell your husband that he's being stubborn, he'll dig in his heels and resist your suggestions. Of course, this is exactly what you're accusing him of. When you use Positive Reframing, you try to view the other person's motives and behavior in a more positive light. You put a positive spin on the situation.

For example, instead of telling yourself that your wife is "irrational," you could tell yourself that she has strong feelings that she wants you to understand, or that she loves you but feels attacked and upset. This change in perspective may help you communicate in a more flattering and respectful manner, so she'll lower her defenses.

I recently presented a new workshop on depression and self-esteem for the first time in Canada. I was a little anxious and hoped that it would be well-received. On day one, a psychologist in the audience was playing devil's advocate. After I'd make an important point, he'd raise his hand and challenge me. He'd say, "But what about this?" or "What about that?" His questions seemed to have a sharp edge. I've learned that arguing with someone in the audience can be a mistake, so I used the Disarming and Stroking Techniques every time I responded to him. I tried to find truth in what he was saying, and let him know that the questions he was raising were extremely important. This seemed to work reasonably well, and his attitude appeared to soften throughout the day.

At the end of the day, when everyone was leaving, he approached me and apologized for being so confrontational during the workshop. I said, "Hey, you don't have to apologize. You made terrific contributions and raised lots of great questions. I have no doubt that many people in the audience were concerned about the exact same things you were wondering about, but they were afraid to raise their hands and speak up. You were really voicing concerns that we've all had. If we're afraid to deal with these issues, we might as well give up on science and start a cult. I was grateful that you were here, and I hope you'll continue along the same vein tomorrow. Your questions made the workshop far more dynamic and interesting for everybody, including me."

He seemed surprised and pleased, to say the least, and walked out of the auditorium beaming. The following day, he didn't make a single critical comment. However, I did receive an e-mail from him several days after the conference. He wrote, "Dr. Burns, you're an awesome teacher! The techniques you presented have already revolutionized my practice."

Why did he become my ally? I had used Positive Reframing. I could have thought about him as a narcissistic complainer who was competing with me. Instead I emphasized that his questions were vitally important, and I said that I'd had similar concerns myself at one time or another. This put us on the same team and transformed a potentially adversarial interaction into one that felt collaborative and rewarding.

You could think of Positive Reframing as a combination of the Disarming Technique and Stroking, but it's more than that. You convey the idea that the conflict is actually a good thing, that no one has to feel ashamed or afraid of what's happening, and that you'll end up feeling closer because of the conflict. You emphasize that something good is happening and that something positive will emerge from the misunderstanding.

Positive Reframing isn't so much a technique as a way of thinking about a conflict. You can view any argument or disagreement as a chance to go to battle or as a chance to form a deeper and more meaningful relationship with the person you're at odds with. It requires creativity, caring, thoughtfulness, and practice.

When you use Positive Reframing, try to think about the other person's motives and behavior in a positive way. For example, if your son says something hostile that hurts your feelings, you could think about his remark as an expression of the hurt, loneliness, and frustration that's simmering just under the surface. After all, if he didn't really love you, he wouldn't be feeling so upset.

Along the same lines, you could reframe your wife's critical comment as the chance to develop a greater appreciation for how she's thinking and feeling, rather than viewing her comment as a prelude to Armageddon or proof that she's just trying to tear you down. And if a colleague seems dogmatic, you could tell yourself that he desperately wants you to understand his point of view.

Positive Reframing has to be genuine or it won't be effective. If you sound false or formulaic, it won't work. Your comments will have to be realistic, too. Think about the psychologist who constantly challenged me on the first day of my new workshop. Was his constant questioning really useful? Or was I just blowing smoke in his face?

I believe that we need more questioning in psychology and psychiatry. There are hundreds of competing schools of therapy, and they all claim to have the answer. But they can't all be right! When I told the psychologist that his skeptical questioning of my presentation was important, I meant it. When I told him that his questions and doubts were valid, I meant it. That's why my response was effective.

If you can set your ego aside, it will become easier to see the other person's nasty or adversarial behavior in a more positive and flattering light. But that can be challenging because it's so easy to feel hurt or threatened by what's happening, so we all tend to get defensive. When you use Positive Reframing, you resist the urge to go to war, and instead try to think about the conflict from a more positive perspective. If you share this vision with another person you're at odds with and convey respect, the positive impact can be dramatic.

Positive Reframing in Business Settings

Of course, Positive Reframing is not just for therapists. This technique can be helpful when you're at odds with your wife, son, neighbor, friend, or colleague—or even a complete stranger. And it can be equally effective in personal or business settings.

I once treated an organic chemist named Babette who was doing drug research at a laboratory in Los Angeles. She was miserable because her boss had disturbing and unpredictable mood swings. She explained that for a month or so, he'd be as sweet as pie. He'd praise everyone in the lab and make creative suggestions to help them with their research. Then storm clouds would gather and he'd become critical and abusive toward everyone in the lab. His dark moods typically lasted for a month or so, and then he'd suddenly switch back and be warm and friendly again. During his moody phases, Babette often went home in tears, humiliated by his hostile comments. She was at her wits' end and wanted to know what she should do.

I asked Babette if she had any pets. She said she loved animals and had a German shepherd. I asked if she'd know how to handle a snarling dog if she ran into one while she was walking in the park.

She said it was pretty simple. All you had to do was remain calm, stand perfectly still, and then slowly back away. She added that sometimes it helped to say sweet, soothing things and talk to the dog in a gentle, admiring tone of voice. She said that she'd actually tried that several weeks earlier when she was jogging, and the dog that was snarling at her calmed down right away. It started wagging its tail and licking her hand like she was a long-lost friend.

"Well," I said, "that's exactly how you handle a snarling boss. You have to treat him like a snarling dog."

I explained that Stroking and Disarming were probably the most useful techniques when her boss was snarling at her, so we practiced these techniques. One of us would play the role of her boss, and the other would play the role of Babette. When I was in Babette's role, I modeled the Disarming Technique and Stroking. We did lots of role reversals and she soon got the hang of it. By the end of the session, she was using these techniques masterfully and was eager to try the new approach the next time she interacted with her boss.

The next day, Babette met with her boss to get feedback on a draft of a paper they were co-authoring. She asked if he'd had the chance to read the paper and what he thought about it. He said that he'd thrown it in the bin because it was the worst piece of rubbish he'd ever seen. Of course, this was the last thing she wanted to hear because the paper represented months of back-breaking, meticulous research.

Babette remembered that she was supposed to treat her boss like a snarling dog, so she replied:

> Gordon, I'm not a bit surprised that you thought the paper was rubbish. To be honest, I had the exact same feeling when I was writing it. I felt like I was rambling on and on. I'm always amazed when I read your papers because they're so incredibly clear and lucid. That's actually one of the reasons I wanted to work with you and why I was so excited when you offered me a position last autumn. The results of our research could be extremely important, and I know that if the paper were well written, it might make a tremendous impact.
>
> The paper may be beyond repair, but I'm wondering if you might have any suggestions about how I could make it better. I want to learn as much from you as I possibly can.

His face instantly brightened, as if the sun had suddenly come out from behind the clouds. He grabbed the paper from the bin and glanced over it, muttering that it was actually a pretty darn brilliant piece of work. He said that all it really needed was a little tightening up here and there, and he made several suggestions, singing her praises the entire time.

Babette submitted the paper to a highly regarded journal, and it was accepted unconditionally on the first submission. She subsequently presented the paper at the New York Academy of Sciences and received a prestigious award for her research.

This was an excellent example of Positive Reframing—Babette thought about a potentially difficult or adversarial situation from a more positive perspective and communicated that vision to her boss. Instead of telling herself that she was a helpless victim who was under attack from a powerful and hostile adversary, she thought about the conflict as an opportunity to develop a more rewarding relationship with him. Her friendly and upbeat attitude was infectious and had an immediate positive impact on him.

You may protest and say, "Babette's comments were false. She wasn't being honest. She wanted to wring his neck." In fact, she probably did feel like wringing Gordon's neck. Most of us would feel the same way. But her statements weren't entirely dishonest because she found a way to talk about qualities she *did* admire: his scientific accomplishments and writing skills. Furthermore, the first draft of her paper wasn't very good.

You could also say, "She shouldn't have to kiss his ass." You'd be right again. She *didn't* have to kiss his ass. But when she conveyed admiration and respect for Gordon, he suddenly changed. He'd probably been feeling frustrated and unappreciated. Most of us feel that way from time to time. Babette's kind response to his hostile comment transformed their interaction and put her in control of the relationship.

What would have happened if Babette had tried to stick up for herself? There would have been an intensely unpleasant power struggle, and Gordon would have gotten even more aggressive. He definitely wouldn't have helped her with her paper, and she might have lost her job as well. All it took was a little Stroking to transform their relationship.

Let's practice. Imagine that your teenage son is mad and says, "You always try to run my life! You're a control freak. Why don't you stop telling me what to do all the time?" How would you respond, using Positive Reframing? Write down your response on a separate piece of paper before you continue reading. You can use any of the Five Secrets of Effective Communication, but remember to put the name of the techniques you're using in parentheses after each sentence you write down, using the abbreviations on page 98.

Answer
Obviously, there isn't any one correct answer, and my response will probably be very different from what you wrote down. You'll notice (PR) at the end of the sentences with Positive Reframing:

> You're right. (DT) I think I have been too controlling. (DT) You're growing up and you deserve more independence. (DT) That's a good thing, and I'm proud of you for feeling that way. (DT; ST; PR) It's embarrassing to hear that I've been trying to run your life too much, but I'm glad that you felt like you could tell me. (IF; TE; PR) It sounds like you're frustrated and mad at me. (FE) Can you tell me more about how you've been feeling? (IN) This is really important. (ST; PR)

Your son has just criticized you. He expects a fight, but you're reframing the interaction as a chance to talk things out and develop greater understanding. Many parents would get defensive and insist that they *weren't* too controlling. If you respond this way, your son will feel even more convinced that you *are* too controlling, because you're trying to force him to view the situation from your perspective. Then things will spiral out of control. He's invited you to battle, and you've taken the bait.

When you use Positive Reframing, you go in the opposite direction. You view the conflict as a golden opportunity to develop a better relationship with your son. How do you do this? You can tell your son that his feelings are important to you, and that you

---

love him. Instead of putting up a wall and insisting that he's wrong, you can welcome his feelings, find some truth in his point of view, and treat him with respect. You can invite him to open up and participate in a more collaborative, mature, and loving relationship with you. Of course, this isn't the way a "control freak" would react, so he'll suddenly experience his relationship with you in a very different way.

Chapter 30

Multiple-Choice Empathy: How to Talk to Someone Who Refuses to Talk to You

M ultiple-Choice Empathy can be very helpful when the person you're trying to communicate with has trouble expressing his or her feelings. When you use Multiple-Choice Empathy, you suggest several possibilities and ask if any of them make sense. For example, you might say, "It seems like you might be feeling hurt, angry, or discouraged right now. Do any of those possibilities ring true?"

Multiple-Choice Empathy can be especially valuable when the other person refuses to talk to you. Adolescents who are upset may glare, cross their arms defiantly, and angrily insist that nothing's wrong. Adults sometimes do the same thing. You may have a friend or family member who pouts, ignores you, and won't tell you what's bothering him or her. What are you supposed to do? If you encourage the other person to talk, he or she will resist even more intensely. Often nothing seems to work.

Instead of feeling frustrated or getting involved in a power struggle, try to put yourself in the other person's shoes and ask yourself *why* he or she doesn't want to talk to you. There are lots of possible reasons. For example, the other person may be:

- Feeling embarrassed or ashamed about something that happened.
- Feeling angry and punishing you with silence.
- Worried about hurting your feelings.
- Afraid of conflicts or disagreements, thinking the problem will go away if he or she ignores it.

The other person may also be afraid that if he or she opens up, you'll:

- Get mad.
- Get defensive and say, "You've got *no right* to feel that way," or "You *shouldn't* feel like that."
- Argue and insist that he or she is wrong.
- Try to "help" or problem solve when all the other person wants is for you to listen and validate his or her feelings.

There's one more reason that towers above all the rest, and it may be a hard pill to swallow. Often, the other person won't talk to you because she's convinced it won't be a rewarding experience. She may feel that when she's tried to talk to you in the past, she's been punished, judged, or hurt.

Most of us tend to blame the other person for not opening up. For example, you might tell yourself that your husband has trouble talking to you because men aren't very good at expressing their feelings, or because he's immature. Although this interpretation may be partially correct, the problem won't get solved if you think about it this way.

Instead, you can use Multiple-Choice Empathy and think about what *you've* been doing that might make it hard for your husband to open up. Ask yourself questions like these: "Have I been judgmental when he's tried to tell me how he feels? Do I have a tendency to be overly controlling? Have I sometimes seemed defensive or holier-than-thou when he's tried to open up?" If you ask him about these possibilities in a kind and accepting tone of voice, he'll be far more likely to open up because you're no longer blaming him for the problem.

This is another example of the Law of Opposites. We've talked about the fact that when you genuinely agree with a criticism that seems totally unfair or untrue, the critic will suddenly discover that the criticism *isn't* true. By the same token, when someone refuses to talk to you, he's also criticizing you, but he isn't putting his criticism into words. He's punishing you with silence. If you acknowledge that you've made it hard for that person to trust you, he'll suddenly begin to trust you. The moment you agree that the other person has a darn good reason *not* to talk to you, he will nearly always open up.

Multiple-Choice Empathy Exercise

A woman named Christine told me that her fourteen-year-old daughter, Audrey, was upset, but when Christine asked Audrey if something was bothering her, Audrey folded her arms defiantly across her chest and snapped, "I don't have *anything* to say!" Can you think of a few reasons why Audrey might be reluctant to talk? Ask yourself, "Why might a teenager who's upset not want to talk to her mom?"

We won't know for sure until Audrey tells us, but there are many possibilities. Maybe Audrey is mad at her mother but feels that she'll get in trouble if she expresses her feelings. Audrey may be feeling ashamed or embarrassed about something that happened. For example, she may be afraid that she's failing English, but knows that her mother will fly off the handle if she tells her. Audrey may also be reluctant to talk because she hasn't had good experiences when she's tried to talk to her mother. She may be convinced that her mother will judge her, criticize her, or make her feel guilty.

Keeping these possibilities in mind, how might Christine respond when Audrey says, "I don't have *anything* to say"? Put your response on a separate piece of paper. Don't continue reading until you've taken a stab at it.

Answer

There's no one correct response, but this approach might be effective:

Audrey, you're telling me that you've got nothing to say. But at the same time, I can see that your arms are crossed and it seems like you're glaring at me. Maybe something happened that's hard for you to talk about. I'm concerned that I might have said or done something that hurt your feelings, but I'm not sure what I did.

I'm also trying to figure out why you don't want to talk to me. I'm worried that I haven't done a very good job of making you feel like you can trust me when you've tried to talk to me in the past. Maybe you're afraid that I won't listen or that I'll get mad at you. Do any of these possibilities ring a bell?

In this response, Christine is commenting on the impasse that's developed. She's acknowledging the tension in the air and trying to understand why Audrey doesn't want to talk to her. Her statement sounds friendly and nonconfrontational.

Christine skillfully disarms Audrey and takes the blame for Audrey's reluctance to talk. But why should she assume the blame for her daughter's childish behavior? After all, Audrey is pouting and acting like an immature teenager.

There's a natural tendency to get into a power struggle with someone who refuses to speak to us. Most of us get frustrated, so we pressure the other person to tell us what's wrong. When she refuses, we subtly blame her and imply that she *should* be more open. This makes her clam up even more.

When you use Multiple-Choice Empathy, you come in from the opposite angle. You disarm the other person and agree that she has a perfectly good reason not to talk to you. Paradoxically, she'll often start talking the moment she hears this message. Of course, your attitude and tone of voice will be as important as the words you use. If you convey curiosity and respect, it will be much easier for the other person to talk to you.

If the other person is still unwilling to tell you how she's feeling, resist the urge to pressure her, criticize her, or make demands on her. Instead, convey caring, respect, patience, and concern. Let her know that everyone has the right to be left alone at times, but that you care about her and hope that you'll get the chance to talk with her later on, when the dust has settled and the timing is better. You can also let her know that you'll check in with her in a day or two to see if she's more in the mood to talk. This reduces the tension and increases the likelihood that she'll share her feelings with you later on.

Appendix

Your Intimacy Toolkit

On the following pages, you'll find copies of some of the tests, forms, and tables in this book. Feel free to photocopy them for your own personal use when you're reading and doing the exercises in this book.*

Some of the forms will be especially useful to you if you photocopy them two-sided. For example, if you photocopy the Relationship Satisfaction Test on page 258 two-sided, you'll be able to take the test four times on each piece of paper. And if you photocopy the EAR Checklist and list of Common Communication Errors on page 261 on the back of the Relationship Journal on page 260, it will be much easier to do Step 3 of the Relationship Journal (Good vs. Bad Communication). Finally, if you photocopy the list of Feeling Words on page 263 on the back of The Five Secrets of Effective Communication on page 262, it will be much easier to do Step 5 of the Relationship Journal (Revised Response). You also will be able to use the Five Secrets and Feeling Words when you're practicing the Intimacy Exercise on page 180.

---

* Therapists who wish to obtain a license to use these and many other assessment and treatment tools in their clinical work can contact me about obtaining the *Therapist's Toolkit*: david@feelinggood.com or visit my website at www.feelinggood.com.

If you photocopy this page two-sided, you'll be able to take the Relationship Satisfaction Test four times on each piece of paper.

Relationship Satisfaction Test (RSAT) Instructions: Use ticks (✓) to indicate how satisfied or dissatisfied you feel about your relationship. Please answer all the items.	0–Very dissatisfied	1–Moderately dissatisfied	2–Slightly dissatisfied	3–Neutral	4–Slightly satisfied	5–Moderately satisfied	6–Very satisfied
1. Communication and openness							
2. Resolving conflicts and arguments							
3. Degree of affection and caring							
4. Intimacy and closeness							
5. Satisfaction with your role in the relationship							
6. Satisfaction with the other person's role							
7. Overall satisfaction with your relationship							

Date:_____ TOTAL ➜ [____]

Relationship Satisfaction Test (RSAT) Instructions: Use ticks (✓) to indicate how satisfied or dissatisfied you feel about your relationship. Please answer all the items.	0–Very dissatisfied	1–Moderately dissatisfied	2–Slightly dissatisfied	3–Neutral	4–Slightly satisfied	5–Moderately satisfied	6–Very satisfied
1. Communication and openness							
2. Resolving conflicts and arguments							
3. Degree of affection and caring							
4. Intimacy and closeness							
5. Satisfaction with your role in the relationship							
6. Satisfaction with the other person's role							
7. Overall satisfaction with your relationship							

Date:_____ TOTAL ➜ [____]

Copyright © 1989 by David D. Burns, M.D. Revised 2005. Therapists who wish to obtain a license to use the RSAT in their clinical work or research can visit my website at www.feelinggood.com for more information about the *Therapist's Toolkit*.

Blame Cost-Benefit Analysis	
Advantages of Blaming the Other Person	Disadvantages of Blaming the Other Person

Copyright © 1984 by David D. Burns, M.D.

Step 1. S/he said. Write down *exactly* what the other person said to you. Be brief:

_____

_____

_____

_____

Step 2. I said. Write down *exactly* what you said next. Be brief:

_____

_____

_____

_____

Step 3. Good Communication vs. Bad Communication. Was your response an example of good communication or bad communication? Why? Use the EAR Checklist or the list of Common Communication Errors on page 261 to analyze what you wrote down in Step 2.

_____

_____

_____

_____

Step 4. Consequences. Did your response in Step 2 make the problem better or worse? Why?

_____

_____

_____

_____

Step 5. Revised Response. Revise what you wrote down in Step 2, using the Five Secrets of Effective Communication (see page 262): Remember to note which techniques you're using in parentheses after each sentence you write down. If your Revised Response is still ineffective, try again.

_____

_____

_____

_____

_____

Copyright © 1991 by David D. Burns, M.D. Revised 2007.

The EAR Checklist

Instructions: Review what you wrote down in Step 2 of the Relationship Journal. Use ticks to indicate whether it was an example of good communication or bad communication.

👂	Good Communication	✔	Bad Communication	✔
E = Empathy	1. You acknowledge the other person's feelings and find some truth in what he or she is saying.		1. You don't acknowledge the other person's feelings or find any truth in what he or she is trying to say.	
A = Assertiveness	2. You express your feelings openly, directly, and tactfully, using "I Feel" Statements.		2. You argue defensively or attack the other person.	
R = Respect	3. You convey caring and respect, even if you're feeling frustrated or annoyed with the other person.		3. You belittle the other person or treat him or her in a cold, competitive, or condescending way.	

Copyright © 2008 by David D. Burns, M.D.

Common Communication Errors

Instructions: Review what you wrote down in Step 2 of the Relationship Journal. How many of the following communication errors can you spot?

1. **Truth.** You insist that you're right and the other person is wrong.	10. **Diversion.** You change the subject or list past grievances.
2. **Blame.** You imply that the problem is all the other person's fault.	11. **Self-Blame.** You act as if you're awful and terrible to prevent the other person from criticizing you.
3. **Defensiveness.** You argue and refuse to admit any flaw or shortcoming.	12. **Hopelessness.** You claim that you've tried everything but nothing works.
4. **Martyrdom.** You claim that you're the innocent victim of the other person's tyranny.	13. **Demandingness.** You complain that the other person "should" be the way you expect him or her to be.
5. **Put-Down.** You use harsh or hurtful language and try to make the other person feel inferior or ashamed.	14. **Denial.** You deny your role in the problem or insist that you don't feel upset when you really do.
6. **Labeling.** You call the other person a "jerk," a "loser," or worse.	15. **Helping.** Instead of listening, you give advice or "help."
7. **Sarcasm.** Your attitude, words, and tone of voice are belittling or patronizing.	16. **Problem Solving.** You ignore the other person's feelings and try to solve the problem that's bothering him or her.
8. **Counterattack.** You respond to criticism with criticism.	17. **Passive Aggression.** You say nothing, pout, or slam doors.
9. **Scapegoating.** You imply that the other person is defective or inadequate.	18. **Mind Reading.** You expect the other person to know how you feel without having to tell him or her.

Copyright © 2008 by David D. Burns, M.D.

The Five Secrets of Effective Communication

Listening Skills

1. **The Disarming Technique (DT).** You find some truth in what the other person is saying, even if it seems totally unreasonable or unfair.

2. **Empathy.** You put yourself in the other person's shoes and try to see the world through his or her eyes.
   - **Thought Empathy (TE).** You paraphrase the other person's words.
   - **Feeling Empathy (FE).** You acknowledge how the other person is probably feeling, based on what he or she said.

3. **Inquiry (IN).** You ask gentle, probing questions to learn more about how the other person is thinking and feeling.

Self-Expression Skills

4. **"I Feel" Statements (IF).** You use "I Feel" Statements, such as, "I feel upset," rather than "You" Statements, such as, "You're wrong!" or "You're making me furious!"

5. **Stroking (ST).** You find something genuinely positive to say to the other person, even in the heat of battle. You convey an attitude of respect, even though you may feel very angry with the other person.

Copyright © 1991 by David D. Burns, M.D. Revised 1992.

Feeling Words

Feeling	Words That Express This Feeling		
Angry	mad resentful upset irate	pissed off irritated furious annoyed	ticked off incensed enraged bitter
Anxious	worried apprehensive panicky nervous	afraid uptight fearful concerned	scared tense frightened uneasy
Bored	uninterested	unmotivated	
Criticized	picked on judged	put down blamed	insulted
Embarrassed	foolish humiliated awkward	self-conscious mortified	flustered shy
Frustrated	stuck exasperated	thwarted	defeated
Guilty	ashamed	at fault	bad
Hopeless	discouraged	pessimistic	desperate
Inferior	inadequate useless second-rate	worthless undesirable defective	flawed intimidated incompetent
Jealous	envious		
Lonely	abandoned unwanted	alone unloved	rejected
Paranoid	mistrustful	suspicious	
Sad	blue depressed hurt disheartened	down disappointed lost low	unhappy despairing dejected miserable
Stressed	overwhelmed pressured	burned out overworked	tense frazzled
Tired	exhausted drained sleepy	weary worn out burdened	fatigued lethargic wiped out
Vulnerable	weak	fragile	exposed

Copyright © 1989 by David D. Burns, M.D. Revised 1992, 2006.

One-Minute Drill: Brief Instructions

Decide who will be the Talker and who will be the Listener first. When you're done, you'll reverse roles: the Talker will be the Listener, and vice versa.

Talker Instructions

You can express your feelings about any topic for approximately thirty seconds. When you're done, your partner will summarize what you said and how you were feeling inside. Rate the accuracy of his or her summary between 0 percent (not at all accurate) and 100 percent (perfect). If your partner's rating is 95 percent or better, you can reverse roles. You'll be the Talker and your partner will be the Listener. If your partner's rating is less than 95 percent, tell your partner about the part he or she missed or got wrong. Now your partner will summarize that part, and you'll give him or her a new rating. Continue this process until the overall rating is 95 percent or better.

Listener Instructions

Say nothing while your partner talks, but listen as carefully as possible. Concentrate on what your partner says. Take notes if you want, jotting down the main points. Sit quietly and respectfully, using good body language. Avoid frowning, raising your eyebrows, shaking your head in a judgmental manner, or folding your arms across your chest defiantly.

When your partner is done, summarize what he or she said as accurately as possible. You can refer to your notes. Your job is not to agree or disagree with anything your partner said. Instead, imagine that you're a court reporter, and your goal is to get it right. Paraphrase what your partner said and how your partner is likely to be feeling inside, given what he or she just said. For example, your partner might be feeling angry, frustrated, lonely, or unappreciated. If your partner gives you a rating below 95 percent, ask him or her to explain the part that you got wrong. Now summarize that information and ask for a new rating. Continue this process until your overall rating is 95 percent or better.

The tone of your summary will be as important as the content. Try to be respectful, even if your partner was angry or critical of you. If your summary sounds sarcastic or belittling, your partner will get upset.

Index

Page numbers in *italics* refer to checklists, forms, and work sheets.

blame *(continued)*
  vs. intimacy, 27, 51–55, 58–59, 233
  and people pleasing, 228
  See also other-blame; self-blame
blind spots, 183
body language, *62*, 74, 130, 181
borderline personality disorder, 61
boredom, *78*
Brenda and Harry case study, 17–22, 24
Broken Record Technique, 228–30
Buber, Martin, 140
Buddhism, 114
burnout theory, 5–6, *7*
Burns, David D.
  bipolar patients of, 95–98
  and Broken Record Technique,
    228–30
  and deficit theories, 8–9
  Feeling Good book and, 95–96,
    103–4, 203–8
  listening vs. helping and, 125–26
  and motivational theory case study,
    9–14
  and positive reframing, 243–44
  and Relationship Journal, 177–79
  Salty, the family dog, 144
  self-pity experience of, 27–28
  and Signe, 102–3
  and Venezuelan family, 104–5
  When Panic Attacks book and, 125
Burns, Signe, 102–3
Burt and Allison case study, 31–36

case studies, illustrating
    communication skills and
    therapeutic techniques
  Broken Record Technique, 228–30
  changing the focus, 238–42
  communication, 71–72, 73, 87–92,
    95–98
  disarming technique, 100–101,
    103–11, 194
  the EAR Checklist, 72–76, 76–77,
    87, 171–72
  empathy, 115–17, 122–25, 203–5
  and "I Feel" Statements, 136–37,
    138–39
  inquiry, 130–31
  multiple-choice empathy, 253–55
  one-minute drill therapy, 31–36
  positive reframing, 243–44, 246–48
  relationship diagnosis, 65–66, 86–92
  stroking, 144–46, 147–49
  See also specific case study
    participants by name

case studies, illustrating problems and
    emotional states
  anger phobia, 210–12
  apologizing, 217–20
  blame, 59–64
  complainers, 151–52
  control, 80–83, 165–68
  criticism, 171–73
  dark side of human nature, 17–22
  disclosure phobia, 199–201
  helping, 203–5
  hidden agendas, 29–30
  jealousy, 168–70
  laziness and stubbornness, 159–65
  motivational theory, 9–14, 31–36
  narcissists, 155–60
  problem-solving, 131–33, 205–8
  resistance to change, 233–34
  self-blame, 59–60
  self-defeating beliefs, 223–27
  See also specific case study
    participants by name
change
  and acceptance, 161–62
  and blame, 54–55, 82
  improving relationships and, 31–38,
    49–50, 88
  and motivational theory, 9–14
  resistance to, 15, 52, 232–34
changing the focus technique,
    237–42
childhood patterns, 8
Chris case study, 95–98
Christianity, 113–14
Christina case study, 61–64
Christine and Audrey case study,
    253–55
closeness. *See* intimacy
codependency, 204, 223
cognitive distortions, 5–6, 15, 61–64
cognitive interpersonal therapy (CIT),
    36–38, 66, 80, 170, 231
cognitive therapy, 4–5, 10, 103–4
communication
  of anger, 72, *78*, 142, 252
  and assertiveness, 71–72, 73, 77–78,
    133
  case studies regarding, 87–92,
    95–98, 100–101
  and changing the focus, 237–42
  common errors of, 4, 73, 75–77, 82,
    261
  and criticism, 105–6, 196, 198
  defensiveness, 73, 82–83, 136
  effective, 95–99, 134–39, 140–49

About the Author

Dr David D. Burns, is an Adjunct Clinical Professor Emeritus in the Department of Psychiatry and Behavioral Sciences at the Stanford University School of Medicine and has served as Visiting Scholar at Harvard Medical School. Dr. Burns has been a pioneer in the development of cognitive behavioral therapy, a drug-free treatment for depression and anxiety that has become the most widely used and extensively researched form of psychotherapy in history.

Dr. Burns has won numerous research, teaching, and media awards, but is best known for his successful self-help books, including *Feeling Good* and *The Feeling Good Handbook*, which have sold more than 5 million copies in the United States alone. In a national survey of American mental health professionals, Dr. Burns's *Feeling Good* was the top-rated book on a list of 1,000 self-help books for people with depression. In addition, American and Canadian mental health professionals prescribe *Feeling Good* for their patients more often than any other self-help book.

In recent years, more than 50,000 mental health professionals have attended Dr. Burns's training programs throughout the United States and Canada. More than 100 articles about his work have appeared in magazines such as *Reader's Digest* and *Psychology Today*. He has been interviewed by numerous radio and television personalities including Oprah Winfrey, Mike Wallace, Charlie Rose, Maury Povich, and Phil Donahue.

Also available from Vermilion by Dr David Burns:

10 Days To Great Self Esteem

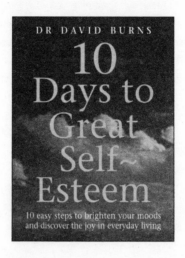

Do you wake up dreading the day? Do you feel discouraged with what you've accomplished in life? Do you want greater self-esteem, productivity, and joy in daily living?

In *10 Days to Great Self Esteem*, Dr David Burns offers a powerful tool providing hope, compassion, and healing for people suffering from low self-esteem or unhappiness. In ten easy steps you will learn specific techniques to enhance self-esteem, productivity and happiness. With easy-to-apply ideas based on commonsense, Dr Burns helps you feel the way you think and change the way you feel, brightening your outlook when you're in a slump for happier everyday living.

£11.99   ISBN 9780091825621   www.rbooks.co.uk

When Panic Attacks

'I just know this plane is going to run into turbulence and crash!'
'My mind will go blank when I give my presentation at work and
everyone will think I'm an idiot.'
'Why am I so shy and insecure? I'm such a loser!'

We all know what it's like to feel anxious, worried or panicky. If
any of these thoughts sound familiar, you can change the way you
feel. *When Panic Attacks* will give you the ammunition to quickly
defeat any kind of anxiety, including chronic worrying, shyness,
public speaking anxiety, test anxiety and phobias without lengthy
therapy or prescription drugs. Dr David Burns will teach you forty
powerful new anti-anxiety techniques and show you how to select
methods that will work for you. The goal is not just feeling a bit
better, but complete recovery. All you need is a little courage and
the techniques in this book.

£11.99   ISBN 9780091929602   www.rbooks.co.uk

FREE POSTAGE AND PACKING

Overseas customers allow £2.00 per paperback

BY PHONE: 01624 677237

BY POST: Random House Books
c/o Bookpost, PO Box 29, Douglas
IsleofMan,IM99 1BQ

BY FAX: 01624 670923

BY EMAIL: bookshop@enterprise.net

Cheques (payable to Bookpost) and credit cards accepted.
Prices and availability subject to change without notice.
Allow 28 days for delivery.
When placing your order, please mention if you do not wish to
receive any additional information.

www.rbooks.co.uk